BRUCKNER

and

MAHLER

SERIES EDITED BY

SIR JACK WESTRUP

M.A., Hon.D.Mus.(Oxon.), F.R.C.O.

MAHLER: THE LAST PORTRAIT
(WINTER 1910–11, U.S.A.)
(By courtesy of Universal Edition, Vienna-London)

BRUCKNER AT THE AGE OF 60
(By courtesy of Universal Edition, Vienna-London)

THE MASTER MUSICIANS SERIES

BRUCKNER

and

MAHLER

by

H. F. REDLICH

Professor of Music in the University of Manchester

With eight pages of plates
and music examples in the text

LONDON
J. M. DENT AND SONS LTD

FARRAR, STRAUS AND GIROUX INC.
NEW YORK

PREFACE

A BOOK bracketing Bruckner and Mahler may well come in for some criticism from continental scholars who have spent much time and effort on the discussion of the divergences of temperament, character and style in these two composers. For the benefit of the English reader, however, the approach to the two great Austrians is determined by somewhat different considerations. For him the similarities of nationality, creed and creative bent in them all but outweigh the indisputable differences of human type and intellectual training; for him the basic fact that both composers are Austrian symphonists of the nineteenth century and in the royal line of descent from Beethoven and Schubert still holds validity. Moreover, the bond linking Bruckner and Mahler is more intimate than that implied by their sharing of a niche in the musical Valhalla of their country. They were, in fact, attached to each other by mutual friendship and high esteem, despite the disparity in their ages. Mahler as a conductor remained to the end a staunch partisan of Bruckner's masses and symphonies, while as a composer he reveals, even in the *Adagio* of his unfinished tenth Symphony, the deep imprint of the older man's style. Both composers, although born in remote provinces of imperial Austria, lived in Vienna during the years of their maturity. The works by which they will be remembered first and foremost were written, planned or completed in the Austrian capital. Both were deeply imbued with the spiritual heritage of the Roman Church. Their music is permeated by folkloristic elements of old Austria in a manner sometimes reminiscent of Schubert, although it is difficult (as in Schubert's case) to identify actual folktunes in their musical subjectmatter. Finally, both composers lived and died during the long reign of Francis Joseph I, who bestowed on them notable signs of appreciation.

I have written this book in England, my adopted country, and in English, my second language from the days of early childhood. Still my familiarity with its subject derives from the fact that I was born in the Austria of Bruckner and Mahler, and that I grew up in Vienna when the posthumous rediscovery of their music was about to reach its apex. As a child I met Mahler in person, and I vividly recall the friendship existing between him, my father and his brother. In the years of my adolescence I was privileged also to meet Mahler's widow, his surviving daughter, his sister Justine Rosé and other members of his family. The unique experience of Mahler's musical personality, coming to life in the shattered world of the defeated Austria of 1918, was finally embodied in my literary apprentice work: a booklet on Mahler I published in December 1919, at the age of sixteen.

My active interest in Bruckner dates from the time of the First World War, when I had opportunities to hear his symphonies in authoritative performances, conducted by his disciples Franz Schalk and Ferdinand Löwe. In the middle 1930s I acted for a time as one of the officers of the Badische Bruckner Bund; it was then that I repeatedly met most of the leading Bruckner apostles.

Apart from the early pamphlet of 1919 I published numerous articles and papers on both composers in English and German. The Bibliography of this book mentions some of these publications, but makes no attempt to list them all. Only two English articles published in recent years and the results of my research undertaken for my article on Bruckner in Grove's *Dictionary of Music and Musicians* (5th edition, 1954) have been utilized for this book.

I am much indebted to Mr Donald Mitchell for unreservedly placing at my disposal new data relating to Mahler's life which were in the first place intended for a future book of his own, *Gustav Mahler and the Twentieth Century*, as also for permitting me to reproduce a page in facsimile from his photostat of the earliest draft of Mahler's *Das klagende Lied*; to Dr Ernest Jones, Sigmund Freud's English biographer, for permission to quote from Freud's psycho-analysis of Mahler and to utilize information on that matter originally imparted to Donald Mitchell only; to Mr Frank Walker for valuable information—partly from unpublished letters—on the personal relations between Hugo Wolf and Mahler, and Wolf and Bruckner; to Mrs Gertrud Staub-Schlaepfer (Zürich) for drawing my attention to new facts and discoveries appertaining to the vexed question of Bruckner's 'original versions'; to Dr Hans Halm, custodian of the music collection of the Bayerische Staatsbibliothek in Munich, for permission to reproduce two pages of an early draft of Bruckner's eighth Symphony which has remained unpublished so far; and to Universal Edition, Vienna and London, for permission to quote from the works of Gustav Mahler published by them. Finally I wish to express especial gratitude to my wife for her unremitting help in correcting manuscripts and proofs.

H. F. R.

1955.

PREFACE TO THE SECOND EDITION

SINCE the first edition of this book, interest in Bruckner and Mahler has increased all over the Western Hemisphere. The issue of LP recordings on a large scale, but also more frequent live performances and broadcasts, have stimulated a closer inspection of their music and its methods. The expiry of Mahler's copyright in 1961 has been responsible for a spate of new editions of his music, some of which are listed in the Catalogue of Works. The hundredth anniversary of his birth and the fiftieth anniversary of his death all but overlapped in 1960–1. Both dates were also responsible for a number of books and papers on the man and his music. Studies of Bruckner's music by Western scholars have also become more plentiful in recent years. Among these new publications two have specially referred to and commented upon the present volume. Both E. Doernberg's *The Life and Symphonies of Anton Bruckner* (1960) and Donald Mitchell's *Gustav Mahler: The Early Years* (1958) are books of scholarly pretensions, as conspicuous by the incompleteness of their information as by the debatable value of their argument.[1] Mitchell's book, however, does contain some important new material which has been

[1] Doernberg's *Bruckner* has been reviewed by me in *Music and Letters*, Vol. 41, No. 4, October 1960, p. 366 ff., and in *Musical Times*, No. 1411, September 1960, p. 555; Mitchell's book on Mahler in *The Music Review*, XX/1, February 1959, and in *Musica*, Cassel, 1959, January issue.

utilized for the text of the second edition. But his book is certainly a far cry from the one originally announced by his publishers, and mentioned at length in the preface to the first edition of the present volume.

Dr Eric Blom, the former editor of The Master Musicians Series, died on 11th April 1959. He took the most active and beneficial interest in the shaping of this volume. The debt of gratitude which I owed him could not be repaid while he was alive for reasons of etiquette. These lines wish to commemorate an inspired and inspiring writer on matters musical.

The revised bibliography makes no attempt to list all books and papers on Bruckner and Mahler (especially those published in German) perused by me since the publication of the first edition. However, some valuable new publications have been included.

1963.
HANS FERDINAND REDLICH, DR. PHIL.
Professor of Music in the
University of Manchester.

CONTENTS

BRUCKNER

MAHLER

Contents

ILLUSTRATIONS

BRUCKNER

CHAPTER I

ANCESTRY—CHILDHOOD

JOSEPH ANTON BRUCKNER was born on 4th September 1824 at the little village of Ansfelden in Upper Austria. Like Schubert he was a schoolmaster's son; but the family were simple country folk, just one degree above peasantry and closely resembling it in their habits. Recent research has traced the family back into the early fifteenth century in the adjacent crown-land of Lower Austria. In its westernmost district an early ancestor of the composer has been traced: one Jörg Pruckner [1] an der Prugk (i.e. living near a bridge), who owned the farm of the Pruckhof. The family seems to have prospered for a time, owning quarries and steadily ascending the social ladder. Some members became aldermen, and one branch even acquired nobility. But in the end the farm was sold. One of Jörg's offspring acquired another at Pyrha near Öd (Lower Austria) by way of marriage. His son, however, Martin Pruckner (1656–1737), had to sell this farm too, and henceforth the family's fortunes were on the wane. From freeholders they dropped in the social scale to broom-makers and innkeepers. It was only Anton's grandfather, Joseph Bruckner, junior (1749–1831), who, starting as a broom-maker's apprentice, improved the family's fortunes through his marriage to Franziska Kletzer, a schoolmaster's daughter. He duly stepped into his father-in-law's shoes, and himself became a schoolmaster at Ansfelden in 1776. His son, Anton Bruckner, senior (1791–1837), the tenth of his twelve children, and the composer's father, seems to have given up broom-making altogether. He started as his father's assistant, and succeeded him in 1823 as village schoolmaster and organist. In the same year he married Theresia Helm (1801–60), the daughter of a local official and innkeeper. She seems to have been a keen and good singer.

[1] The spelling used by the composer seems to have been adopted by his paternal grandfather.

The lot of the poorly paid Austrian village schoolmaster, who generally held the ancillary posts of organist and sexton, was not eased by his proverbial procreative faculties. Bruckner's father was no exception. He must have found it very difficult at times to support his numerous family adequately. Anton, the composer, was the first-born of a family of eleven children, five of whom died in infancy. With three sisters—Rosalia, Josefa and Maria Anna— and one younger brother, Ignaz (died 1913), he grew up in the tiny rural community of Ansfelden, in the Traun district of Upper Austria (or Viertel ob der Enns, as it was still called at the time of his birth). It lies in the fertile plain of the crown-land, bordering in the west on Bavaria and in the north on Bohemia; confined by the rivers Traun and Enns, and leading up to the slopes of the Salzburg Alps, whose northernmost peak, the Traunstein, becomes visible on a clear day. It is a region rich in tradition and folklore, and the district between the rivers Traun and Enns receives an added cultural stimulus from the presence of beautiful, medieval fortified towns such as Enns and Steyr, adorned by cathedrals and surrounded by opulent monasteries.

Not far from Bruckner's birthplace is the provincial capital of Linz. The sphere of his early life is the western area of the crown-land, bordering on Lower Austria, whence his family came. In this country of simple, hardworking and hard-bitten peasant folk, proficient in local dance and music, devout worshippers of the Roman Church, Bruckner spent his childhood. The date of his birth makes him a subject of the Emperor Francis II (died 1835) and an educational product of the so-called *Vormärz*.[1] It is important to realize that Bruckner's education and early experience occurred before the great change of 1848 and its liberalizing influences. Bruckner's lifelong attitude of servility towards his social superiors, his decidedly old-fashioned epistolary style and quaint manners, his cautious and circumspect approach to life in general, are characteristics of the age into which he was born.

Country people in the Austria of those days thought but little of

---

[1] The period preceding the liberal revolution of March 1848.

things of the mind, and treated the humble intellectuals in their midst—schoolmasters and organists—with a mixture of condescension and harshness. Bruckner's father must have belonged to this select minority, for he soon discovered little Tonerl's musical gifts. He gave the boy his first musical tuition and encouraged him to play the organ and the 'spinet,' [1] In the spring of 1835 Tonerl, aged eleven, was in turn discovered by his godfather-cousin, J. B. Weiss, a well-informed musician and experienced composer of church music, who took the boy to Hörsching (near Linz) and instructed him more systematically in thorough-bass and organ playing. It was there that, encouraged by Weiss, young Anton started to compose little organ preludes and became acquainted with the rural Austrian musical traditions of the Mass. Bruckner retained an ever-grateful memory of his first teacher, who ended his life prematurely by committing suicide in 1850.

In the autumn of 1836 young Bruckner had to return to Ansfelden as deputy for his father, who had fallen seriously ill. The following year—worn out too early by his ill-rewarded labours, the father died of consumption on 7th June. A few weeks later his widow and the family moved to Ebelsberg, nearer to Linz. It was the resourceful and far-seeing cousin Weiss who suggested that Tonerl, who wanted to become a schoolmaster like his father, should become a pupil and chorister in the famous monastery of St Florian, the oldest-established Augustinian foundation in the crown-land, re-nowned for its wealth, its famous library and its architectural beauties, by whose atmosphere and influence his future development was to be largely determined. With this momentous step he estab-lished his lifelong close association with the Church, with the organ and with the music of the Roman service.

The St Florian foundation, not far from the town of Enns, and close to the border of Lower Austria, was built after the last invasion of the Turks, i.e. in the last quarter of the seventeenth century. Its artistic highlight, the magnificent baroque church, was completed shortly before 1700 by the Milanese brothers Carlone. The organ, one of the greatest on the Continent, had been built in 1771 by the

---

[1] Doubtless a square piano, not a harpsichord.

Slovene priest Krismann. It boasted four manuals, a pedal with 30 keys and comprised 94 stops and 4,993 pipes.[1] The largest pipe, the Contraprinzipal, had a width capable of concealing a heavily built man. With its four 32-ft. and twelve 16-ft. stops this organ outshines all others in the Austrian monasteries. This was Anton Bruckner's organ, the instrument from which he was to receive inspirations of beauty and grandeur, the instrument in the shadow of which he lies at rest to-day.

For the next three years (until 1840) young Bruckner, like Haydn and Schubert before him, led the secluded but thoroughly musical existence of a chorister, receiving tuition in turn from his house-master, Father Bogner (thorough-bass), from the principal organist, Kattinger (organ and piano), and from the administrative official Gruber (violin). Bruckner's zeal and energy in the pursuit of know-ledge was becoming noticeable. With the help of an assistant teacher he mastered a considerable curriculum that made him eligible for an examination at a higher school. He passed it with distinction and became an assistant schoolmaster on 1st October 1840. After that he duly enrolled for the *Präparandenkurs* at Linz, a one-year training-college for elementary school teachers. Despite his love of the organ and his conspicuous talent for composition, Bruckner's chosen profession remained schoolmastering until his thirty-first year. So long did it take him to reach the decision to become a professional musician. For many years he continued to waver between teaching and becoming a civil servant. Even at Linz, after his appointment as cathedral organist, he still toyed with the idea of studying law and entering the civil service. No great musician—Heinrich Schütz excepted—ever took up the professional calling of his art with greater hesitation than Bruckner.

At Linz, Bruckner continued to study harmony and counterpoint with the distinguished theorist A. Dürrnberger, and to add to his still rather patchy general knowledge. After a further successful examination on 30th July 1841 he was declared fit to teach as an assistant at elementary schools.

[1] It was later reconstructed by Mauracher of Salzburg.

CHAPTER II

BRUCKNER'S first educational appointment was that of assistant schoolmaster at the miserable little village of Windhaag, in the north-east corner of the crown-land (October 1841). The place was quite near the frontier of Bohemia, and not far from the little town of Freystadt. This first assignment provided useful if bitter experiences. Bruckner received a very paltry salary, and was asked to undertake numerous menial jobs in the fields, in addition to his gratuitous services as deputy organist and sexton. His superior evidently disliked his enthusiasm for the organ and for composition, and resented his reluctance to work in the fields. He made things as difficult as possible. Life seemed bearable only thanks to the haven of friendship offered him by the family of the musical weaver Sücka. With them Bruckner eventually formed a dance band in which he played second fiddle. They were asked to play at country inns, especially for dance entertainments and wedding celebrations. The local peasantry was as much bewildered by Bruckner's musical accompaniments on the organ as by his absent-mindedness and concentration on intellectual pursuits.

When finally his superior, Fuchs, denounced him for his refusal to work in the fields, he was summoned before the prelate Arneth of St Florian, who sized up the situation very fairly. He transferred Bruckner in January 1843 to the even tinier village of Kronstorf near Steyr. But this was no disciplinary action, for Kronstorf proved a great improvement. It was half-way between Linz and Steyr, both possessing beautiful organs and inhabited by more enlightened people. Steyr even had a Krismann organ, like St Florian, and at Enns was a master-organist, Leopold von Zenetti, who soon became Bruckner's first authoritative musical mentor. On an old piano, discovered in an attic at Kronstorf, Bruckner practised Bach day in,

7

day out. He made friends with the parish rector of Steyr. He frequently practised the organ at the parish church there, and played Schubert's piano duets with Karoline Eberstaller, who had played them twenty years before with the composer himself.

Bruckner's intellectual range now widened considerably and made him more self-confident. On 29th May 1845 he successfully passed the *Konkursprüfung*, and thus acquired the status of a fully salaried schoolmaster.

As an organist he distinguished himself. On 25th September 1845 he was appointed teacher at St Florian, which he had left five years earlier as a schoolboy. This appointment carried the meagre annual salary of 36 fl., and he was to remain in that humble position, teaching mainly the two lowest forms, for a whole decade. However, he was also appointed assistant organist of the monastery, becoming deputy to his old teacher Kattinger, who encouraged the eager young man to perfect himself in organ playing, free improvisation (which was to become his speciality at the organ) and religious composition.

After the political excitements of 1848, to which Bruckner reacted mildly by temporarily enrolling in the National Guard, his first ambitious compositions—the Requiem in D minor and the 'Missa solemnis' in B flat minor—quickly brought him to the fore. He was appointed temporary organist of St Florian in 1849, and became chief organist in 1855.[1] In the meantime he continued his private studies with an eye to raising his educational qualifications. He even began to learn Latin, and started a two years' course at the Unter-Realschule of Linz (1850–1). In 1851 he also took up work in the district law-courts of St Florian as a temporary assistant and clerk. These bureaucratic experiences led him in 1853 to apply for a permanent job in the civil service, for which he professed to have felt a vocation for a considerable time. Fortunately for posterity this ill-advised application was unsuccessful.

Soon afterwards, on 25th–26th January 1855, Bruckner, having passed the highest examination at Linz, became a fully qualified

[1] E. Schwanzara (see Bibliography); not 13th September 1851, as other biographers state.

senior-school teacher. He had outstripped the modest achievements of his grandfather and his father; yet he felt strangely dissatisfied. Meanwhile, in 1851, he had undertaken the long and trying journey to Vienna (railways were still in their infancy in Austria), and called on Ignaz Assmayer, Michael Haydn's pupil and Schubert's one-time friend and colleague, a distinguished composer of masses and oratorios. To him he dedicated his Psalm CXIV, one of the works presaging future greatness, which was successfully performed at St Florian shortly after its completion (*c.* 1854). In a letter to Assmayer, dated 30th July 1852, Bruckner complained bitterly of his position at the foundation, and of its rulers' scant interest in matters musical. His isolation, coupled with the personal disappointments of repeated rebuffs from young girls with whom he fell in and out of love, drove him in 1854 to undertake a second journey to Vienna. On 9th October 1854 he asked three outstanding Viennese organists and theorists, Assmayer, Sechter and Preyer, to examine him as an organist. Meanwhile the Mass in B flat minor had been successfully performed (on 14th September 1854), and Bruckner had obtained another eulogistic testimonial from Robert Führer, a well-known master organist from Prague (27th April 1855). With the score of the Mass and Führer's testimonial he went a third time to Vienna (July 1855) to call on Sechter who, clearly impressed this time, accepted him at once as a pupil.

But before Bruckner was able to begin his regular studies under Sechter matters at home came to a head. On 9th November 1855 Wenzel Pranghofer, the first organist of Linz cathedral, had died. Four days later a preliminary competition took place at the organ of the cathedral to find a temporary successor. Bruckner, neither invited nor ready to compete, but happening to be present, joined in at the last moment, and beat his competitors easily with an improvised strict fugue. He was immediately appointed. Although, unde-cided, diffident and abnormally shy as he was, he neither applied for the fixed appointment nor even announced his intention to parti-cipate in the main competition of 25th January 1856, he decided at the last minute to compete and won again on all counts against formidable opponents. The definite appointment was confirmed on 25th April 1856. It meant an annual salary of about 520 fl., with free lodgings, and at long last released Bruckner from the drudgery of teaching and the pettifogging duties of St Florian. It also transferred him forcibly from monastic seclusion to the livelier surroundings of a provincial capital and bishopric. What is more, it brought him into professional, human and spiritual contact with the Bishop of Linz, Dr Franz Josef Rudigier—the most forceful personality to cross the modest organist's path. This was the man whose fiery temperament was to help in releasing the divine spark in Bruckner's humble soul.

CHAPTER III

SLOW AWAKENING (LINZ, 1855–68)

BISHOP RUDIGIER was a man of iron will-power (as he was to show later in his head-on clash with the Austrian Government), but also of deep-seated humanity, and endowed with a genuine love of music. He accorded Bruckner preferential treatment from the start. He liberally sanctioned his frequent and prolonged journeys to Vienna, and deeply appreciated his skill at the organ. He often invited him to play privately for him on the cathedral organ in times of tribulation and preoccupation. It was Rudigier, also, who sent a priest to look after Bruckner during the months of his nervous breakdown, and while he was taking the waters at Bad Kreuzen. Most important of all, he commissioned the *Domkantate* and the Mass in E minor, both composed for the bishop's cherished new cathedral and its votive chapel. Rudigier was so strongly impressed by Bruckner's D minor Mass (1864) that he confessed he had felt unable to pray during the performance because of its artistic fascination. Bruckner continued to venerate this great priest even after he had left Linz for good. He composed his austerely beautiful antiphon *Tota pulchra es* especially for the occasion of Rudigier's twenty-fifth anniversary as a bishop in 1878.

Actually Bruckner was in sore need of the bishop's benevolence. He had undertaken a prodigious amount of work, which often came into conflict with his double duties as official organist at the cathedral and at the parish church of Linz. Reflecting on the Linz period later, he said he had studied seven hours daily, in addition to giving many piano lessons, by which he was obliged to augment his income, constantly drained by the costly journey to Vienna.

Apart from these local duties, he travelled once or twice a year to Vienna for as long as six or seven weeks, spending every day from

11

morning to night in Sechter's house. His studies with Sechter were the core of Bruckner's intellectual existence. Renouncing free composition for nearly seven years, he went through the whole gamut of Sechter's musical theory from 1855 to late November 1861. The tuition progressed in four stages: 1855-8, harmony; 1859, simple counterpoint; 1860, double counterpoint; 1861, canon and fugue. Each stage was concluded by an intermediate examination, to the evident delight of Bruckner, who, as we have seen, was an avid collector of testimonials. So indefatigable was he in studying Sechter's long-winded treatises, and contriving numerous solutions for every problem, that the dry pedant finally had to restrain him because he became worried about his pupil's health. Sechter declared he had never had a more industrious disciple.

After Bruckner had passed the final examination with distinction on 20th March 1861, Sechter expressed his complete satisfaction by dedicating to him a fugue composed to commemorate the occasion. On his own confession Bruckner felt 'like a watch-dog who has broken his chain.' Immediately after the termination of his studies with Sechter he applied for admittance to the final examination at the Vienna Conservatory in order to become eligible later on for appointments as a teacher of harmony and counterpoint at conservatories throughout the monarchy. It may be assumed that Sechter, who was on the teaching staff of Vienna Conservatory, supported this step. Bruckner's exercises with Sechter were submitted; they were passed by the examiners in highly flattering terms. However, to give Bruckner an opportunity for special distinction, he was invited to improvise a fugue on a given subject on the organ of the Piarist Church in Vienna. The commission of examiners—Hellmesberger, Herbeck, Dessoff and Sechter—was so overwhelmed by Bruckner's prowess that the enthusiastic Herbeck epitomized their feelings in the words: 'He should have examined us! If I knew one-tenth of what he knows I'd be happy!' The final testimonial o 22nd November 1861 is a memorial to Bruckner's prodigious perseverance and industry.

The prolonged abstinence from composition, imposed on him by Sechter, might have seriously affected his development as a creative artist. Fortunately a short cut to practical music was just then provided by fate: Bruckner's connection with secular music was established at Linz through the choral society 'Frohsinn.' He joined it in 1856 as a singing member, but became librarian and finally conductor (1861). In the latter capacity he conducted the men's choir at competitive festivals at Krems and Nuremberg with some success; and it was at a founders' day concert of the 'Frohsinn' that he made his début as a composer at Linz, when his seven-part *a cappella* offertory, *Ave Maria*, was sung on 12th May 1861. Together with the offertory *Afferentur* with accompanying trombones (first performed on 14th December 1861 at St Florian) this marks Bruck-ner's successful resurrection as a composer. Shortly afterwards he met the young conductor Otto Kitzler at Linz and studied orchestration, secular composition, sonata form, etc., with him until 1863.[1] It was through Kitzler that he became first acquainted with Wagner's *Tannhäuser*, as well as with Liszt's symphonic music. On 10th July 1863 Kitzler solemnly declared Bruckner a master, and with that day the abnormally long period of his musical apprenticeship came to a happy end.

The release of original creative power, suppressed for so long, was close at hand. The miracle of Bruckner's seemingly sudden trans-formation into a front-rank composer (with the Mass in D minor) is clearly foreshadowed by the remarkable activity starting soon after the final examination of November 1861. The *Domkantate* of 1862, Psalm CXIV, *Germanenzug* and—last but not least—the symphonic essays conceived while still working with Kitzler are milestones on the road to mastery.

In the years between the termination of his studies with Sechter and Kitzler, and his appointment in Vienna, Bruckner came into personal contact with Wagner and his partisans. He may have attended one of Wagner's concerts in Vienna about 1862; he certainly met him in person for the first time at Munich in June 1865, on the occasion of the first performance of *Tristan*. It was then that he also

---

[1] A definite date is difficult to establish. These studies cannot have started until well after the examination of November 1861.

became acquainted with Hans von Bülow, who was much impressed with the still unfinished score of Symphony I. Bruckner had already paid a visit to Munich in 1863, when he had called on Franz Lachner, the leading conductor (and Wagner's later adversary), who took an interest in Bruckner's *Studiensymphonie*, in F minor. Probably on the advice of Kitzler's successor at Linz, Ignaz Dorn, Bruckner made every effort to establish contact with progressive composers. He met Berlioz and Liszt in Vienna and Budapest, and attended performances of *La Damnation de Faust* and *The Flying Dutchman*. However, his relations with Liszt and Bülow remained inconclusive. In later years Bülow was to turn increasingly critical when referring to Bruckner's music, and Liszt even as late as 1884 treated him very condescendingly. Not so Wagner, who apparently sympathized with Bruckner from the first, and even allowed him to perform the final scene of *Die Meistersinger* with the 'Frohsinn' choir on 4th April 1868, before the production at Munich. Later on he accepted the dedication of the third Symphony, and he repeatedly praised Symphonies II and III—the only ones he ever saw in manuscript. It is difficult to decide whether Wagner was serious when he promised Bruckner later to perform his symphonies at Bayreuth. Cosima Wagner's letters to Bruckner, the fact that she invited him to play the organ at the funeral ceremony of Liszt in 1886,[1] as well as Bayreuth's official reactions to Bruckner after his death make it seem not wholly unlikely. There may have been patronage and even an element of teasing in Wagner's intercourse with Bruckner, whose adoration knew no bounds and often became fulsome, but he certainly entertained a high opinion of him as a symphonist.

Immediately after the termination of his apprenticeship Bruckner started his efforts to obtain official recognition and to secure an appointment more in line with his stature as a composer, conductor and organist. Despite his local successes at Linz—with the first performances of the D minor Mass (1864) and of Symphony I (1868) under his own direction—he felt the need of a wider field of musical activity. In 1861 and again in 1868 he applied unsuccessfully for

---

[1] On that occasion he based his improvisation on a theme from *Parsifal*.

the post of cathedral conductor and director of the Mozarteum at Salzburg. He was equally unlucky with his application (1862) for the post of *Expektant* (organist-designate) at the imperial court chapel in Vienna. Finally he failed in his efforts to be appointed teacher of composition in the Faculty of Philosophy of Vienna University (November 1867). It was then that he first encountered the hostility of Eduard Hanslick, the pugnacious music critic of the *Neue Freie Presse*, who happened to be also professor of musical aesthetics at the university, and put every obstacle in Bruckner's path from that time onwards. However, the two lines of approach last mentioned show a curious prescience: Bruckner was to obtain both appointments in years to come.

Meanwhile Bruckner's health had seriously deteriorated. A complete nervous breakdown with peculiar pathological symptoms —probably resulting from overwork as much as from rigorous continence—necessitated a three-months' cure at Bad Kreuzen (May–August 1867), which gradually restored him to health. He badly needed the stimulus of a big commission or of a spectacular appointment. It was Sechter's death (10th September 1867) which at last offered him an opening for a musical career in Vienna. He repeated his earlier application for the post of court organist on 14th October 1867, and now it was Johann Herbeck's turn to transform Bruckner's life decisively. He was to become in 1868 for the mature artist what Bishop Rudigier had been for the striving organist in 1856. Herbeck, who had been Bruckner's sincere admirer ever since the examination of 1861, and had just performed his D minor Mass in the court chapel (1867), decided to secure his services for the capital. He personally went to Linz on 24th May 1868 to persuade the ever-hesitant Bruckner, who, filled with dark forebodings, was reluctant to give up his secure appointment in exchange for a poorly paid teaching-post in Vienna. Then, as later, he tried to avoid a transfer to Vienna. He even pleaded with Bülow to get him a commission at Munich through Wagner's influence. But at last the negotiations with Vienna came to a positive conclusion, thanks to Herbeck's tenacity and his generous understanding of Bruckner's psychological make-up. In a letter of 23rd July 1868, addressed to the Vienna Conservatory, Bruckner at last consented to become Sechter's successor, and to start on 1st October. But it is thoroughly characteristic of his suspicious nature and his lack of self-confidence that even at this late hour he persuaded Bishop Rudigier to retain him in his post as cathedral organist for the time being. Not till two years later, safely installed in Vienna, did he at last relinquish the old Linz appointment.

CHAPTER IV

TRIAL AND FULFILMENT (VIENNA, 1868-96)

THE history of Bruckner's life in its final period is embodied in the history of his symphonies. His personal life settled down, after the passing excitements of the transfer from the provinces to the capital, to a rather rigid routine of academic and scholastic duties. Their scope, variety and emoluments form a telling contrast to the modest appointments at Linz. Yet, Bruckner was never satisfied and tried more than once to obtain a post abroad. He continued to complain bitterly of his financial position, which was affected by the expense incurred by the copying and performing of his manuscript sym-phonies. Bruckner never received any fees for his compositions, and was able to publish them only by degrees in the last decade of his life, supported by the Emperor of Austria, the Austrian Government and the King of Bavaria, and with the help of donations collected by his friends and disciples. It may have been partly due to this comparative financial insecurity that he was driven to struggle for public recog-nition on a larger scale. His tenacious striving for a lecturership at the University of Vienna, as well as his constant endeavours to obtain an honorary doctor's degree from any academic body may have been prompted largely by financial considerations.[1] However, these efforts may also have been a naïve expression of his lifelong desire for intellectual distinction.

When Bruckner took up his appointment on 1st October 1868 his professional and financial position seemed secure enough. As Sechter's official successor he became professor of thorough-bass, counterpoint and organ at the conservatory (under Hellmesberger's

[1] In the early 1880s Bruckner tried repeatedly to obtain a Mus.D. degree from British and American universities. The strange affairs in connection with his appetite for academic titles are amusingly described by F. Klose (see Bibliography), pp. 114 ff.

directorship) with an annual salary of 800 fl., which was soon augmented by a further 240 fl. The duties involved were sixteen hours'
teaching per week. Through Herbeck's good offices he also received
a stipend of 500 fl. from the Ministry of Education. Herbeck further
succeeded in securing him at least a foothold in the imperial court
chapel. On 9th September 1868, while Bruckner was still at Linz,
he received the appointment of organist-designate at the chapel.
This post, however, was merely honorary, and Bruckner only
deputized for Pius Richter, the holder of the full appointment. In
return he was permitted to bear the title of *k.k. Hoforganist*. He was not
a success at the court chapel, was but rarely asked to assist on great
occasions and still less often was he given an opportunity to show his
art of improvising. The emperor and his family alone expressly
invited him to play at private festival occasions. As an organist he
was dogged by further misfortune. In 1877 he applied in vain for
the post of conductor at the church 'am Hof'; also, he had to wait
fully ten years as unpaid *Expektant* before, in 1878, he was at last made
a proper member of the court chapel, with an annual salary of 800 fl.
Even then his opportunities for a worthy display of his faculties as an
executant remained disappointingly rare.

To improve his financial position Bruckner accepted a further
appointment as piano teacher at the seminary for women teachers,
St Anna, with 500 fl. a year. His annual income in 1871 was therefore in the neighbourhood of 2,080 fl., but unfortunately it tended to
fluctuate. In St Anna Bruckner suffered from singularly bad luck.
He became involved in a disciplinary action following a denunciation
by two women students who alleged they had been insulted by him.
It seems likely that his rough peasant dialect and rural manner
had caused a regrettable misunderstanding, but the composer was
harassed for weeks, pilloried in the Viennese gutter press—although
his innocence was soon established—and was finally transferred to
the male section of the seminary with a severe drop in his income.
In 1874 he lost that position altogether because the post itself was
scrapped for reasons of general economy. In consequence he had to
borrow money with interest, and to restart his frantic efforts to obtain
an appointment outside Austria.

Once he was definitely installed in the capital, Bruckner also renewed his application of 1867 for a university appointment. He started to launch petitions again in 1874, but it took nearly two years until at last he secured from the Ministry of Education an appointment as unpaid lecturer in harmony and counterpoint at Vienna University. His formidable opponent in this case was Hanslick. Originally the powerful critic had been quite friendly towards Bruckner, and had even hailed the Mass in F (first performed under Bruckner's direction in the Augustinian Church in 1872) as a masterpiece. Of Bruckner's academic ability, however, he had no high opinion, and said so in a rather venomous official letter to the ministry. But thanks to Minister von Stremayr's sympathy for Bruckner, which was evidently shared by the faculty, Hanslick was finally overruled. The appointment was a great and lasting success despite the lecturer's rather unacademic mode of speech and free and easy manners. Bruckner soon became a truly popular figure among the undergraduates. He seems to have begun his lectures on 24th April 1876, although there is no absolute certainty about the date. Late in 1880, after many applications and memoranda, the ministry consented to pay him a paltry annual salary of 800 fl. for his academic work, in acknowledgment of which he dedicated his fifth Symphony to Stremayr. Harmony and counterpoint were discoursed on by him at his lectures in a thoroughly systematic if popular manner, with occasional illustrations at the piano.

The monotonous regularity of Bruckner's life in Vienna was agreeably interrupted by frequent journeys, suggested by Herbeck, who was anxious that Bruckner's prowess as an organist should not be allowed to rust. The earlier journey to Nancy (April 1869), where Bruckner created a sensation at the organ of the new church of Saint-Epvre, seems to have originated in a suggestion of Hanslick's. Bruckner was duly invited to Paris, to play on the organ of Notre-Dame. The French press was enthusiastic, and so were the organ-building firms of Cavaillé-Coll and of Merklin-Schütze, whose new instruments Bruckner had put on the map by his improvisations. He met César Franck, Saint-Saëns, Gounod and even the aged Auber on that occasion and appears to have made a lasting impression.

His subsequent journey to England (August 1871) he undertook as official delegate of the Vienna Chamber of Commerce, and participant in an international organ competition on the new instrument just installed in the Albert Hall. Bruckner's first recital was set down for 2nd August 1871. Its programme is worth reproducing as clearly showing his strong points as well as his limitations as an organist:

Programme of the Music

To be performed

On the Organ in The Royal Albert Hall

By Herr Bruckner, Court Organist at Vienna (First Appearance)

On Wednesday, August 2nd, at Twelve O'Clock

1. Toccata (in F major) . . . . *Bach*
2. Improvisation upon the foregoing.
3. Fugue (in D minor) . . . . *Handel*
4. Improvisation (Original).
5. Improvisation on Fugue (in E major) . . *Bach*
6. Improvisation on English melodies.

Herr Bruckner's strong points are Classical Improvisations on the works of Handel, Bach, and Mendelssohn.

The English press apparently was less easily satisfied than the French, and the *Musical Standard* made no bones about thinking little of Bruckner's interpretation of Mendelssohn's first Sonata. He seems to have played some of the great organ fugues by Bach, but his improvisation on *God save the Queen* was evidently the highlight of the recital. Plans were hatched for a big concert tour through England, to take place in the following year, but they never materialized. In a letter to his friend Moriz von Mayfeld of Linz, dated 23rd August 1871, and written from Seyd's Hotel, Finsbury Square, London, E.C., Bruckner sums up his London achievements. According to his report he gave six recitals in the Albert Hall and five in the Crystal Palace. He claims to have played at one of these concerts to an audience of 70,000, and expressly mentions that

Manns, the conductor, invited him to come again and to introduce himself as a composer. Nothing remained of this stimulating experience except a permanent nostalgia for England and the feeling —unwarranted, as it was to turn out—that his music would meet there with more appreciation than in his home land. His repeated efforts later on to renew contact with England through diplomatic personalities doubtless re-echo the pleasant memories of August 1871.

In later years journeys to Bayreuth became a kind of fixture in Bruckner's holiday time-tables. He went five times altogether, first in September 1873, when Wagner accepted the dedication of the third Symphony; next in the summer of 1876 for the first performance of the complete *Ring*; then in 1882 on the occasion of the first *Parsifal*. This was the last time he met Wagner, whom he may also have seen during his stay in Vienna in 1877. After Wagner's death Bruckner returned to Bayreuth in 1886, to hear the first Bayreuth *Tristan*. It was then that he played the organ at Liszt's funeral. In the summer of 1892 he paid his last visit—praying long and devoutly at Wagner's grave.

The rest of Bruckner's travels were divided between relaxation and duty. For the former's sake he regularly went to his native Upper Austria, revisiting the monasteries of St Florian and Kremsmünster, where he had intimate friends among the ecclesiastics, and conducting his masses at Linz and Steyr. Journeys undertaken for the sake of his symphonies led him repeatedly to Munich (where No. VII scored a veritable triumph under Hermann Levi in 1885), to Prague (where he played the new organ at the Rudolfinum in 1886), to Berlin (in 1891 and 1894), where Siegfried Ochs gave glorious performances of the *Te Deum*. Only once, in 1880, did Bruckner undertake a purely recreational journey in the manner of Brahms: he went to see the Passion play at Oberammergau and toured Switzerland. Travel slowed down after 1890, and ceased altogether after his last journey to Berlin in January 1894. In his last two years Bruckner was so ill that he could not even attend the first performance of the fifth Symphony at Graz under Franz Schalk's direction (8th April 1894).

Bruckner's relations with his famous musical contemporaries in Vienna continued to remain stiff and uneasy. While he was worshipped by all the young and ardent, such as Hugo Wolf, Gustav

Mahler, Hans Rott and the brothers Schalk, official musical Vienna remained cold and unconvinced to the bitter end. Hanslick's hostility increased in proportion to the growing number of Bruckner's symphonies. He and his henchmen Kalbeck and Dömpke tried for decades to create an unfavourable prejudice in the minds of the Viennese audiences against Bruckner and his music. On the other side much unnecessary bitterness was caused by the provocative behaviour of the Wagner Verein, who championed Bruckner's cause to the intense irritation of Brahms and his clique. Helm, Wolf and a few similar uninfluential critics took up the cudgels for Bruckner, while intelligent connoisseurs like Speidel preferred to sit on the fence. Repeated attempts to establish a better personal contact between Bruckner and Brahms misfired.[1] Hans Richter tried to have the best of both worlds. In later years he conducted many first performances of Bruckner, but in the 1870s his attitude was often insincere. In a letter to W. Tappert, dated 12th October 1877, Bruckner went so far as to call Richter 'the generalissimo of deceit.' The date of this letter is characteristic. Those were the years when Brahms's first three symphonies came out and Richter conducted their first performances. Richter even went to the length of declaring at that time that Wagner's style had no claim to the concert platform, which by right belonged to the composer of classicist outlook (i.e. Brahms). However, Richter's attitude improved considerably after Levi and Nikisch had triumphed with Bruckner's fourth and seventh Symphonies and after Brahms had given up composing symphonies himself. Between 1886 and 1894 Richter conducted the first performances in Vienna of Bruckner's Symphonies I, II, III, IV, VII and VIII, in addition to the first orchestral performance of the *Te Deum*.

With regard to public recognition the tide turns perceptibly after the successes of Symphony VII at Leipzig and Munich, and of the *Te Deum* (1884–5); Bruckner's sixtieth birthday was still no more than a provincial celebration at Vöcklabruck (September 1884), but

[1] As late as 9th February 1885 Bruckner complains of Brahms's 'almost insulting behaviour' towards him. Cf. Briefe, II, No. 147 (see Bibliography). For further details see also the Mahler section of this book, pp. 114–17.

in July 1886 the composer was honoured with the Franz Josef order, together with an increment of 300 fl.

He was also received by the emperor personally,[1] who liked to listen to his organ playing when visiting Ischl, and who later on accepted the dedication of the eighth Symphony. In 1887 Bruckner was created an honorary member of the Dutch Maatschappij tot Bevordering der Toonkunst. Two years later he became an honorary member of the Richard Wagner Verein, and on 30th October 1891 the Upper Austrian diet voted him an honorary stipend of 400 fl. At last, on 4th July 1891, the University of Vienna bestowed an honorary doctorate in philosophy on Bruckner—a much-coveted prize, won only after years of subtle wire-pulling and of sundry plots and counterplots.

It was on the occasion of the official drinking-bout held in Bruckner's honour by the Akademische Gesangverein on 11th December 1891 that the then Rector Magnificus of the university, the famous physicist Exner, addressed the new Ph.D. in these memorable words:

... Where science has to call a halt, where insurmountable barriers bar its progress, there the realm of art begins which is capable of expressing those experiences from which knowledge remains excluded. Thus I, the Rector Magnificus of Vienna University, pay humble homage to the former assistant teacher of Windhaag. ...

This address marks the climax of Bruckner's official career. Actually, these tardy signs of public recognition did not come a moment too soon. Since 1890 Bruckner had been a sick man. In the spring of that year he suffered from a chronic catarrh of the larynx, besides displaying features of an abnormal nervous condition in general. In the autumn of the same year he was relieved of his duties as organ professor at the Conservatory, and on 15th January 1891 he retired as professor emeritus of that institution. In the following year he left the service of the imperial court chapel; in 1893 he became an honorary member of the Gesellschaft der Musikfreunde. In that year also he completed his last secular composition: the symphonic

[1] The story goes that on the occasion of this audience Bruckner tried to enlist the emperor's help against Hanslick's intrigues.

23

chorus *Helgoland*, which followed hard on Psalm CL, and the first two movements of Symphony IX. Between the completion of *Helgoland* and its first performance in Vienna on 9th October 1893 he fell gravely ill with dropsy, and so poor was his condition considered to be by the end of that year that his will was made on 10th November 1893. His physical strength was progressively sapped by the exhausting labours of revision and publication of his masses and symphonies. It seems like a miracle that the ailing man could summon up courage and energy to continue with the composition of Symphony IX, the *Adagio* of which was tackled in 1894.

Surprisingly, Bruckner rallied once more, and early in 1894 even went to Berlin, in Hugo Wolf's company, where Symphony VII, the *Te Deum* and the string Quintet were performed with enthusiastic and general acclamation. If he was too ill to travel to Graz for the first performance of Symphony V on 8th April of that year, he was well enough to celebrate his seventieth birthday at Steyr among friends and fellow countrymen who took the opportunity of presenting him with the freedom of Linz. His last lecture at the university was given on 5th November 1894. He had resumed his academic activity only a week earlier and now had to give it up altogether. He was evidently sinking fast. Yet, undaunted by the shadows of approaching death, he completed the glorious *Adagio* of Symphony IX on 30th November 1894, starting the finale in December.

The Ministry of Education and the emperor evidently tried to alleviate Bruckner's personal situation, now sadly aggravated by his growing physical disabilities. In addition to a subsidy of 150 fl. he received in 1895 a donation of 600 fl. The emperor also offered him free lodging at the palace of Belvedere in the so-called *Kustoden-Stöckel*. Bruckner moved into this pleasant abode—surrounded by a lovely public garden—in July 1895, giving up his old flat at Hessgasse 7, where he had lived, high up on the fourth floor, by candlelight and in scant comfort, ever since 1879, looked after by his faithful housekeeper, Kathi Kachelmeyer. Throughout 1895–6 Bruckner worked fitfully on the finale of Symphony IX. On 12th January 1896 he heard his own music for the last time: it was his favourite work, the *Te Deum*.

ST FLORIAN: THE COLLEGIATE CHURCH
(By courtesy of Universal Edition, Vienna-London)

The Final Years—Illness and Death

During the last months his friends and disciples noticed a sinister change in Bruckner's mental condition. He grew apathetic about the fate of his works (except Symphony IX), and pathological obsessions, as in the cases of his earlier breakdowns of 1867 and 1887, began to cloud his mind. The spectre of religious mania lurked in the background. Neither Franz Schalk nor Hugo Wolf could conduct a rational conversation with him during those final weeks. A pupil who brought him flowers heard him murmur distinctly: 'Alone—quite alone—no music any more. . . .' This seems to indicate that Bruckner must have had moments of complete mental clarity, and that his condition must have been subject to tidal fluctuations. The flame of musical creation flickered until the very last day.

Bruckner died in the afternoon of 11th October 1896, after a walk in the park, having worked at the finale of Symphony IX in the morning hours. The funeral ceremony on 14th October took place in the Karlskirche, near the Grosse Musikvereinssaal, in which so many of his symphonies had had their first performance. It was an impressive ceremony, attended *inter alia* by the ailing Brahms, doomed to follow Bruckner into the grave in barely six months. Bruckner's faithful friend and admirer Hugo Wolf was not admitted, as he failed to produce the necessary invitation by ticket.

As early as 1893 Bruckner had obtained permission from the prior of St Florian for the interment of his mortal remains in the church of the monastery with which he had been so closely connected. That permission was granted only after the opposition of some of the prebendaries, who evidently resented the burial of a layman within the precincts of their church, had been overcome. Bruckner's remains were duly transferred to St Florian. There his coffin rests under the great organ which had once been the prime source and fountain of his musical inspiration.

CHAPTER V

BRUCKNER must have cut a strange figure: ambling along, as in a day-dream, on the populous boulevard-like pavements of the elegant, new-built Ringstrasse with its brand-new Parisian opera-house of 1868, both the visual symbols of Vienna's irrepressible gaiety, frivolity and sensuousness, even after the recent defeat of Sadowa. . . . A stockily built figure, carrying an imperious head on broad peasant's shoulders; a profile whose aquiline nose recalled a Roman emperor rather than a provincial organist from the backwoods of Upper Austria; clad in garments of strangely old-fashioned cut, black, with short, baggy trousers of grotesque width (apt trouser-legs for one contending with organ pedals); with a broad-brimmed slouch-hat (instead of the customary topper) and with a huge red, tobacco-stained handkerchief flapping from one of the bulging coat-pockets; in his hand the inevitable snuff-box (in place of the customary elongated 'Virginia' cigar); close-shaven (save for a ridiculously small suggestion of a moustache right under the nose) and the hair closely cropped (instead of the flowing locks and picturesque beard worn by artists and intellectuals); the mighty profile with the Roman nose and the deep-seated eyes expressing at once childish surprise and, as it were, a permanent silent quest. . . .

In the sparkling turbulence of the Vienna of Johann Strauss waltzes and decorative boulevards built in mock-Renaissance style, the appearance of Anton Bruckner must have struck the casual observer as a picture of typically provincial maladjustment. In fact Bruckner's appearance, so ill matched with its surroundings, was but the external side of his character's stubborn conservatism. Born of peasant stock, if not actually of peasants, he remained rustic at heart and in social behaviour. He clung to the usages and manners of his youth, and never overcame the servility of his early days. Yielding to intellectual pupils and fashionable conductors in practical details, he refused to be deflected from the preordained groove of his humble beginnings. Although the artist in him was elevated into the rarefied atmosphere of the later symphonies, the man continued to live, to pray, to write letters, and to speak in the vernacular as in the far-off days of his youth. It is possible that the frivolous atmosphere of the Vienna of *Die Fledermaus* and *The Gipsy Baron* stirred his deep-seated if inarticulate powers of resistance. Bruckner remained an un-assimilable 'original,' a slightly ridiculous outsider, considered almost a simpleton by casual acquaintances.

In an attempt to assess his character one is struck at once by its paradoxical nature. A sturdy peasant body with a healthy appetite for country fare and good Pilsen beer, a naïve joy in the simple pleasures of native dance and song, an iron constitution able to withstand years of poverty, ill-paid teaching jobs and even the grim austerities of Sechter's counterpoint—that is one side of him. A delicate, nervous sensibility (visible in his beautiful hands with their long tapering fingers) always threatening to disturb the balance of his mind; a firmly rooted piety and love of God; a sincere, almost fanatical attachment to the Roman Catholic creed and ritual; and lastly the indisputable fact of his innumerable affairs of the heart, continuing until well past his seventieth year—that is the other.

The paradox may perhaps best be explained in the idiom of his younger fellow countryman, Siegmund Freud: his is a case of sexual inferiority complex, in need of powerful compensatory satisfactions. Indeed, the peculiarities of Bruckner's psychology and the entanglements of his emotional life can all be traced back to that cause.

Throughout the earlier part of his life Bruckner's instinctive craving for fatherly protection may be easily observed. It was in fact one of the most powerful though carefully hidden agencies of his life. The boy of thirteen, bereft of paternal protection with tragic suddenness, found it first in his cousin, J. B. Weiss. But not till he went to Linz did he find the supreme father-figure and protector, Bishop Rudigier, under whose stern benevolence the shy and diffident organist began to unfold his wings. Only at the very end of this period did the Bishop of Linz, who inspired Bruckner's composition and actively supported his studies under Sechter, have to yield his spiritual influence to the master of Bayreuth and to the director of the Vienna Opera, who both succeeded in secularizing Bruckner's approach to life and art, while still satisfying his lifelong craving for powerful fatherly guidance. In the end Bruckner cut himself loose from the bondage of an unduly protracted father-attachment, leaving the protective sphere of the Church and transplanting himself into the metropolitan soil of Vienna. The eventual loss of his two secular protector-figures, Wagner and Herbeck, at last made Bruckner spiritually independent at the ripe age of sixty. But he often felt lost in the hostile wilderness of the capital, and the craving for fatherly protection never left him completely.

Bruckner was far from being the deliberate celibatarian some of his more mawkish biographers have tried to make of him. If he had remained chaste throughout life, of which we have no proof whatever, then continence would have been forced on him by a certain in-sufficiency in his relations with women rather than by religious vows. My own conviction is that celibacy was the outcome of his dis-appointments with the fair sex, not of a moral principle. That he was throughout his life strongly attracted by women and harboured a deep desire for the sexual consummation of love is proved not only by the opinions and reports of his pupils and friends, but by the events of his life. He fell continuously in and out of love, the objects of his infatuation being invariably young girls under twenty. It was in the first place physical attraction that prompted him to press his suit, and induced a man well past fifty to attend all the customary dance entertainments of Vienna, dancing innumerable polkas, waltzes and quadrilles with young ladies in and out of fancy dress.

In his diary two antithetical forces in him can be seen in head-on clash. The same diaries in which he conscientiously lists how many quadrilles he has danced with a certain young lady at the annual *Concordiaball*, contain strange abbreviations of repeated A's and V's, often heavily underscored, standing for the daily number of 'Ave Maria's' and 'Pater nosters' (*Vater unser*) he had prayed.[1] Un-doubtedly there is a psychological link between his unsuccessful love affairs and the strangely fanatical side of his religious worship.

[1] A fascimile of one page of the diaries is shown by M. Auer (see Biblio-graphy, 1934), opposite p. 289.

The Roots of his Inferiority Complex

That Bruckner was singularly unsuccessful with women is a well-known fact. A spate of clumsy letters exists with pathetic suggestions of marriage. He seems to have been unattractive to the fair sex, especially to pretty young girls who could not take seriously this prematurely old-looking man of indeterminate age whose methods of courtship aroused their mirth or their rage.[1] Yet he never learnt, and his entanglements became an ever-recurrent part of his life and an object of good-natured raillery on the part of his friends. Late in life, when he was nearly seventy, he fell into the trap of a wily chamber-maid at a Berlin hotel who succeeded in extorting a promise of marriage from him, and to whom he actually became engaged for an afternoon. He had to be extricated from her clutches by Siegfried Ochs, who manfully undertook the distasteful task of buying off the would-be bride with a considerable sum. Bruckner's undaunted hope of marriage during lifelong years of bachelorhood curiously resembles the case of his great adversary Brahms, who also remained unmarried and yet so strangely expectant of late matrimonial bliss up to the end of his days. The cry for human companionship, the pain of isolation and solitude, resound through all the length of Bruckner's correspondence. Not yet thirty, he writes from St Florian to a friend: '. . . I sit always poor and forsaken and deeply melancholy in my little room. . . .'

The unsuccessful struggle for a loving mate, the thwarted attempts to obtain emotional satisfaction, are coupled with a striving for perfection in his art and for recognition as a musician. Yet that striving for artistic perfection only led to a deeper insight into musical matters, and thus to a self-dissatisfaction that drove him to seek training in the skill of counterpoint. What it never led to was a broadening of his mental horizon. Intellectually Bruckner remained the little assistant teacher up to the last day of his life, never acquiring new points of view, never developing an interest in anything beyond the spheres of music and religion. He was unaffected to the last by literature, poetry, philosophy, science and politics. The galaxy of Vienna's theatres held no lure for him, nor did the bookshops and

[1] To one of his sweethearts Bruckner gave a prayer-book as a present. It was flung down the stairs in contempt.

29

well-stocked libraries of the metropolis. The narrow circle of his interest was drawn pitifully tight. In the place of intellectual penetration into other spheres of human interest or artistic hobbies Bruckner pursued certain manias, recurring cyclically and indicative of the great nervous strain under which he intermittently laboured. He had several serious nervous breakdowns, two of which at least (the collapse of 1867 and his mental condition during the last two years of his life) brought him in tidal waves near the brink of insanity. Minor periodic recurrences may also be traced in between, the worst of them perhaps occurring in the years 1887–9 under the impact of the shock caused by Hermann Levi's refusal to accept the original draft of Symphony VIII for performance.

Bruckner's symptoms in each of these cases were similar. They might be divided into a harmless and a clearly pathological phase. In the first group may be classed the fascination exercised by H. von Payer and his polar expedition as well as by the fate of the Emperor Maximilian of Mexico. Bruckner was avid for any information he could obtain on these two famous Austrians, and he became a voracious reader of books on polar expeditions and on Mexico's troubled history. The pathological side is represented by his unhealthy interest in corpses and by his obsessional urge to count windows, weathercocks, church crosses, dots, buttons and ornamental figures. How closely both these groups of obsessions were interlinked is proved by a letter written shortly after his breakdown of 1867 and referring to his 'pet,' the recently executed Emperor of Mexico, whose body had just been brought back to Austria:

. . . Even during my illness this was the only thing that was dear to my heart: it was Mexico, Maximilian. I'd give anything in the world to see the body of Maximilian. Be so kind, dear Weinwurm,[1] as to dispatch a completely trustworthy person into the imperial palace; perhaps best inquire at the office of the Imperial Chamberlain, if the body of Maximilian is likely to be on view (i.e. open in a coffin or visible in a glass frame), or if only the closed coffin will be visible. Please, inform me kindly by telegram, so that I may not come too late. . . .

---

[1] Rudolf Weinwurm (1835–1911), an intimate friend of Bruckner's and a distinguished musical educationalist and choral conductor.

Bruckner's veneration for Beethoven led to a similar excess when he insisted on witnessing the exhumation of Beethoven's remains (to be transferred to another grave) and when he inspected them so closely that he lost a glass out of his pince-nez in that act of morbid curiosity.

The mania of counting inanimate objects was really a mania of repetition, i.e. a musical obsession, comparable to Schumann's obsession with certain rhythmic patterns.[1] This repetition-mania, which finds its creative reflex in Bruckner's predilection for a frenzied repetition of short motives (e.g. the five-note motive propelling the scherzo of Symphony VIII), is particularly evident in the sphere of religious worship. Mention has already been made of Bruckner's diaries, keeping a day-to-day account of the nature and number of his prayers. A friend relates how Bruckner, praying with him at the open bier of his late friend Traumihler, the *regens chori* of St Florian, repeated the words 'Thy will be done' nine times and how he recited in a loud voice the prayer 'Our Father which art in Heaven' five times in succession. In moments of a more than usually troubled mental and spiritual condition (as, for instance, in the years 1887–9) the obsession with repetition and focusing morbid attention on the number and character of inanimate ornamental objects refused to be canalized into the purely musical or religious sphere alone. It began to inundate his everyday life, threatening his reason, as may be gathered from the following typical letter of 12th August 1889 to his later biographer, A. Göllerich:

Excuse me, one more request: I'd so very much like to know the material from which the two pointed finials above the cupola of the two municipal towers . . . are made. Next to the cupola is (*a*) the pommel: then (*b*) the weathercock with ornament, isn't it? then . . . (*c*) a cross ?? and a lightning conductor, or what else? Is there a cross?

What is on the tower of the Catholic church? I believe only a weather-cock without a cross?

Many apologies, and many thanks in advance. Please, write it all down; in the autumn I shall ask for clarification. . . .

---

[1] 'The walrus and the carpenter' rhythm in the first movement of Symphony I or the finale of the *Études symphoniques*, for instance.

The mania for counting and adding up figures is probably co-responsible with Bruckner's lifelong habit of counting through every composition, numbering each bar and even indicating the general harmonic trend after each stave through so-called 'directs' at the turn of each page. Bruckner's pedantic insistence on counting every bar may also be responsible for his clinging to the rigours of 4+4-bar periods and for his partiality for rather stiff regularities of periodization—a tendency that brought him sometimes dangerously near to rhythmic monotony and to a structural four-squareness comparing unfavourably with the rhythmic flexibility of the Viennese classics.[1]

That adding up figures, maniacal repetition in every department of life and a morbid interest in inanimate objects may have played a kind of compensatory part in Bruckner's emotional life in which the spheres of sexual satisfaction and of intellectual pursuit (outside the sphere of musical creation) remained severely undernourished, is also borne out by his strange craving for examinations. He passed no less than nine major ones, insisting on written testimonials in each case, and celebrating every one as a major event. The urge for repetition was equally strong in the case of his evident craving for self-assertion and self-confirmation, obviously being under constant threat from the permanent undercurrent of his lifelong inferiority complex. Taking all this into account, one is bound to come to the conclusion that at times Bruckner's reason must have been threatened as much as Schumann's or Wolf's. What saved him was his emotional attachment to the Church and his music, which enabled him after 1863 to objectify his obsessions and internal conflicts in creations of overpowering eloquence.

This character sketch would remain sadly incomplete if it did not include a few words on Bruckner as a musical executant and as a theorist. Although he studied the piano and the violin with Kattinger and Gruber at St Florian, it is chiefly as an organist that posterity remembers him. It is very difficult to form a conclusive

[1] F. Klose (see Bibliography), pp. 55 ff., was aware of that deficiency of Bruckner's, which he believed to be typically Teutonic. It is certainly also noticeable in Wagner's style.

opinion on that particular side of his musical activity. Reports on his playing and on the degree of his technical proficiency vary greatly. There is no tangible clue to his organ style. Like Palestrina, Hof-haimer, Schütz and Fux before him, he never composed seriously for the instrument. This is all the more remarkable as he seems to have relied more on his powers of improvisation than on a concert repertory based on Bach and Mendelssohn. That he must have shown remarkable powers as an improviser, especially on given fugue subjects, is proved by the sensational results at the competition in Linz cathedral on 25th January 1856, and also later on at the final examination in Vienna on 19th November 1861. His successes as an organist in France and England (1869–71) are undeniable. How-ever, even the disparaging reports of the London press seem to indicate that his free fugal improvisations were more appreciated than his rendering of an organ sonata by Mendelssohn.

There is ample documentary evidence for the fact that Bruckner studied Bach, but little to show that he became deeply affected by Bach's organ music or that Bach meant to him as much as Palestrina and Gallus. It is also a fact that his appointment as one of the organists of the imperial court chapel was not successful. He seems to have lacked skill in the accompaniment of singers and orchestras, and Liszt complained of his dragging accompaniment on the occasion of the performance of one of his oratorios. His superior at the court chapel also curbed his inclination for free improvisation, which could have expanded more freely in the Lutheran service. How much Bruckner as organist must have left to chance and to the inspiration of the happy moment emerges even from the full scores of his masses, in which no separate organ part is included, although it is known through the testimonies of Wöss and Ochs that Bruckner himself played the organ in a later performance of the Mass in E minor, and evidently expected it to be employed in the F minor Mass also. That professional critics occasionally had a poor opinion of him as an organist transpires from R. Heuberger's obituary of Bruckner.[1] On the other hand it is undeniable that the organ as such—especially

---

[1] *Neue Freie Presse,* Vienna, 13th October 1896.

a mighty specimen such as Krismann's organ at St Florian—left its indelible imprint on his musical imagination. Perhaps Bruckner's symphonic style and his peculiar orchestral lay-out would never have become so organistic and so strongly flavoured with the atmosphere and the dynamism of the organ if he had attempted to compose for the instrument of his choice as Bach did before him and Reger after him.

Neither as a pianist of rather old-fashioned technical habits nor as a violinist did Bruckner seem to have been more than an average performer. As a vocalist he acquired some useful experience when he became a member of the *Liedertafel* 'Frohsinn.'

He was only moderately successful as a choral and orchestral conductor. Although he did not do too badly when conducting his men's chorus at the festivals of Krems and Nuremberg, friend and foe agreed that the first performances of some of his symphonies suffered rather under his erratic baton.

If Bruckner's performing talents were not always equal to the occasion and certainly vastly inferior to his creative genius, his educational powers must have been considerable. As a teacher he was splendidly equipped. None of the great composers of his century can boast of such a thorough contrapuntal training, none of them had laid so firmly the foundation for later imparting knowledge to others. Although he was not happy at the seminary of St Anna, and seems to have clashed occasionally with his colleagues at the Conservatory, he certainly enjoyed tremendous popularity as a lecturer at the university, and was worshipped by his private pupils. One cannot speak of a Bruckner school in the sense in which Liszt created a tradition of pianism or Arnold Schoenberg a school of composers. Bruckner was too one-track minded as a composer, too little interested in musical problems outside the limited world of his own artistic experiences; but he could boast of a formidable array of fine musicians who proudly hailed him as their mentor. Among them were the conductors Franz Schalk and Ferdinand Löwe, the musicographer A. Göllerich, the theorist Heinrich Schenker, the composer F. Klose, the writers E. Decsey and F. Eckstein.[1]

[1] E. Decsey (see Bibliography), pp. 67 ff., enumerates more: among them the composers Camillo Horn and Cyrill Hynais, the conductors

Teacher and Pupils

It is also a remarkable fact that the gist of Bruckner's teaching has been preserved in several formidable publications by F. Klose (1927), E. Eckstein (1923) and E. Schwanzara (1950). The last-named reproduced the complete script of several university lecture courses on harmony and counterpoint, held by Bruckner in the early 1890s and regularly attended by the editor. They all agree that Bruckner as musical theorist accepted Sechter's Rameau-inspired doctrine of the fundamental bass (which is made to accompany any modulation in a silent chain of falling fifths) as 'Holy Writ,' and that he reproduced it in a very original simplification during his lectures. Sechter's chief publication of 1853 (*Die Grundsätze der musikalischen Komposition*), as well as his unpublished but preserved manuscript on counterpoint, remained throughout his life the basis for theoretical teaching. They also agree on the incompatibility of Sechter's scholasticism with Bruckner's own free composition and on the uselessness of Sechter's fundamental theory for a relevant analytical approach to the chromaticized harmony of Liszt, Wagner and, indeed, Bruckner himself. They all finally testify that Bruckner studiously refrained from teaching 'free composition' (just as Sechter had banished it from Bruckner's own curriculum) and that he never quoted an example from his own works. Bruckner's teaching (especially on the subject of harmony) seems to have resulted in excellent if at times fussy part-writing, and in a deeper understanding of the intricacies of canon and fugue. It evidently never aimed at raising young, experimentally minded composers with creative ideas of their own, as Schoenberg later on so brilliantly succeeded in doing. Bruckner the teacher was concerned with fundamentals only, with elementary problems of musical combination, not with their application in the struggle for individual artistic creation in an individual musical idiom.

Krzyzanowski, Marschner, Mottl and Nikisch, and the pianist Emil Paur. To these should be added Hans Rott (cf. Mahler section of this book). Mahler himself does not strictly belong to Bruckner's personal pupils.

CHAPTER VI

THE COMPOSER AND HIS CENTURY

ANTON BRUCKNER is undoubtedly the most considerable composer of symphonies and of music for the Roman Church emerging after Beethoven and Schubert, and sharing their national, cultural and religious environment. Yet his general recognition was so long delayed that his claim to eminence in those two special fields is still contested outside the German-speaking communities. Although only thirteen years younger than Liszt and less than nine years older than Brahms, Bruckner did not begin to make an impact on his contemporary world till the later 1870s, when Liszt's creative work was all but completed, and when Brahms had firmly established himself as the leading instrumental composer in the classical tradition. The chief reasons for this belated emergence of Bruckner as a front-rank composer may be found in the peculiarities of his personal character, in the circumstances of his musical development and also in certain stylistic features of his music. Both the man and his work are at odds with the typical musician of the later nineteenth century. In time Bruckner belongs to the generation of sophisticated and in-tellectually alert composers anticipated by Berlioz, Mendelssohn and Schumann, and culminating in Liszt and Wagner, but compared with these brilliant contemporaries he appears like a throw-back into an earlier phase of musical development. He has but little in common with the average romantic composer of his century, although many critics continue to classify him as such.

In an epoch of profuse song composition he hardly wrote more than a few lyrical trifles of no artistic value. Nor did he seem to share the delight of the romantics in the various branches of chamber music. He remained totally unaffected by Liszt's fertilizing idea of the one-movement symphonic poem, and Wagner's music-drama affected him only as a new world of sound, for it remains doubtful whether the poetic and philosophical side of Wagner's art ever became intelligible to him. Like his antagonist Brahms, Bruckner never seriously contemplated the composition of an opera. On the other hand, Bruckner is perhaps the only great composer of his century whose entire musical output is determined by his religious faith.[1] Also, there are very few composers of his time who received a contrapuntal training of such excessive thoroughness as Bruckner's six long years of musical apprenticeship under Simon Sechter (1855–61). Finally, with the sole exception of Max Reger, Bruckner is the only German-speaking composer of importance in his century to become a universally acknowledged virtuoso on the organ. With all these features Bruckner's artistic personality seems to link him with the age of the Renaissance and the Baroque era rather than with the epoch of Liszt and Wagner.

If we compare Bruckner with great composers of the past, we come upon some significant parallels. His lifelong devotion to the theoretical concepts of Sechter reminds one of the manner in which Bach's educational precepts were canonized by some of his pupils. In his stubborn insistence on a thorough theoretical training, as well as in his ability to integrate archaic processes into the progressive idiom of his own mature music, he resembles Schütz, with whom he also shares two further peculiarities: a late start as a professional composer and the absence of any work for the instrument of his choice—the organ.

Although Bruckner's earliest essay in composition dates from 1836, when he was barely twelve, and his first four-part Mass was composed as early as 1844, he is a very late starter in large-scale composition. The first work which fully revealed his artistic personality, the Mass in D minor, was written at the age of forty. A veritable chasm separates the numerous compositions of his youthful years from the works composed in 1863–4 and after. It is almost impossible to detect an evolutionary link between these early essays in provincial church music, interspersed with occasional secular partsongs of very

[1] The nearest resemblance may be found in César Franck, although he had a more developed worldly side, especially as a composer of unsuccessful operas.

limited literary ambition, and the eleven symphonies and five large-scale church compositions which constitute the core of his later output.

Bruckner's really important compositions may be easily divided into two main sections: vocal music for the church and instrumental music for the concert-room. Of the former all but two that matter (the *Te Deum* of 1881-4 and Psalm CL of 1892) were composed before the removal to Vienna. Of the latter all but two (*Studien-symphonie* in F minor and Symphony I [Linz version]) were written during the Vienna period (if not always in the Austrian capital itself). A later chapter will reveal the high degree of affinity and interdependence between these two categories, which express an identical basic experience on different planes of artistic expression and through different albeit closely related media of sound.

That Bruckner should have focused his main creative energies on a monumental conception of the symphonic mass and simultaneously on a type of monumental symphony, at a time when both were at a discount in Central Europe, is surely one of the strangest aspects of his artistic career and the one chiefly responsible for the slowness of general recognition accorded to him. The symphonic mass of Bruckner's conception, modelled on Beethoven's *Missa solemnis* and on Cherubini's Mass in C (1816),[1] but also cross-fertilized by the masses of Palestrina, Gallus (Handl), Caldara, Fux and others, was as much contrary to the *Zeitgeist* as his monumentalized symphonic type. Masses accompanied by an orchestra of symphonic dimensions were becoming increasingly unpopular after the Caecilienverein had been founded in 1867, whose main *raison d'être* was the restitution of plainsong and the exclusion of orchestral accompaniments in the music for the Roman service, enforced in 1903 by the *Motu proprio* of Pius X. The great symphony of Beethoven's and Schubert's conception was practically dead and buried when Bruckner emerged as a symphonist at the turn of 1863-4. Wagner in his theoretical writings had declared the species extinct, and Mendelssohn's and Schumann's 'monumentalized' chamber music [2] could only confirm Wagner's

[1] Of this work a copy in Bruckner's hand exists in the Vienna National Library; cf. R. Haas (see Bibliography, 1934), p. 34.

[2] Paul Bekker, *Die Symphonie von Beethoven bis Mahler*, Berlin, 1918.

conviction. Liszt's and Berlioz's ambitious symphonic canvases differed from the classical symphony by virtue of their programmatic affiliations, and none of Brahms's symphonies had yet been written. There seemed to be no place for symphonic music of a Beethovenian stature, a circumstance which may explain the reluctant attitude publishers displayed towards Bruckner until the late 1880s. When at last Brahms's symphonies were published between 1874 and 1886 their obvious stylistic connection with the restricted romantic type of Mendelssohn and Schumann, as well as the serenade-like character of their middle movements, made it easy for audiences to associate them with the music of the early nineteenth century. Bruckner's symphonies, on the other hand, appeared like anachronistic monstrosities: Brahms in one of his least generous moods called them 'symphonic boa constrictors.'

Despite isolated successes, Bruckner's large-scale works made but little headway in the general esteem as long as the music remained in manuscript. By January 1885 only two main works—Symphony III (second version) and the string Quintet (1879)—had become available in print, and the majority of the symphonies and masses were published only from about 1890 onwards. Even at the time of Bruckner's death two symphonies were still unpublished and unperformed. It is thus not difficult to understand that a fair assessment of Bruckner's music seemed an impossible task even for the sympathetic student to undertake in the composer's lifetime. This peculiar situation also goes a long way to explain why a more general popularization of Bruckner had to wait until the twentieth century, and why his music failed to affect the minds of younger generations until long after his death.

CHAPTER VII

THE TEXTUAL PROBLEM

ANY approach to Bruckner's music, any attempt to assess its merits and to reach an authentic standard of interpretation has been immeasurably complicated by the gradual publication since 1934 of the so-called *Originalfassungen* (original versions, O.V.[1]) of Symphonies I–IX, and of the great Masses, based on the autograph scores which Bruckner bequeathed to the National Library in Vienna. His will stipulated that these manuscripts should be put at the disposal of the firm of J. Eberle & Co., which later became amalgamated with the Universal Edition, Bruckner's exclusive publishers from 1909 to 1931. The heated arguments aroused some twenty years ago by the question of 'O.V. versus R.V.' and their respective authenticity have been continued ever since, to the embarrassment of conductors, musicologists and biographers who have tried to establish contact between Bruckner's music and the public. The case is unique in musical history, and therefore of special interest in so far as Bruckner seems to have been the only major composer whose scores, though published during his lifetime, do not necessarily represent his ultimate artistic convictions. The question uppermost in the mind of any performer is simply whether O.V. or R.V. represents the truly authentic version. The answer, which unfortunately is far from simple, is formulated on the following pages.

The composition of a symphony or a mass was usually a painfully long process for Bruckner, sometimes taking as much as fifteen or twenty years, and involving nearly every work in repeated revisions

---

[1] This is the correct expression, not *Urfassung*, as used in many German text-books as a somewhat misleading and imprecise term. The abbreviations O.V. and R.V. will be used hereafter for original and revised versions.

BRUCKNER IN HIS FORTIES
(*By courtesy of Universal Edition, Vienna-London*)

and transformations. This laborious striving after perfection was due as much to Bruckner's hesitancy and lack of faith in his own powers, confirmed by the often unduly critical and cavilling attitude of his fellow musicians, as to the well-intentioned suggestions of his first conductors and his own disciples, who were anxious to secure an easier passage for these lengthy and unusually difficult works. This dual psychological pressure from outside produced an abnormally self-critical attitude in him and made him yield only too willingly to the wishes of his early interpreters. The situation was aggravated by the fact that some of the symphonies (i.e. I, II, III—second published version—IV, V and VIII) and the three great Masses were published (in ' revised versions') only during the last six years of his life, when, constantly ailing and heavily preoccupied with his titanic struggle with the finale of Symphony IX, he was neither inclined to nor indeed capable of supervising the processes of printing and publication.

However, two characteristic reactions of Bruckner's to these revisions shed some light on the curiously roundabout way in which his mind worked. In the case of Symphony VIII (first published and performed in 1892) he wrote to Weingartner, who intended to perform the work at Mannheim in 1891, but had to give up the idea because of his sudden appointment to Berlin:

Please apply radical cuts to the finale, as indicated; for it would be much too long and is valid only for a later age and especially for a circle of friends and cognoscenti. . . .

Yet in his very next letter to Weingartner the composer adds, a trifle anxiously:

Please arrange everything to the liking of your orchestra; however, I beg you not to alter the score; also in the case of publication to leave the orchestral parts unaltered.

It seems pretty clear from the foregoing that Bruckner hoped to publish the eighth Symphony later on in accordance with his autograph score rather than in a revision. Such alterations and cuts as he sanctioned were intended merely to ease the initial difficulties encountered by conductors and orchestras. At the same time it is undeniable that he was always ready for any temporary concession that seemed expedient. Even more ambiguous were his reactions in the case of the famous cymbal clash in the *Adagio* of Symphony VII (R.V., Eulenburg min. score, letter W, p. 87), which is so significantly absent from the score of O.V. (ed. R. Haas, Leipzig, 1944, min. score, letter W, p. 69).[1] Shortly after the first performance of this Symphony under Nikisch (30th December 1884) and before its publication (Gutmann, Vienna, 1885) Joseph Schalk wrote to his brother Franz (10th January 1885):

... Recently I went with Löwe over the score of Symphony VII with regard to some changes and emendations. ... Perhaps you do not know that Nikisch has insisted on the acceptance of our desired cymbal clash in the *Adagio* (C major, $\frac{6}{4}$ chord), as also on triangle and timpani, which pleases us immensely. ...

The facsimile reproduction of that addendum to the autographs (to which Bruckner seems to have acceded only with reluctance), published by R. Haas, however, reveals Bruckner's 'second thoughts' on the matter. Before sending the autograph to the engraver his 'editors' took the precaution of cancelling three significant question marks in Bruckner's hand in the margin of the extra leaf containing the parts of the newly introduced percussion instruments. But in later years the ageing Bruckner added a note in pencil, 'not valid,' which unmistakably countermands the whole addendum.

The textual situation of Bruckner's symphonies may be thus presented in tabulated form.

ORIGINAL VERSIONS

on the basis of autograph scores

Symphonies V, VI, VII, and IX . .	One version each.
„ I and VIII	Two versions each.
Symphony II	Three versions, none of which represents Bruckner's ultimate intentions.

---

[1] It has been restored in L. Nowak's revision, 1954 (cf. p. 69, letter W).

Symphony III . . . . . Four versions.

" IV . . . . . One version only, but with alternative movements for scherzo and finale.

REVISED EDITIONS

(published in Bruckner's lifetime), for which the composer is responsible, at least in part

Symphony I . . . Bruckner's own revision of 1891, publ. 1893.

" II . . . B.'s last revision of 1891, publ. 1892.

" III . . . B.'s four revisions, No. 2 publ. 1878; No. 4 publ. 1890.

" IV . . . B.'s 4th revision of 1881, publ. 1889.

" VIII . . . B.'s 3rd revision of 1888–90, publ. 1892.

REVISED EDITIONS

published without Bruckner's consent

Symphony V . . . Publ. 1896, shortly before the composer's death; engraving supervised by F. Schalk.

" VI . . . Publ. posthumously in 1899, engraving supervised by Cyrill Hynais.

" IX . . . Publ. posthumously in 1903, edited by Ferdinand Löwe.

FIRST EDITIONS

published in Bruckner's lifetime

Symphony III . . . B.'s 3rd revision, first publ. 1878.

" VII . . . First publ. 1885. An edition which does not always conform to O.V., as has been pointed out in this chapter.[1]

The three great Masses, as well as the two late choral works (*Te Deum* and Psalm CL) and the string Quintet, were likewise subject

[1] A list of the hitherto published scores of O.V. is given, with bibliographical particulars, in Appendix B (Catalogue of Works).

to numerous revisions. It seems difficult in their case to exonerate Bruckner from responsibility, for they were clearly published under his supervision between 1887 and 1892.

Generally speaking, a careful collation of the published scores of O.V. with those of R.V. reveals considerable differences in orchestration and structural proportions. The changes are particularly far-reaching in the cases of Symphonies V, VI and IX, which, as already mentioned, were published posthumously and therefore without the composer's participation. The orchestral lay-out of nearly every bar of them has been radically altered, with the result that Bruckner's original conception of a, so to speak, terraced, organ-like orchestral sound has had to give way to an orchestration based on Wagner's principle of mixed colours. In several instances the editors did not hesitate to cut single bars or even to alter the rhythmic contours of a motif and to invent new accessory parts, especially in accompaniments. In addition huge cuts were made in Symphonies V and VI, particularly in the finale of the former, which tend to change entirely the formal conception of the respective movements. For this editorial surgery Franz Schalk and Ferdinand Löwe—two of Bruckner's most trusted disciples and lifelong apostles—have been made responsible, although opinions differ about the precise share of their responsibilities. However, Schalk himself admitted that the separate brass band intoning the chorale in R.V. of the finale of Symphony V was his own idea, and that he had obtained permission from the ailing composer to perform the Symphony in this fashion at Graz (1894). In the case of the posthumous publication of Symphony VI Cyrill Hynais is generally believed to have acted as self-appointed editor *a posteriori*. In the case of Symphony IX, left incomplete at Bruckner's death and first performed by Löwe in 1903, Löwe acted as editor of its full score, first published later in the same year by J. Eberle & Sons. The Symphony was then presented as in three movements only. The principle of Wagnerian orchestration was here put into effect with even less restraint than in Symphonies V and VI. There is no shred of evidence that Bruckner would have endorsed editorial interference on so vast a scale. Löwe's edition can only be called an unauthorized and arbitrary arrangement which should no longer be performed.

Two musical examples from Symphony V showing the difference between O.V. and R.V. so eloquently illustrate the nature and extent of these interferences as to speak for themselves:

Ex. 1

Symphony V, finale (bars 1–16), O.V., publ. 1939, Vol. V of Coll. Ed. (ed. Robert Haas).

Ex. 2

Symphony V, finale (bars 1–14), R.V., publ. Vienna, 1896.

Symphony V (O.V. and R.V.)

While the question of the respective merits of both versions seems to leave little room for differences of opinion in this instance, the editorial problems present a somewhat different aspect in the cases of R.V. of Symphonies I (1890), III (1878, 1890) and VIII (1892), all of which were undertaken by Bruckner himself, admittedly on the basis of critical suggestions from conductors and disciples. The publication of Symphony VIII, in particular, reflected Bruckner's shaken self-confidence after Hermann Levi's rejection of its second version (1887). Even if some of the far-reaching redraftings in those scores of R.V. which in time became the first published versions of Symphonies I, III and VIII may have been inspired by Bruckner's executants and pupils, it is difficult to absolve him wholly from responsibility for them. They must be taken seriously as representing his second thoughts on problems of structure and orchestration, and they certainly have a right to retain their place among his authoritative publications.

One thing clearly emerges from the foregoing: the inadmissibility of the posthumously published scores of Symphonies V, VI and IX, and the doubtful value of the first score of Symphony VII (publication 1885). In these four cases performances as well as analyses should be based exclusively on the scores of O.V. But in the cases of Symphonies I, II, III, IV and VIII several versions with conflicting claims to authenticity confront the bewildered student. A later analytical chapter will attempt to assess their merits and to assign them their legitimate place.

A brief account of the latest phase in the history of Bruckner editions remains to be given. Shortly after the end of the First World War steadily increasing interest in Bruckner led to the formation of a Bruckner League in Vienna, the nucleus of a later International Bruckner League (4th November 1925), which in turn ultimately resulted in the foundation of an International Bruckner Society, the incorporation of which was achieved, after many intermediate setbacks, on 17th February 1929. Among its guiding spirits were the Bruckner biographer Max Auer and the conductor Franz Moissl. The latter had already stimulated interest in Bruckner's little-known early works by his first performances of the Symphonies in F minor, in D minor (No. 'O') and the Overture in G minor between 1921 and 1924. Full scores of the two last-mentioned works were issued by the Universal Edition. Rumours that the hitherto published scores of Bruckner's symphonies did not represent the composer's original intentions began to circulate in the early 1920s. How far O.V. could differ from R.V. was at last revealed when on 2nd April 1932 O.V. of Symphony IX was performed for the first time, conducted by Siegmund von Hausegger. The impression it created was so profound, and the discrepancies between the two versions were considered so startling, that the Bruckner Society decided there and then to recommend its use for future performances. Meanwhile the I.B.S. had started its activity with the launching of a complete and critical edition, the publication of which was entrusted to a new firm, the Musikwissenschaftlicher Verlag of Vienna. Publication started in 1930 with two early choral compositions (Requiem in D minor and Mass in B flat minor), edited by Robert Haas, the chief editor of the Collected Edition, except for vol. ix (containing Symphony IX), which was edited (together with the preserved sketches for its incompleted finale) by A. Orel (1934). The ensuing arguments on the merits of the respective versions increased in intensity with the gradual appearance of the volumes of the Collected Edition. The chief editors of R.V., Franz Schalk and Ferdinand Löwe, being then dead, the disputes were tempered by no restraint. Up to 1950 all the symphonies had been reissued in O.V., in addition the early Masses of 1849 and 1854, the sketches for the finale of Symphony IX and the second O.V. of the Mass in F minor.

The I.B.S. and its Viennese publishing house became entangled in Hitler's *Kulturpolitik* soon after 1933. Nazism recognized the society as a fitting object for nationalist cultural propaganda—in flagrant violation of the society's statutes of 1929. This led to its ultimate disruption and to a transfer of its activities to several independent firms of publishers. Haas's removal from his post as custodian of the Music Department of the National Library in Vienna in 1945 also terminated his editorial connection with the Collected Edition, which is now being directed by his successor L. Nowak.[1]

[1] The new critical and complete edition, sponsored by the Austrian

The numerous volumes of the earlier Collected Edition, with their scholarly commentaries, issued by Haas over a period of more than fifteen years, represent a staggering achievement of editorial scrupulosity and insight into the secret processes of Bruckner's mind. The sum-total of his research has been epitomized in his critical biography —so far the most scholarly attempt to assess the man and artist.

Ministry of Education and by the Administration of Upper Austria, is published by the directors of the Austrian National Library and by the International Bruckner Society. Its general editor is Professor Leopold Nowak, Director-General of the Music Collection of the Austrian National Library, Vienna. Under his editorship thirteen volumes have been issued up to 1963. (Cf. Appendix B.)

CHAPTER VIII

FUNDAMENTALS OF STYLE

AFFINITY OF MASS AND SYMPHONY. To compare Bruckner's eleven Symphonies and three grand Masses with Beethoven's nine Symphonies and two great Masses (a suggestion which might strike a Central European as not altogether blasphemous) is to discover two fundamental differences. Beethoven's symphonies show a steady development coupled with a general tendency to lengthen each movement, to increase the orchestral sonorities, and to vary the formal planning. This tendency moves from the Haydn-like simplicity of the first Symphony to the manifold complexities of the ninth. Bruckner's symphonies, on the other hand, have a single formal pattern with but little variation. Permanent characteristic features of his style may be discovered in his earliest symphonic essays, the so-called *Studiensymphonie* in F minor and the 'Zero' Symphony in D minor. They are, as it were, blueprints for the official set of nine symphonies. Again, Beethoven's two Masses are conceived in a distinctly different emotional and stylistic vein from his symphonies, despite an occasional symphonic bias noticeable in the *Missa solemnis*. In Bruckner's case the interrelationship between mass and symphony is so close that the one cannot be satisfactorily considered without the other. It is a fair guess that Bruckner's archetype of grand 'festival mass,' as seen in the two masterpieces in D minor and F minor, left its imprint on his particular brand of monumentalized symphony. The extended proportions of the 'Gloria' and 'Credo' sections of these two Masses may also have subconsciously determined the length of the first two movements of the three early symphonies. The masses in turn are indebted to certain liturgical habits attributable to the Austrian *Landmesse*. In their emotional pictorialism they seem to re-echo Haydn's latest masses as well as Mozart's *Requiem*; their contrapuntal ingenuities draw on Cherubini's church compositions and, farther back, on the vocal polyphony of Palestrina and Gallus, Fux and Caldara.[1]

[1] On Bruckner's close knowledge of the works and composers mentioned here see Haas (see Bibliography), pp. 33 ff., 73 ff.; E. Decsey (see Bibliography), pp. 120 ff.

The basic pattern of Bruckner's symphony, evolved at the very beginning of his creative maturity (1863–4), remains essentially unchanged. Its four unusually extended movements owe much to the structure and thematic treatment in Beethoven's ninth Symphony and in his late string quartets.[1] Each symphony is in four movements, three of which move slowly and, by virtue of their solemn mood and monumental development, closely resemble the four principal sections of the setting of a mass. Only the scherzos are frankly secular music of a rustic type. The other movements could easily be transformed into sections of a mass by way of 'parody,' in the technical sense of the ecclesiastical practice in earlier centuries.

One of the most characteristic features of a Bruckner symphony is the close thematic and structural affinity between its outer movements. This surely is as much a result of his patient striving for thematic integration as it is an exact parallel to the interrelationship between the 'Kyrie' and 'Dona nobis pacem' in his masses. This affinity may be one of actual thematic substance, as it becomes operative in the first and last movements of Symphony II:

Ex. 3

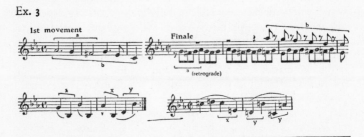

---

[1] See Schalk, *Briefe*, etc., p. 89; F. Blume, *Die Musik in Geschichte und Gegenwart*, II, col. 370. It is doubtful if they owe anything to Schubert's great C major Symphony and to his 'Unfinished,' with which it is unlikely that Bruckner became familiar, since they did not appear till 1839 and 1865 respectively, and were far from popular in Bruckner's formative years. Schubert's indisputable influence on Bruckner came through the medium of his songs and choral compositions, with which he seems to have been thoroughly acquainted at an early date.

This might be compared with the exact reappearance of the principal 'Kyrie' subject in the final 'Dona' of the D minor Mass (1864):

Ex. 4

The affinity may also be one of episodic reminiscence of earlier movements, evidently modelled on the finale of Beethoven's ninth Symphony and its episode of thematic quotations. There are cases of this in Bruckner's Symphonies III, IV, V and VIII. This process frequently leads to a piling-up in a final contrapuntal agglomeration of considerable complexity, as in the finale of Symphony VIII:

Ex. 5

Thematic affinity between the two outer movements may even lead to a new thematic character in the finale, as in the special case of Symphony V. In it both the outer movements culminate in a mighty chorale resorting frequently to a fugal method of thematic deployment. The thematic association between the relevant passages in the first movement and the finale indicates the high degree of organic development controlling the growth and treatment of Bruckner's thematic subject-matter in general:

Ex. 6 (*a*)   (*b*)

These chorale-like climaxes and contrapuntal knots occur invariably in the finales, less frequently in the first movements (see
Symphonies III, V, VII and VIII). Their position within the
structure of the movement, resembling a mountain-peak, can be
approached only across long stretches of gradual thematic development
or by way of huge dynamic contrasts, obtained by treating the
orchestra like a monster organ. Such thematic conditions and
methods of symphonic treatment explain the forbidding length of
these finales, which surpass those of any symphony of their century in
their lumbering slowness of motion and inexorable cyclic rotation of
their thematic subdivisions.

Both the chorale as harmonic crystallization of contrapuntal
energies and the fugue as a polyphonic texture made subservient to
symphonic development are rooted in church music, and both appear
in Bruckner's masses at psychological turning-points comparable to
their location in the symphonies. Moreover, fugal treatment has its
historical place in the tradition of the Austrian mass. It occurs
inevitably in Bruckner's church music at the final sections of the
central movements of the mass setting: the 'Gloria' in all three great
Masses, the 'Credo' in the F minor Mass, the final section, 'In te,
Domine, speravi,' in the *Te Deum* and the fugue at letter L in Psalm
CL. These fugal episodes utilize rigorous contrapuntal texture for
the purpose of heightening the mounting tension. This is finally
eased by the appearance of the chorale itself, majestically enunciated
by the brass. By analogy to its application in the masses fugue is
exclusively reserved for finale movements in the symphonies (Symphonies V and IX; also string Quintet).

Symphony III (*Thematic Analysis*)

GENERAL SYMPHONIC PATTERN. The following pages will discuss the general pattern of Bruckner's symphony type as exemplified in the representative case of Symphony III (final version of 1890, second printed version). This work seems especially eligible, as it were, for the dissecting-table, not only because it is closely related to some of Bruckner's most important works by virtue of its principal thematic subjects and its principal key (Mass in D minor, Symphony No. 'O,' Symphony IX), but also because work on it spread over practically the whole period of Bruckner's maturity (1873–90).[1]

One of the essential features of Bruckner's first movements are their primordial character and their gradual emergence from the sonorous nebulae of fundamental harmony. The comparison of the first subject-group of Beethoven's ninth Symphony with Bruckner's openings has often been made, although it is doubtful if Bruckner had heard that work before 1867, i.e. before his three early symphonies, in all of which these features of style may be observed, were more or less definitely committed to paper. Bruckner's first movements almost invariably emerge from tonal obscurity and indefinite motion, usually contrived with background harmonies in the strings, produced *tremolando* (viz. the openings of Symphonies III, IV, VII, VIII and IX). This is to be observed particularly in Symphony III, which in turn utilizes the beginning of the earlier Symphony 'O' and is closely related to the two o her principal works in the same key, the Mass in D minor and Symphony IX, as well as to an early forerunner of them, the *Missa solemnis* in B flat minor (1854).

Symphony III, then, begins like Beethoven's ninth Symphony with the indeterminate interval of a bare fifth, from which emerges, as it were by rotation and multiplication, a subject given out by the trumpet which impressed even Wagner with its elemental grandeur:

Ex. 7

---

[1] Cf. the author's comprehensive preface to his 1962 revision of this work (see Appendix B).

This theme might be called a 'signal-tune' of Bruckner's music in general, for it contains all the typical characteristics of this kind of invention peculiar to him. It is dualistic (x and y); it functions twice within the ambit of an octave; it contains the intervals of the falling fifth and fourth (cf. x 1 and x 2); it further comprises the interval of the minor third, ascending and descending (z) and cast in triplet rhythm, thereby establishing—though only by implication so far —Bruckner's unmistakable sign-manual, the quintuple rhythm

♩ ♩ ♩ ♩ ♩. This is a rhythmic pattern utterly alien to the classics, and evidently derived from experiences of plainsong and from the late medieval polyphonists.

We have seen that the expository sections of Bruckner's first movements are usually modelled closely on Beethoven's exposition of themes in the first movement of the ninth Symphony. This becomes especially evident in the first movement of Bruckner's Symphony III, which shares with Beethoven's ninth not only the principal key but many particulars of thematic treatment and key-relationships. The dualism of Beethoven's first theme is reflected in Bruckner's, consisting of a visionary antecedent (Ex. 7) and this passionate consequent:

Ex. 8

The movement's delicious *cantabile* section (*Gesangsperiode* was Bruckner's technical term for his lyrical episodes), for which he chose the key of the mediant (F) where Beethoven preferred the submediant (B♭), floats on the wings of the composer's favourite rhythm—the symbol of exuberance and passion—accompanied by a deliberately Meistersingerish counter-subject in the violas:

Ex. 9

Spun out to great length, this finally produces a subject for the codetta, growing out of the twofold thematic elements of Ex. 7 (*a* and *b*). The end of the exposition is slow in arriving. It forms a lengthy para-graph, the great extent of which explains why Bruckner's symphonies take so much longer to get to their preordained destination than even Beethoven's last Symphony. It begins with a new chorale melody in the trumpets (seven bars after letter G) which closes into a restatement of the inverted principal tune (Ex. 7) in the distant key of E major and, continuing in chorale-like meanderings of woodwind and horns, finally trails off mysteriously into a quotation from the 'Miserere' section of the Mass in D minor (cf. 'Gloria,' four bars after letter D). This quotation from a mass, to be repeated literally at the end of the *Adagio* of Symphony IX (O.V., letter T), is characteristic not only of the close interplanetary connections between Bruckner's choral music and his symphonies, but also of the organ-like orchestra-tion found in all the symphonies by this organ-inspired composer, who yet never composed anything for the instrument of his choice.

The liturgical character of this transition is further emphasized by a sequence of triads in root position, recalling the opening of Pales-trina's *Stabat Mater*. The inversion of the join (Ex. 7, *y*) by the flute and the root motive of the falling fourth and fifth within an octave (Ex. 7, *x* 1 *x* 2) act as a thematic bridge leading into the development section (letter I). This is one of Bruckner's most accomplished feats of thematic integration. Besides utilizing all the thematic matter quoted above, it develops important new motives and focuses attention on a splinter-motive such as Ex. 8, *x*, which, together with its inversion nine bars after letter M, becomes the chief agent of an irresistible climax, which culminates in a mighty enun-ciation of the trumpet motive (Ex. 7), crashing out in stark octaves. In chorale-like harmonies and telescoped rhythms the music is then driven to a further climax in the remote key of E major—touched upon, as we know, at the very tail-end of the exposition. The end of the development (even in the considerably tightened-up version of 1890) is again emphasized by a lengthy transition based on a reminiscence of the *cantabile* subject (Ex. 9), linked up with the recapi-tulation by a cadence in the heavy brass, evidently modelled on similar transitions in the Mass in D minor and recurring literally in Symphony IX at a similar pivotal point between recapitulation and coda. The former progresses on orthodox lines and the coda is again unmistakably inspired by the coda of Beethoven's ninth Symphony, movement 1, even using Beethoven's chromatic *ostinato* bass as a propelling agent.

If the character of the first movement has been pugnacious and militant, interrupted by episodes of exultation and liturgical solemnity, the mood of the *Adagio* is one of solemn adoration and abject humility throughout, interspersed with episodes of passionate desire for the unattainable. More than any other part of this Symphony it comes closest to the spirit of the mass. Indeed it is not surprising to detect in all Bruckner's slow movements frequent thematic reminiscences from the masses. Such meaningful self-quotations already occur in the *Andante* and finale of Symphony 'O.' The former alludes to the passage 'Qui tollis peccata mundi' from the E minor Mass (1866), while the latter utilizes the 'Osanna' from the early *Requiem* in D minor (1849) in its *cantabile* section, and later on quotes the seven-part *Ave Maria* (1861) in the transitional bridge leading from the development to the recapitulation. Such quotations become especially noticeable in the *Andante* of Symphony II (1871-2), with its copious quotations from the 'Benedictus' of its liturgical sister-work, the grand Mass in F minor (1867-8). They continue in that Symphony's finale, which quotes extensively from the 'Kyrie' of the same Mass. Quotations finally assume almost programmatic significance with the appearance of the 'Non confundar in aeternum' motive from the *Te Deum* at the climax of the *Adagio* of Symphony VII, and they add a bitter-sweet flavour to the coda of the *Adagio* of Symphony IX. That last *Adagio* of Bruckner's was his avowed farewell to life, in which reminiscences from Symphonies VII and VIII mingle with the melancholy strain of the 'Miserere' from the D minor Mass.

The liturgical connotations in this *Adagio* of Symphony III are mainly supplied by the *Marienkadenz*, a familiar turn of Bruckner's, first used in his settings of the four-part *Ave Maria* of 1856 and the seven-part one of 1861, and also introduced into the *Agnus Dei* of the Mass in F minor. It occurs frequently in eighteenth-century masses, especially in Haydn's and Mozart's music of a devotional character. Here it is as it appears in Bruckner's third Symphony:

Ex. 10

The simplicity of its form is typical of the emotionalism of Bruckner's slow movements in general. Like all of them this one is in ternary form (A—B—A), the recapitulation (at letter H) presenting A in a highly ornate variant leading up to a visionary climax (with a new melodic turn in the trumpet, an afterthought of the version of 1890), and fading away in a mysterious coda with a faint but noticeable allusion to the 'sleep harmonies' in Wagner's *Walküre*.[1]

The scherzo is one of Bruckner's most successful dance movements, happily inspired by the musical folklore of his native Upper Austria. It shows the high degree of thematic integration to which he aspired even at the outset of his career as a symphonist. Despite its rustic trappings, the thematic as well as the emotional connection with the stark violence of the first movement are apparent in both manifestations of its main subject, the cumulative dynamics of its introduction as well as its ultimate thematic shape.

The hollow sound of the empty fifths, blaring out in an ominous *crescendo* in the introductory bars, links this high-spirited *Ländler* scherzo with the primordial beginnings of the two outer movements. This process of thematic integration and unification is carried a step farther in Symphony V. There the ambivalent motive of the melancholy *Adagio* is transformed into a bustling scherzo theme by a process of rhythmic 'stream-lining.'

[1] The Symphony's first version (1873) contained many more thematic allusions to *Tristan* and *Walküre*. They were already eliminated in the second version of 1877. (See footnote p. 55.)

The finale of No. III gathers momentum exactly as movements 1 and 3 did, i.e. with the interval of the bare fifth screaming in the orchestra's top register (bars 1–8), enlivened by a repetitive little figure in the strings. Its main theme, given out in the heavy brass with something like deliberate Wagnerian swagger, is closely modelled on the rhythmic and thematic contour of Ex. 7, while its sharpened chord of the seventh, combining the leading-note (C♯) and the flat supertonic (E♭) steer back to the tonic D minor. This had already been anticipated in the scherzo's thematic exposition (bar 11, after letter A).

The *Gesangsperiode* shows a poignancy of emotional contrast unparalleled in Bruckner's work and naïvely explained by the com-poser as being expressive of the stark dualism of this world. Sorrow and joy, existing, as it were, cheek by jowl, are here symbolized by the gaiety of a 'polka' (*a*) and the solemnity of a chorale (*b*), inter-twined in the following paragraph (bitonally spelt by Bruckner himself):

Ex. 11

The harshly syncopated unison of the codetta (letter K) reminds us as much of its corresponding point in the first movement (letter G) as the organ-like cadences of horn and woodwind, building a bridge to the tempestuous and much revised development section, recall the 'Miserere' quotation in that movement. Remarkable about this section is the fact that development and recapitulation are, as it were, telescoped (letter P)—a process of structural integration characteristic of Bruckner, recurring in the later symphonies (especially VIII and IX) and strongly impinging on the conception and shape of Mahler's finale movements. The final return of the *Leitmotiv*, Ex. 7, in radiant D major, is duly prepared. The Symphony ends logically with a climax representing the unresolved tension as expressed in the dissonant interpretation of the main thematic subjects of movements 1 and 4. This is going to become the generally adopted pattern of Bruckner's final unravellings.

TONALITY AND COUNTERPOINT. Discussing Bruckner's one and only published work for chamber music, the string Quintet in F major, on the occasion of its performance in 1881, the Viennese critic, Ludwig Speidel, called it an Odyssey of keys. Thus was Bruckner's orignal conception of progressive tonality announced to a musical world which still experienced the greatest difficulty in appreciating Wagner's and Liszt's revolutionary harmonies. Actually, Bruckner's attempt to widen the ambit of tonality in this work, as in his later symphonies, appears to-day as the logical result of Beethoven's and Schubert's exploits in that particular direction and as a creative echo to his teacher, Simon Sechter's, little-known, Rameau-inspired theory of 'interdominants.' In combination with the elements of plainsong and modal polyphony in his ecclesiastical music Bruckner's concept of harmony and his processes of key-relationships were bound to become revolutionary and in some ways anticipatory of more recent developments in that field.

An investigation into the problem of tonality, as presented by the string Quintet—written for a restricted medium, but closely related to the world of symphonies—may prove Bruckner's importance as a link between the Viennese classics and the twentieth century. Of its four movements the first is in the principal key of F major.[1] The second (*Adagio*), however, is in the flattened supertonic (Gb major), and this was considered a breach of tradition in the 1880's, although its employment is clearly foreshadowed in the first movement of Beethoven's 'Appassionata' Sonata. Bruckner's (as well as Beethoven's) predilection for that distant key is, of course, determined by its cadential power as the chord of the Neapolitan sixth. It seems a foregone conclusion that Bruckner, for whom the Neapolitan cadence always retained its attraction (e.g. the chorale in the finale of Symphony V, Ex. 6 (*b*)), composed the second movement of the Quintet as one extended Neapolitan complex. The scherzo is in D minor, the

[1] The author has published a more detailed analysis of the Quintet in *Music and Letters*, July issue, 1955 (see Bibliography).

relative minor of F major, modulating frequently into the distant
sharp keys of A and E major. The main section ends in D major
and is followed by a slower trio in E flat major, which must have
baffled the critical pundits of the 1880s. Yet this again is nothing
else but the Neapolitan sixth of D, and the whole trio is thus only a
cadential parenthesis between the scherzo proper and its recapitulation. The finale, which in the published version of the Quintet
follows the *Adagio* in G flat, whereas in O.V. it came after the D
major conclusion of the scherzo, is 'officially' in F minor, but it only
reaches that key after a devious excursion into dependencies of G flat.
It thus continues logically where the *Adagio* left off. Its very first bar,
with its bustling, Beckmesserish motive in the second viola, is based
on the chord of the ninth, leading back to G flat. In bar 13 G flat is
touched in passing, only to be jockeyed into a position where it could
be used as a cadential starting-point for steering into the home tonic
of F. This intriguing situation is illustrated by the false relations
between the first violin and the second viola (Gb against G), signalling
the slackening of tempo in bars 16–17. Bar 17 contains an implicit
dominant preparation for F minor, but that key is reached only in a
pizzicato passage later on. The sudden *volte face* of harmony in these
two bars contains in a nutshell the gist of Bruckner's modulatory
innovations:

Ex. 12

If Bruckner's concept of harmony and modulation owes its extension of range to a subtle interpretation of Sechter's theories, as well as
to a highly original use of the Neapolitan cadence, deriving perhaps
from the Wanderer scenes in Wagner's *Siegfried*, his counterpoint
draws special inspiration from Palestrinian polyphony. Bruckner's

employment of contrapuntal devices is quite unacademic and un-
obtrusive. Nothing can make his point of view clearer than the
following passage from a letter, dated 22nd April 1893, referring to
a performance of the Mass in D minor:

... Who on earth has mentioned the pedal-point of the Brahms *Requiem*
in the critical report of the *Steyrer Zeitung* of April 6th? I am no
pedal-point pusher and don't care a fig for it. Counterpoint is not inspiration by genius, but only a means to an end. ...

In the 'Sanctus' of the E minor Mass (which tries to live up to the
purist conceptions of the Cecilians) Bruckner builds up a dazzling
canonic edifice, based on a theme from Palestrina's *Missa brevis*. This
'Sanctus,' composed in the spirit of medieval workmanship, and
perhaps nearer to the polyphony of the Renaissance than any composition written after 1750, consists of a perpetual chain of four two-
part canons in the lower fifth, evolved from Palestrina's motif:

Ex. 13

If in that Mass the arts of Flemish imitative polyphony are revived for
the purposes of solemn praise, the devices of chorale and fugue are
employed in the colossal sonority scheme of the *Te Deum* (1884).
Its psychological climax is reached by the intonation of Bruckner's
signal-tune *par excellence* (which is to play such an important part in
the *Adagio* of Symphony VII) on the words 'Non confundar in
aeternum.' The tune is first given out by the sopranos (with orchestral
accompaniment and with a bass foreshadowing its later hymnic
harmonization):

Ex. 13 (*a*)

It then forks out into the exposition of a double fugue, proliferating from its thematic substance as in nearly all vocal fugues in Bruckner's mature church music. The tune finally crystallizes into a chorale conclusion in the trombones and leads up to the final unison climax. Fugal technique, chorale verticalization and polyphonic radiation of thematic matter all served Bruckner in turn to express the religious idea of his composition which begins, as it ends, with the archaic magnificence of plainsong unison.

CHAPTER IX

VOCAL MUSIC

THE extent, scope and character of Bruckner's vocal music was largely determined by his relations with the Church and with choral societies. Surpassing his instrumental compositions in sheer weight of number it approximately equals them in actual bulk. Two categories of vocal composition much favoured in the romantic period are all but excluded: Bruckner wrote no opera and hardly ever a song with piano accompaniment. The anachronistic nature of his creative personality seems vividly expressed by his almost exclusive concentration on choral music for the Roman liturgy and on the part-song with or without instrumental accompaniment. The greater part of these compositions are *pièces de circonstance* either commissioned by church dignitaries (e.g. the Mass in E minor) or suggested by secular authorities for a festive occasion (e.g. Psalm CL). Others again, like the first large-scale secular composition, *Germanenzug*, were written for competitive choral festivals. However, some of the greatest among these works owe their existence to the promptings of Bruckner's genius alone.

The greater part of this music was written while Bruckner kept in close touch with cathedral choirs and secular choral societies. It belongs to the first half of his life (i.e. before 1868), spent mainly in Upper Austria as teacher, chorus-master and organist, and thus represents in the main a man of under forty-five, whose musical apprenticeship extended well into his forties and who only then began to strike out on a creative path of his own. Once Bruckner had exchanged the organ-loft of Linz Cathedral and the conductor's rostrum of the *Liedertafel* 'Frohsinn' for the lecturership in harmony and counterpoint at the Vienna Conservatory, his interest in choral composition in general and in works for the Church in particular began to diminish. In the last twenty-eight years of his life only two major choral works of a devotional character were written: the *Te Deum* of 1881–4 and Psalm CL of 1892. Neither of them is intended for a religious service. Only a handful of smaller, motet-like compositions, composed mainly for specific occasions, appeared during these later years in Vienna. Among them are the austerely modal antiphon *Tota pulchra*, composed in 1878 for a jubilee of Bishop Rudigier, and the magnificent trombone-accompanied hymn *Ecce sacerdos*, written in 1885 for the jubilee of the Linz diocese, and re-echoing the barbaric splendour of the *Te Deum*. Bruckner's creative activity was now almost exclusively directed towards the symphony. In this connection it is interesting to observe that he never reverted to the mass once he was installed in Vienna. Only a brief sketch for a *Requiem* dated from 1875. His ardent concentration on the symphony, especially from the time of Symphony II onwards (1871–2), is unparalleled in his century and not unworthy of comparison with Wagner's equally exclusive devotion to the music-drama.

Bruckner's vocal compositions divide easily into a larger ecclesiastical and a smaller secular group. Only a small number of them is of importance to-day and truly representative of his genius at its best. In the former category are a few large-scale works which continued to rank among his finest and may be regarded, so to speak, as the pedestal of his later symphonies: the three great Masses, in D, E and F minor, the Latin *Te Deum* and its vernacular parallel, Psalm CL. But no less than seven masses by Bruckner are extant, if the *Requiem* of 1849 is included; and some fragments and sketches dating from the years of schoolmastering in Kronstorf (1844–5), as well as from the early days of his St Florian appointment (1846), prove that at least four must have been planned and may even have been completed before 1846.

The first two of the complete masses of this early period—the short chorale Mass in C major for contralto, two horns and organ (Windhaag, 1842), and the equally short *a cappella* Mass for four-part chorus, in F major (Kronstorf, 1844)—evidently belong to the provincial species of the Austrian *Landmesse* or *missa brevis,* in which parts of the 'Credo' are usually cut and other parts telescoped for the sake of brevity. The poverty and culturally low standard of Bruckner's early environments are poignantly reflected in the paucity of musical means at his disposal. The Mass in C is monodic—like Viadana's *Missa Dominicalis* of 1607—and accompanied mainly by a figured bass to be performed on the organ. However, in the preserved fragment of the Mass in E flat major Bruckner's natural bent towards the colossal already finds expression in a richer orchestral palette, as also in a more ambitious choral lay-out with antiphonal responses for soloists and *tutti*. Yet nothing in the musical substance of these early masses seems to foreshadow future distinction, still less greatness. Bruckner's mental and spiritual development continued to proceed at a snail's pace. The two largest creative efforts of the St Florian period—and incidentally the only two ambitious works composed before the eight-year period of training under Sechter and Kitzler, during which the outlet for free composition seemed all but completely blocked—were the *Requiem* in D minor and the *Missa solemnis* in B flat minor. Both works are a landmark in Bruckner's development. Despite their immaturity, the conventionality of their thematic matter, the hide-bound traditionalism in the treatment of the liturgical text and the short-windedness of their single structural sections, they anticipate the future type of Bruckner's symphonically conceived festival mass, which in turn anticipated his later type of monumentalized symphony. Both Masses are in minor keys, one even in D minor, the key of Bruckner's loftiest inspiration; both point to a careful study of certain masses by Haydn and Mozart. The D minor *Requiem* is thematically and structurally dependent on Mozart's famous work in the same key, while Haydn's 'Nelson,' 'Heilig' and 'Harmony' masses were models for the Mass in B flat minor, not to mention certain sections of the grand masses of Bruckner's early maturity.

The *Requiem* was first performed two days after its completion, on 13th March 1849, at St Florian under the composer's direction. Like all Bruckner's works written before 1878 it remained in manuscript, was revised as late as 1894 by the ageing composer, who had a particular weakness for it, and was eventually published in 1931. The influence of Mozart is even more noticeable in the later Mass in B flat minor, which was first performed under Bruckner's direction on 14th

September 1854 on the occasion of the installation of the composer's patron, Friedrich Mayr, as provost of the chapter of St Florian.

The volcanic eruption of Bruckner's creative energy in the three great Masses in D, E and F minor coinciding more or less with the drafting of his first mature symphonic essay (Symphony I, Linz version), and extending from the summer of 1864 to the early autumn of 1868, may be regarded as a convulsive psychological reaction following on the fallow years of contrapuntal studies. A pent-up urge to create and unrelieved continence made these critical years in Bruckner's life, leading him to the brink of self-destruction and insanity, but also lifting him high above his former self by the miracle of musical originality, first manifested in the score of the D minor Mass of 1864.

It is easy to-day to recognize Bruckner's three masses as the most potent post-classical church music, outdistancing Liszt's mass compositions of 1855 and 1867, as well as Verdi's *Requiem* of 1874, by the authenticity of their religious fervour as well as by the fact that they remained ecclesiastically negotiable in spite of their episodic byways, whereas Liszt occasionally expands into the long-winded rhetoric of the oratorio and Verdi skirts the boundaries of opera. In their own time, however, they seemed to fall between two stools. Taking the solemn masses of Haydn, Mozart and Beethoven as models, yet inspired also by the spirit of plainsong and cross-fertilized by the technique of Palestrinian polyphony, the Masses in D and F minor employed a full orchestra enlivened by the harmonic audacities of Wagnerian romanticism and attuned to the taste of a great organist. It was the symphonic grandeur of these masses which displeased the musical purists in the Roman Church, whose antagonism ultimately drove Bruckner, like Liszt, into the camp of the opponents of Cecilianism. That Bruckner was well aware of the musical crisis dividing the Roman Church at that time is borne out by the fact that he clearly aims in the E minor Mass at conforming more closely to the pattern of officially 'desirable' liturgical music, as propounded so vehemently by the Cecilians under the leadership of Franz Xaver Witt. The contrast of style between the two symphonic masses in D and F minor and the more modestly conceived work in E minor

(scored for eight-part chorus and wind instruments only) expresses
the general cleavage of opinion as to the admissibility of orchestral
colour and symphonically extended sonata form into the music for
the Roman service. Bruckner's three attempts at a solution of this
problem compete in greatness of conception, originality of thematic
substance and profundity of religious feeling with Beethoven's *Missa
solemnis,* Cherubini's two *Requiem* masses and Liszt's church music,
all of which contributed to his conception of the 'symphonic mass.'

The Mass in D minor, composed between 4th July and 29th
September 1864, first performed under the composer's direction on
20th November of the same year at Linz Cathedral, drastically
revised in 1876, 1881-2 and again in 1884 and finally published
under Bruckner's supervision in 1892, is one of the most remarkable
self-revelations of musical genius at the comparatively late age of
forty. It succeeds (where Liszt fails) in integrating elements of
plainsong and progressive harmony into the traditional festival mass
of the classics. This may be observed particularly in a tendency to
treat the central sections of the mass setting (i.e. 'Gloria' and 'Credo')
as sonata movements with freely inserted dramatic episodes. The
work presents, as in a nutshell, all the typical features of Bruckner's
later symphonic style. Its general importance as thematic reservoir
for later works is shown by the quotations from it in Symphonies
III, VII and IX.

Like its successor in E minor, the D minor Mass is observant of
liturgic requirements by leaving the opening words of the 'Gloria'
and the 'Credo' uncomposed and by thematically adjusting the
choir's entry, 'Et in terra pax,' to the plainsong style of the priest's
preceding intonation. Yet it is also revolutionary in the use of a
descriptive orchestra ('Resurrexit,' letter K). It handles distant key-
relationships with powerful imagination (the F sharp major section of
'Et incarnatus est') and achieves a high degree of formal integration
through thematic affinities, linking 'Et vitam venturi' with the first
'Dona nobis pacem' entry, and again by treating the 'Dona' as the
recapitulation of the initial 'Kyrie.' [1]

[1] This tradition of linking 'Kyrie' and 'Dona' is discussed in Chapter
VIII, p. 52.

If the Mass in D minor is a happy, even exuberant work, that in F minor is a conception of Beethovenian grandeur and ruggedness. It is planned on an ambitious scale as a concert mass, including the initial words of the 'Gloria' and 'Credo' in the choral setting, and it succeeds in dramatizing these middle sections into pictures of awe-inspiring monumentality. Its thematic material is fertilized by plainsong to an even greater extent than that of the preceding mass, and it is closely organized by virtue of a common root-motive of unmistakably liturgical flavour, a falling or ascending fourth that determines the thematic subject-matter in all parts of the work: [1]

Ex. 14

Symphonic features abound in this Mass, which matured between Symphony I and Symphony 'O,' at a time when Bruckner quickly acquired full mastery in the handling of a modern orchestra. The long *cantilena* preceding the choral entry in the 'Benedictus'—one of Bruckner's loveliest melodies—becomes the pattern and matrix for the *adagios* of the symphonies, just as the orchestra's vivid pictorialism in 'Et resurrexit' (letter F) utilizes the hollowness of bare fourths and fifths, which are the interval-elements of Symphonies 'O' and III, to express the miracle of resurrection. The style of this gigantic episode, with an orchestral background woven by the persistent figure:

Ex. 15

---

[1] It shows a curious resemblance to the corresponding motive in the first section of Verdi's *Requiem*.

is a pointer towards the equally persistent motive:

Ex. 16

in the orchestral tapestry of the *Te Deum*.

The climax of Bruckner's technical achievements in this work is reached in the breath-taking double fugue on the traditional fugal text of 'Et vitam venturi.' Of special interest in this fugue (which represents a kind of detachable symphonic coda to the 'Credo') is the shape of its subject, to which, as a legitimate thematic appendix, the 'Credo' motive is tacked on, acting as counter-subject and providing regular chordal interpolations in the imposing flow of choral polyphony:

Ex. 17

Et vi - tam ven - tu - ri   sae - cu - li. A - men.   Cre - do, Cre - do.

The root-motive of the falling (or ascending) fourth also determines the final section of the Mass, the 'Agnus Dei,' whose 'Dona nobis pacem' part—in conformity with the two preceding masses—represents a complete recapitulation of the introductory 'Kyrie.' It is here transposed into the tonic major, thus conforming to the traditional usage of sonata composition. The Mass expires with the oboe's final sigh, giving out the motive of the falling fourth (Ex. 14, *x*) with tender determination and finality. The Mass in F minor, which is Bruckner's longest choral work, was composed at the very end of the Linz period, and partly overshadowed by his serious nervous breakdown of 1867. It was begun on 14th September 1867, and completed a year later, on 9th September 1868, at Linz. It was subjected to repeated revisions in 1872, 1876, 1881 and 1883 (mainly in connection with repeat performances under Bruckner's direction in the imperial court chapel). Its first performance took place on 16th June 1872 in St Augustine's Church in Vienna under the composer's direction; it had already been preceded by a preliminary revision of the whole score. Brahms attended that performance and was deeply moved by it, as were Hellmesberger, Herbeck, Hanslick, Dessoff and the cream of musical notabilities of Vienna. In the final revision undertaken shortly before its publication, the number of horns was increased to four. Robert Haas believes that the published score of this R.V. of 1890 contains many unauthorized changes. His own publication of O.V. (based mainly on the autograph of 1867–8, and on the early revision of 1881, and published in 1944 by the Brucknerverlag of Wiesbaden) clearly reveals considerable discrepancies between both the published scores. The orchestration of O.V. is thoroughly consistent with that of O V. of the symphonies; so are phrasing and articulation. Surely the arbitrary excision of the soprano solo in the R.V. shortly before the recapitulatory part of the 'Kyrie' cannot claim authorization from the composer. The score of O.V. as presented by Haas carries conviction in every bar: it alone should be used for performance.[1]

Bruckner's third mass written during the Linz period, the Mass in E minor, reflects in its stylistic contrast to the preceding one in F minor the uncertainty of his relations to the musico-liturgical authorities of his time. He was at heart quite antagonistic to Cecilianism and deeply resented F. X. Witt's high-handed corrections in his *Pange lingua* of 1868. On the other hand he tried to serve the Church and its requirements to the best of his ability, and to provide it again and again with music inspired by plainsong and eschewing orchestral theatricalism. How far he was prepared to go in that direction— at least in a piece of restricted scope and size—is shown by the gradual *Os justi,* composed and published in 1879, which he dedicated to his friend Traumihler, the chorus-master of St Florian and an ardent Cecilian to boot. In a letter to him of 25th July 1879 Bruckner writes with surprising self-denial:

. . . I should be very pleased if you found pleasure in the piece. It is composed without sharp and flat, without the chord of the seventh, without a $\frac{6}{4}$ chord or chordal combinations of four and five simultaneous notes.

The result of all this austerity is a completely non-chromatic piece

[1] According to L. Nowak (cf. the preface to his revised edition of 1962) Bruckner made some more changes in the orchestration of the Mass between 1890 and 1893. They are incorporated in his revision only.

in the Lydian mode, revealing an uncompromising asperity of polyphonic conception which links it with the devotional music of the
twentieth century.

If the *Os justi* and *Pange lingua* represent the extreme to which
Bruckner was prepared to go in occasional pieces for the Church, the
Mass in E minor stands for the golden mean. This deeply inspired
and organically conceived Mass completely succeeds where the
exuberant and experimental pictorialism of the two preceding masses
failed. It creates a musical idiom nurtured by the great polyphonic
tradition of the past, yet fully conscious of the tremendous development in harmonic subtlety taking place in Bruckner's own period.
It relegates the orchestra to the background, yet enables it to take a
working part and to support the chorus in its adventurous meanderings
through distant key-relationships. The work is indeed a miraculous
achievement, reviving, as it does, Palestrinian imitative polyphony and
letting it coalesce with Bruckner's own progressive harmony; creating
an atmosphere of medievalism yet never steering into the shallows
of historical pastiche, as Brahms does in his *a cappella* motets, Op. 110.

The E minor Mass is scored for eight-part chorus and an orchestra
of wind instruments. It starts in the Phrygian mode and returns to
it in the usual recapitulatory section of the 'Dona nobis pacem.' The
'Kyrie' is an *a cappella* piece by nature (the orchestra is expressly
marked *ad libitum*); however, in the 'Gloria' the bassoons intone an
undulating motive of plainsong provenance which is destined to act
as a motoric agent for the whole movement. The 'Sanctus' is
woven round the 'res facta' of Palestrina's *Missa brevis* in the manner
and technique of a *missa parodia*. The 'Benedictus,' however, floats
in the luxuriant atmosphere of Wagner's *Tristan*. Bruckner's
emotionalism, ever ready to give of its best in the 'Benedictus' sections
of his masses, draws inspiration from the mysterious four chromatic
semitonal steps of the *Tristan* prelude:

Ex. 18

This Mass was written in the autumn of 1866, completed on 25th November and revised in 1869. It was dedicated to Bishop Rudigier, who commissioned it, and first performed at the consecration of the new votive chapel in the cathedral of Linz. The performance took place in the open air, in front of the chapel, on 29th September 1869, and Bruckner conducted. The work was repeatedly revised (especially in 1883 and 1885 for performances at the imperial court chapel) and finally published in 1890. The chief variants between the different versions are in the instrumental parts. It is reported that Bruckner played the organ at a second Linz performance, but, as in the somewhat similar case of the F minor Mass, there is no provision made for this instrument in any full score of the work.[1] In the D minor Mass alone is an independent part, and even there it is confined to a mere eight cadential bars, which help to bridge the gulf from 'passus et sepultus est' to the tempestuous orchestral prelude to 'Resurrexit' (letter K). A definite solution of such problems of performance will have to wait until critical editions of O.V. of both masses have become available. It is possible that future performing practice will pool the results of the different revisions. The alternative solution in the case of the E minor mass of replacing the wind band by an organ seems completely justified by the reported action of the composer himself. It would certainly increase the chances of more frequent performances of this beautiful work.

Bruckner's last two religious compositions for chorus and orchestra have so many features in common that they may be discussed together. Both the *Te Deum* and Psalm CL are based on the same hymn of praise, the psalm 'Praise ye the Lord,' the former on the Latin, the latter on a German version. Both works are in the key of brazenly triumphant C major, a key but sparingly used by Bruckner in general. Both are scored for a big orchestra and chorus, including four horns, three trumpets, three trombones, organ *ad. lib.*, four-part chorus and soloists. Both keep to quadruple rhythm, propelled by a ubiquitous motive combining the elemental intervals of the fifth and the fourth. In both works thematic matter as well as harmony (the

[1] There are plenty of signs that Bruckner, at times at least, contemplated the participation of the organ in both masses.

latter showing a marked modal tendency) are determined by motive-cells derived from plainsong. In the *Te Deum* two contrasting sections in F minor, sung by soloists ('Tu ergo' and 'Salvum fac'), interpose between the main choral portions, throwing the stridency of the home tonic into even stronger relief. A third contrast for the solo quartet ('In te, Domine, speravi') prepares for the final peroration of 'Non confundar in aeternum.' Both works culminate in a free double fugue, leading up to a shattering *fortissimo* climax. In the *Te Deum* the climax is reached only after the dual fugue subject has been replaced by the chorale melody of the 'Non confundar,' scaling the heights with a wrenching dissonance (thirteen bars before letter Z). In the Psalm the fugal theme, intoned by the choral basses, is immediately shadowed by an elaborate counter-subject in the violins, a contrapuntally rather involved start, characteristic of Bruckner's unorthodox methods of fugal procedure:

Ex. 19

Both works are inspired and indeed carried away by an almost pagan feeling of triumph, an almost barbaric enjoyment of crashing sonorities, a naïve pleasure in noisy acclamations of the Lord. The *Te Deum*—to which Psalm CL appears like a creative afterthought—was Bruckner's special favourite. Fery Beraton painted a portrait with the composer proudly sitting at the piano, the full score of the *Te Deum* open on the instrument's desk. This work expresses Bruckner's personal faith more succinctly than any other; he therefore dedicated it, with all the naïve sincerity of his fervent soul, to his 'dear God,' as he was to do later on with his last symphony. The *Te Deum*'s majestically ascending chorale motive, 'Non confundar,' gloriously re-echoed in the *Adagio* of Symphony VII, exhales a faith at once childlike and omniscient, rocklike and incandescent, a faith that may move mountains. Mahler, perhaps its most eloquent interpreter, who conducted it in 1892-3 at Hamburg, characterized it aptly by cancelling in his copy the description 'for chorus, solo voices and orchestra, organ *ad. lib.*,' and replacing it by the words 'for angelic tongues, for God-seekers, tormented hearts and for souls purified in flames.'

The *Te Deum*, originally suggested by Hellmesberger, who had already encouraged Bruckner to compose the string Quintet, took long to mature, despite its shortness. Work on it started on 3rd May 1881; the first draft of 1881 was replaced by a much more elaborate version of 1883-4, completed on 7th March 1884, in which the final fugue was introduced; this version was first performed with piano accompaniment on 2nd May 1885 in Vienna, under the auspices of the Wagner Verein; its first orchestral performance took place on 10th January 1886 under Hans Richter—the score had been published in December 1885.[1] Its success was instantaneous. There were twenty-six performances of it in the two years preceding Bruckner's death, one at Cincinnati, under Theodore Thomas, on 26th May 1892.

Psalm CL was composed between March and 29th June 1892 as a *pièce de circonstance* for the Allgemeine Deutsche Musikverein music festival in Vienna, which was cancelled in the end. It was eventually performed there under Gericke on 13th November 1892, and published in the same year.

The shorter choral works of a devotional character do not add much to Bruckner's stature as a composer, nor do they afford new aspects of his musical personality. Their comparative insignificance clearly indicates how Bruckner's creative energies became wholly absorbed in his monumental conceptions in the fields of the festival mass and the symphony. His numerous secular partsongs for men's voices and his fewer cantatas for mixed choirs with or without instrumental accompaniment were written mainly in the earlier part of his life and hardly call for detailed discussion in a short book in English, a language into which it is safe to say they will never be translated. They are for home consumption only.

[1] On the considerable differences between the two versions of 1881 and 1884 see R. Haas (see Bibliography), pp. 89 ff.

CHAPTER X

THE SYMPHONIES

AMONG the strange anomalies of Bruckner's development is the fact that he wrote no large-scale instrumental composition before the age of thirty-eight. Various explanations have been offered: his 'arrested development' in general; his lack of opportunity to hear orchestral music in his provincial backwater; his ecclesiastical surroundings; the six years of austere study of strict counterpoint under Sechter. Probably all these circumstances contributed in equal measure to this strange hesitancy in approaching what later was to become his most personal means of expression. Bruckner is reported to have tried to explain the late appearance of his first great orchestral compositions with a phrase of characteristic humility: 'Ich hab' mich nicht getraut' ('I didn't dare'). He certainly lacked a deeper knowledge of sonata and symphony (sternly excluded from Sechter's almost medieval curriculum), both of which he only began to study with the new opera conductor of Linz, Otto Kitzler, the last of his tutors and fully ten years younger than his middle-aged pupil. Bruckner worked under him from the end of 1861 to 1863. As Kitzler's pupil he insisted especially on the subjects deliberately neglected by Sechter: form and orchestration. Instinctively he had chosen the right person, for Kitzler was as progressive as Sechter was ultra-conservative. He was the first to perform Wagner's *Tannhäuser* at Linz, and he thus acquainted Bruckner for the first time with a Wagner score at the turn of 1862-3. The essays in composition dating from this time are, with the sole exception of a string Quartet in C minor, orchestral. They vary in quality and comprise four pieces for orchestra, two marches for military band, an Overture in G minor and a complete Symphony in F minor.

The Overture is Bruckner's symphonic prentice-work *par excellence*. It is in fact a fully fledged symphonic first movement, scored for an orchestra with double wind and three trombones. It begins with the slow introduction traditional in the Lullian 'French overture,' popular with Haydn and occasionally used by Mozart and Beethoven, but not at all characteristic of the later Bruckner, who only once resorted to it again (Symphony V). The boldness of its chromaticism and harmonic suspensions would seem to link this introduction with Liszt and Wagner, were it not that Bruckner did not become familiar with them till shortly after its completion—a fact which proves the inherent originality of his creative mind.

The Symphony in F minor, classified by the composer himself as a 'school work' and received by Kitzler with but tempered approval, is much less satisfactory as a work of art. It was conceived in close proximity with Psalm CXIV and the secular choral piece *Germanenzug*, and was actually written between 15th February and 21st May 1863. Haas rightly believes that it was cross-fertilized by Sechter's peculiar conception of harmony as well as by Kitzler's emphasis on orchestral colour. These somewhat antagonistic principles may well have caused a kind of creative deadlock, shown by the melodic insignificance of the Symphony's thematic matter as well as by certain conventionalities of instrumental style (especially in the *Adagio*), not noticeable in the earlier Overture. However, even here the grandeur of symphonic lay-out, the unusually generous proportions, as well as the bold and picturesque use of the brass, are pointers towards the future. In addition there are already chorale-like episodes for the heavy brass and other idiosyncratic elements of Bruckner's personal musical language.

It is the Mass in D minor (1864) rather than those early instrumental works which paves the way to the conception of a type of symphony with decidedly religious connotations, augmented proportions and organ-like colours, found in the next four works, composed within eight years, i.e. between January 1865 and 31st December 1873, in this order:

Symphony I, C minor (1st version)	January 1865–14th April 1866 (Linz)
Symphony 'O,' D minor	24th January–12th September 1869 (Vienna)

| Symphony II, C minor (1st version) | 11th October–11th September 1872 (Vienna) |
| Symphony III, D minor (1st version) | Early February–31st December 1873 (Vienna) |

THE 'MASS' SYMPHONIES (1865–73). This earliest batch of Bruckner's mature symphonies shows a close proximity in date, style and even thematic matter with the three great masses. The psychological background of these symphonies is in fact determined as much by the overwhelming experience of writing the masses as by the events in Bruckner's personal life. Between 1865 and 1873 Bruckner met Wagner, Liszt and Hans von Bülow, heard *Tristan* at Munich (June 1865) and Beethoven's ninth Symphony under Herbeck (Vienna, 1867). He brought his three masses to performance at Linz and in Vienna, and his first Symphony at Linz (1868). Of his greater compositions he published for the first time *Germanenzug,* in 1865, and became professor at the Vienna Conservatory as well as prospective organist at the imperial court chapel (1st October 1868). He celebrated his greatest triumph as an executant, playing the organ at Nancy, in Paris (1869) and later in London (1871). He experienced his first and most critical nervous breakdown (1867) and saved himself from melancholy and perhaps insanity by writing his most magnificent choral work, the Mass in F minor (1867–8). Finally, and most important of all, he effected the greatest change in his mental and spiritual climate by moving to Vienna and all but terminating his church appointments, thus secularizing his environment as well as his sphere of interest. It is against this background of cross-currents and fluctuations that the following works must be assessed.

Symphony I, in C minor, is surely one of the most remarkable 'first' symphonies ever conceived by a great composer. It is original to excess, and completely justifies the loving nickname bestowed on it by the ageing composer, *'s kecke Beserl* ('the saucy little besom'). It exists in two versions of equal authenticity: the early 'Linz' version, composed between January 1865 and 14th April 1866, and first performed on 9th May 1868 at Linz under the composer's direction;

and the final version of 1890–1, completed on 18th April 1891, and first performed under Hans Richter in Vienna at a Philharmonic concert on 13th December of that year. That second version was published under Bruckner's supervision in 1893. The published score, however, contains discrepancies with the autograph of R.V. of 1890–1, among them a serious one: Bruckner's tempo indication 'C' of 1865 *and* 1890–1 has been changed to *alla breve*. It should be put on record that it was the unrevised 'Linz' version (remaining more or less intact until approximately 1890) which in turn had captivated Hans von Bülow (as early as June 1865, during the final rehearsals of *Tristan* at Munich), Hans Richter and Hermann Levi, who pleaded as late as 1891 for its *unrevised* publication.

The first movement, with its stubborn march rhythm and the rugged jauntiness of its principal subject, has become the ancestral blueprint for a certain type of introductory march movement in a minor key, favoured later on by Mahler (Symphony VI) and Alban Berg (*Marsch*, No. 3 of *Drei Orchesterstücke*, Op. 6). The enormous interval skips of its first trombone entry (Linz V., letter O) anticipate the *Wiener Spannungen* (Viennese tensions) in the thematic material of Arnold Schoenberg and his school. The rustic ferocity of the scherzo, in G minor, creates a type of vernacular symphonic *Ländler* which is to re-echo frequently in Mahler's earlier symphonies, and the fiery finale ends with a chorale apotheosis in the horns, exulting in the dissonance of its upward-leaping seventh:

Ex. 20

The differences between O.V. and R.V. are not inconsiderable; clearly they are the outcome of Bruckner's honest attempt at tightening up the structure. The gradual change of his approach to the intricate problems of symphonic form can best be studied by a comparison of the trio section of the scherzo (both versions) with its many subtle variants in harmony, contrapuntal treatment and scoring. Also, the very end of the work has been thoroughly revised, especially from letter

P onwards. The whole orchestration and the phrasing-marks have been carefully overhauled in many instances, with the result that the passionate, almost violent character of the Linz version has been some-what modified, not to say watered down. In sharp contrast to the other three symphonies of its period, No. 1 not only contains no thematic allusion to the masses, but seems rather to revel in the secular character of its passionate thematic material. Not even the beautiful *Adagio,* with its preconceived *Tristan* harmonies and its devotional 3-4 middle section, contains any noticeable reminiscence from the world of ecclesiastical music which Bruckner was rapidly outgrowing with this unique work. It was this Symphony's final version that Bruckner dedicated to the University of Vienna in return for the honorary doctor's degree bestowed on him in the year of its first performance.

Very different is the aspect of Symphony ' O,' in D minor, the step-child of traditional Bruckner biography. It is chiefly the mistaken assignment of the date of its origin which led to the almost universal underestimation of this second symphonic essay of his—not counting the early ' study ' symphony. For a deeper understanding of Bruckner the symphonist a thorough knowledge of this work is all the more indispensable since the composer used it later on as a thematic quarry for some of his later symphonies, though at the same time this is the reason why it is not counted as a ' number.'

It is difficult to determine this Symphony's date of origin precisely. Göllerich and Auer relegated it to the winter of 1863-4, thus making it an immediate successor to the Symphony in F minor. Their assumption is based on Bruckner's vague remark, on being con-fronted with the manuscript on the occasion of his removal to the Belvedere in 1895, that it belonged to his Linz period. It was then that Bruckner wrote on its cover: ' Symphony "O," quite invalid (only an attempt). . . .' But—and this seems to point to his real feelings—he refrained from burning the manuscript, as he did in the case of many other manuscripts before his removal, and bequeathed it in his will to the Oberoesterreichisches Landesmuseum at Linz. According to the dates in the manuscript the Symphony was actually written between 24th January and 12th September 1869. The trio, which can bear comparison with the famous trio in the scherzo of

Symphony VII, was certainly composed on 16th July 1869. Further proof of the late date of the actual composition is to be found in a letter addressed by Bruckner to his friend Moriz von Mayfeld at Linz, dated 15th July 1869, which unmistakably proves that a large portion of the second movement was composed during July of that year. The *Andante* represents a very mature standard of composition. It already contains Bruckner's typical features of style: rapid harmonic progressions in the quaver motion of the strings, offsetting a daring two-part counterpoint in horn and oboe, comparable to the 'Et incarnatus' section of the Mass in F minor.

Bruckner's letters contain further proof. On 21st January 1865, writing to his friend R. Weinwurm, he refers to 'the score of my symphony.' This can only be the 'study' Symphony in F minor, whose completion he had announced to Weinwurm on 1st September 1863. Eight days later, i.e. on 29th January 1865, he tells the same friend: 'I am just working on a C minor Symphony (No. 2) . . .' which Max Auer quite correctly identifies as the later Symphony I (Linz version). If Bruckner had sketched another symphonic work in the meantime—i.e. between the completion of the F minor Symphony (September 1863) and the start of this new C minor Symphony —he would certainly have mentioned it to Weinwurm and would not have referred to the new work as 'No. 2' only eight days after alluding to the full score of his earlier F minor Symphony. It is of course possible, technically as well as psychologically, that Bruckner worked on portions of No. 'O' some time during the winter of 1863-4, but it is not very likely. He had completed Psalm CXII and *Germanen-zug* by September 1863 (in addition to the F minor Symphony) and was to embark on the D minor Mass early in July 1864. Between that date and September 1868 he composed the three great masses and Symphony I. He could hardly have found any time for No. 'O' during that period of Herculean creative labour. Also, a great part of the winter and spring of 1866-7 was lost to composition because of his nervous breakdown.

All this evidence goes to show that the decisive creative effort for No. 'O' must have been made between January and September 1869 —that is to say, well after the disheartening experience of the critical reactions to the first performance of Symphony I (Linz, May 1868), and as an unmistakable psychological reaction to it. Bruckner is known to have performed the first movement of 'O' in Vienna in the presence of Otto Dessoff, the influential first conductor of the Court Opera, who asked candidly: 'Where is the principal subject?' That question clinched the matter, and the score was definitely laid aside. Bruckner would not have presented an immature work to Dessoff, on whose goodwill he counted at the start of his own activities in Vienna.

Surely the best proof for the true value of this neglected Symphony No. 'O' must lie in the fact that its first theme (precisely the one which Dessoff could not or would not identify) supplied the thematic underlay for the glorious trumpet theme of Symphony III, in D minor. Many more motives of No. 'O' were re-employed in later symphonies. The beginning of the coda in its first movement reappears literally in the finale of Symphony VI, while the continuation motive in its own finale constitutes a most important element in the first group of themes in the first movement of Symphony III. But perhaps the most convincing proof, albeit adduced only from internal evidence, of the Symphony's late origin is the twice-repeated quotation (in the *Andante*) of a mournful motive sung to the words 'Qui tollis peccata mundi' in the 'Gloria' of the E minor Mass (composed in 1866). This quotation, surely, would lose much of its significance if it were merely anticipated in an early sketch of 1863–4, i.e. long before the Mass was composed; on the other hand it is very significant if understood as the outcome of Bruckner's spiritual and mental crisis during 1866–7. Indeed, the after-effects of that crisis may have determined the conceptual pattern of the whole work which, if composed after Symphony I, and the E minor and F minor Masses, appears in many respects like a retrograde step after the boldness of Symphony I. Self-imposed restraint is clearly reflected in smaller theme-groups and shorter bridge-passages as well as in a more lyrical and introspective general mood. This deliberate curbing results in many felicities of style, especially in the *Adagio,* whose devout first motive curiously resembles the beginning of the slow movement of Brahms's Serenade No. 1, Op. 11, in the same key (B♭ major). The seraphic atmosphere of certain portions of the three masses returns not only in the actual quotation from the E minor Mass, but also in more distant allusions, as for instance the *cantabile* group at cue 30, and in the Brahms-like return of the first theme over *pizzicato* basses. The finale begins in the mood of a 'Sanctus' from one of Bruckner's early masses. These ecclesiastical associations in the critical movement of the whole work may well be deliberate; they are repeated at letter A, when the 'Osanna' end from the 'Benedictus' of the early *Missa solemnis* in B flat of 1854 is literally quoted,[1] and they culminate most impressively before the recapitulation in a quotation from the seven-part *Ave Maria* (1861) at bars 120-30. The first movement with its indeterminate exposition (justifying to a certain extent Dessoff's wonderment) and its straggling development, propelled by the *staccato* quavers from the 'Gratias' section of the F minor Mass, is the least satisfactory part of the Symphony.[2] However, in the part composed last of all, the trio, Bruckner's struggle for close thematic integration scores a remarkable success, for the trio is linked to the scherzo by a common motive (x):

Ex. 21

Its ferocity in the scherzo is beautifully transformed into the lyrical gentleness of the trio. Such purple patches more than counter-balance undeniable weaknesses of structure and thematic treatment, especially in the two outer movements.

[1] A passage completely misunderstood by R. Haas (see Bibliography), p. 105. The whole Symphony has been analysed with little sympathy by M. Auer (see Bibliography, 1934), pp. 94 ff.

[2] In both cases these *staccato* quavers accompany the contrasting section of the *cantabile*, thus establishing a customary usage in Bruckner's symphonies (cf. Symphonies IV and V, where these ubiquitous but also slightly numbing quavers turn up again).

Symphony ' O ' and Symphony II

The 'Zero' Symphony had to wait for its first publication (edited by J. von Wöss, Universal Edition) as well as for its first complete performance until the year of the hundredth anniversary of Bruckner's birth (12th October 1924). Since then it has asserted in increasing measure its evolutionary importance for an understanding of the early stages of Bruckner's career as a symphonist.

Symphony II, in C minor, shares, curiously enough, its principal key with its predecessor, Symphony I, to which it otherwise forms a psychological contrast even more startling than that between Symphonies I and 'O.' Its conception is still determined by the reaction caused by the unrestrained outburst of Symphony I, the general misunderstanding of that work by critics and first audiences and no less by the unfavourable reception of Symphony 'O' at the hands of Dessoff and the critical pundits.

The spectre of shapelessness began to haunt Bruckner, whose symphonic patterns, determined largely by the proportions of the musical setting of the mass, refused to be pressed into the Procrustean bed of classical form. The self-imposed restraint which had led to unequal and inconclusive results in Symphony 'O' now led to an emphasis on lyricism and a manner of formal circumspection fundamentally alien to Bruckner. It is obvious that he was in two minds about future symphonic composition at that time. Although he started work on Symphony II on 11th October 1871, a plan for a very different Symphony in B flat major interrupted these beginnings as early as 29th October. The preserved sketch of some sixty-seven bars indicates a more optimistic work, almost in the jaunty mood of the first movement of Symphony I; but this fleeting mood was destined to vanish and to be swallowed up by the elegiac beauty of Symphony II. This work, composed with such care for the traditional rules of sonata form, has been nicknamed 'Pausensymphonie' (symphony of rests) because of the caesuras which the timorous and self-doubting composer inserted at every pivotal turning-point of its structure. With as much justification it might be called the 'Mass-Symphony' because of the extensive quotations from the F minor Mass in its *Adagio* as well as in the finale. Such self-quotations counterbalance with their episodic freedom the formal regularities of

85

a symphony which suffers much less than others from the composer's habitual *longueurs*.

The work had a chequered history, vividly reflecting Bruckner's initial difficulties in the Austrian capital. Although composed in a comparatively short span between 11th October 1871 and 11th September 1872, it was revised again and again[1] until it was published in December 1892 in a version very different from O.V. of 1872, and containing cuts of rather doubtful authenticity. The first performance took place on 26th October 1872 under Bruckner's direction. It was his first symphonic *première* in Vienna, where he was still treated like a provincial stranger. The Philharmonic Orchestra had disdainfully turned the work down, so that Bruckner had to hire its services. The concert, taking place at the very end of the Vienna World Exhibition, received an added attraction through Bruckner's playing Bach's organ Toccata in D minor and a free improvisation. He had an enthusiastic reception, in the end even from the recalcitrant orchestra. However, when he attempted in all humility to dedicate the work to the Philharmonic players, they cold-shouldered him again. Much later he dedicated the Symphony to Liszt, whose letter of acceptance (29th October 1884) sounds rather reserved. When Bruckner discovered that Liszt had left the score carelessly behind on travelling to Budapest, he was deeply hurt and withdrew the dedication. Meanwhile Symphony II, a special favourite of Johann Herbeck's, received another performance (20th February 1876), which was commented on with marked hostility by Hanslick and his henchmen representing the Brahms faction of the Vienna press. Rather late in the day the Philharmonic Orchestra made amends by performing R.V. under Richter at one of its regular concerts (25th November 1894), but after that it waited nearly another twenty years before putting the Symphony on again: under Weingartner, 23rd November 1913.

In the third Symphony, in D minor,[2] Bruckner evidently rallied by

[1] R. Haas counted four versions: 1872, 1873, 1876–7, and 1892 (R.V.). F. Blume believes that Bruckner never reached the stage of a conclusive final version.

[2] See Chapter VIII, where a detailed analysis of this Symphony is attempted as a general study of Bruckner's symphonic procedure.

returning to the monumental conception of Symphony I and utilizing thematic material from Symphony 'O' (first movement) as well as quotations from his religious music. But more than anything else it is, as we have seen, the experience of Beethoven's ninth Symphony which inspired the work. These fertilizing Beethovenian elements are powerfully counterbalanced by the music of Wagner, which appears in naïve quotations from *Tristan* and *Walküre*. They occur for the first time in a score of Bruckner's and were probably inserted as soon as he had formed the plan of dedicating the work to the master of Bayreuth. They were completely expunged from the later versions, a clear indication of Bruckner's ever watchful self-criticism.

Like its predecessor, Symphony III was subjected to several far-reaching revisions, and it has the distinction of being the first major work of Bruckner's to be published. Here follows the story of its *gradus ad Parnassum* in tabulated form:

Version 1, composed 1873 (completed 31st December 1873), improved in 1874.

Version 2, composed 1876–8, first performance in Vienna, 16th December 1877, under Bruckner.

Published (in score and in a piano duet arrangement by Mahler) by Th. Rättig, Vienna, 1878.

Version 3, 1888–9, based on the published score of 1878; first performance 21st December 1890 in Vienna (Richter).

Published 1890, Vienna (Th. Rättig).

The third Symphony (in its incomplete first version) was seen by Wagner at Bayreuth in September 1873, alongside a score of No. II. Wagner was much impressed, especially by the trumpet motive in the first movement, which later served to provide Bruckner with the nickname 'Bruckner, the trumpet' in the house of Wahnfried. After careful perusal Wagner accepted the offered dedication, and he seems to have entertained sympathies for the work until his death. The Vienna Philharmonic Orchestra twice refused to include the work in its programmes; finally Herbeck, Bruckner's generous patron, arranged a performance for 1877–8, but he died before it took place on 16th December, and Bruckner himself had to conduct. Although its reception was disastrously hostile, it was published in the following year. The ruthless third revision was evidently under-taken under the impact of Levi's temporary refusal to perform it in O.V. (1887), when Bruckner's self-confidence was at its lowest ebb. The influence of the brothers Schalk, who sympathized with Levi's criticism, is even more noticeable. F. Oeser has shown that much new material, inserted into this third version, belongs to the stylistic orbit of Symphony VIII, and does not really coalesce with the sub-stance of Bruckner's early symphonic style of 1873-4. The structure of the monumentally planned finale has especially suffered in this third revision.[1] Although the second version (1878) is often long-winded and self-repetitive, it is a much more natural growth, with even its smallest bridge-passage drawing substance from genuine thematic source material. Compared with it the third version (1890) seems laboured, artificial and essentially inorganic, with its frequent abrupt caesuras replacing natural transitions and despite the luxuriant sound-cushion of Wagnerian horns and trombones. As in the case of Symphony II no really satisfactory final version of this work exists. It seems possible that, as in the case of modern performances of Gluck's *Orpheus*, future performing practice may resort to a process of fusing the different versions of both these symphonies. That the method of scoring and indeed the whole harmonic atmosphere is much more consistent and of a piece in the third version (1877) of Symphony II, as well as in the first printing of Symphony III (1878), can no longer be in doubt.

THE 'ROMANTIC' SYMPHONIES, 1874-81. The symphonic urge continues with unabating intensity in this third stage of Bruckner's development as a composer of large-scale instrumental music, which comprises Symphonies IV-VI and the Quintet. It does not yet tolerate temporary deflection into the calmer waters of religious music and keeps straight to its course even when temporarily transferred to the alien medium of chamber music. The four works under discussion

[1] Cf. the ugly gap of 53 bars (R.V. before letter U). See Oeser (see Bibliography) on the doubtful instrumental changes in the setting of the chorale motive, 9 bars after letter T.

here are not lumped together merely because of their proximity in date; like the four of 1865–73, they form a coherent group by virtue of their common musical climate. Symphonies I–III and the 'Zero' Symphony had been composed in the tragic and mysterious keys of C and D minor—keys fraught with mystical or religious associations ever since Beethoven and Schubert. The following four works are all in the major keys of E flat, B flat, F (string Quintet) and A. They are optimistic, romantic (No. IV, a description appearing already in the earliest sketch), fantastic (No. V, Bruckner himself called this his ' Fantastic ' Symphony) or joyful (No. VI, Bruckner is reported to have said of this 'Die Sechste ist die Keckste' ['the sixth is the sauciest']). They completely lack ecclesiastical self-quotation—they are secular in a way reminiscent of Symphony I—and in their most popular work, Symphony IV, they reveal Bruckner's deep attachment to nature in a mystical, not in a descriptive-senti-mentalizing sense. Their history is even more involved than the story of the vicissitudes of the earlier group of symphonies. The appearance of these works coincided with the summit of Brahms's career as a composer of symphonies and large-scale chamber music. Ruthless competition between the two composers was an unpleasant but inevitable consequence of the general artistic situation in Vienna, in those days still the musical nerve-centre of Europe.

The fourth Symphony, in E flat major, the 'Romantic,' should not be misunderstood as a belated attempt on Bruckner's part to write symphonic programme music in the manner of Liszt. Unfortu-nately the composer in his childlike naïvety provided unsuspecting biographers with all the material for exactly that kind of misinter-pretation. He attempted, *a posteriori,* to describe the first movement as a medieval mood-picture *à la Lohengrin* (Act II, medieval city—morning dawn—morning call by trumpets—the knights gallop into the forest—forest murmurs, etc.). In addition he called the scherzo (second version) 'Hunting of the Hare,' and its charming trio in G flat major, 'Dance-melody during the Huntsmen's Repast.' Finally he labelled the finale (first version) 'Popular Festival.' All these interpretative attempts *post festum* carry but little conviction. On the other hand nobody will want to deny that the mystical opening call on the horn, emerging from the golden-green depth of an E flat major chord, played *tremolando* in the strings, suggests almost forcibly the majesty of alpine forests, and nobody will grudge the charming 'Vogel Zizi-Be':

Ex. 22

—Bruckner's own description—admission to the symphonic aviary presided over by Beethoven's equally persuasive yellow-hammer.

The fourth Symphony's especially happy melodic inspiration has made it a favourite among modern audiences. Its popularity is fully deserved: Bruckner is never more lovable than when his music assumes a native Austrian tone. This peculiar landscape atmosphere emanates from every bar of the work: its romantic chorale in the heavy brass (first movement after letter K, R.V.) no less than the almost Schubertian elegy of the peripatetic *Andante*, and perhaps most of all its jaunty continuation in the violins with its irresistibly Viennese lilt and its echoes of *Burgmusik* (letter E, O.V.). The Symphony shows, especially in its first version, a high degree of thematic integration, which in some ways has been weakened in its later revision. The integration becomes particularly noticeable in the employment of the quintuple motive ♩♩ ♩♩♩ from the scherzo in the introduction to the finale (O.V., cue 30) and even more so in the final resolution accorded to the Symphony's mysterious initial bars.

The story of this Symphony's genesis is more complicated than ever. Its gradual progress is best given in tabulated form again:

Version 1, composed 2nd January–22nd November 1874 (autograph only partly preserved).

Version 2, 1878, composed 18th January–5th June 1880.

Version 3, 1879–80, with completely new 'hunt' scherzo and a new finale (all but replacing the original 'Volksfest' of 1874).

The amalgamated version 2–3 (with the new middle movements) had its successful first performance in Vienna (under Richter) on 20th February 1881.

Version 4 (final version) 1887–8; first performed 22nd January, under Richter.

This final Version 4 alone was published (Gutmann, Vienna, 1889).[1]

It is not easy to assess the respective merits of the two published scores, each reproducing in a fashion the autograph of Bruckner's final intentions, particularly as the publication of 1890 occurred at a time when he was in good health and spirits. It seems pretty certain that the cymbal-clash (finale, three bars after D, Gutmann score), as well as its *pianissimo* echo later on (finale, six bars before letter T, Gutmann score), represent interpolations by the Schalk brothers, and that some of the cuts most probably reflect suggestions from Herbeck and possibly also from Richter. The differences between these two published scores are in no way comparable to the discrepancies between the two published scores of Symphony III. A restoration of Bruckner's *Urfassung* of Symphony IV (and here alone perhaps this much-abused term is applicable), presenting the original scherzo and finale ('Volksfest') in a performable version, might be an interesting and enlightening venture.[2] In whatever guise it appears this 'Romantic' Symphony will continue to remain Bruckner's most lovable, most popular and most easily performable work.

With the fifth Symphony, in B flat major, and its sorry fate, we have reached the nadir of Bruckner's personal misfortunes, poignantly enough expressed in the seeming hopelessness of his situation in

[1] But the published version differs in many respects considerably from the autograph of the final version of 1887–8, which has been published only recently with the version of 1874 and the hitherto unknown finale of version 3 of 1879–80 in the Complete Edition, ed. R. Haas, 1936; reprint of the final version alone by Brucknerverlag, Wiesbaden, 1949, and (utilizing newly discovered source material) in Vol. IV, II of the Complete Edition, by L. Nowak, Vienna, 1953.

[1] F. Blume (*Musik in Geschichte und Gegenwart*, II) speaks of two O.V. with two different scherzos and finales.

Vienna, where he was fated to compose vast symphonies—lonely, misunderstood, misrepresented—in utter contrast with the frivolous gaiety of the city of Johann Strauss, jun., and confronted with the north German, Protestant austerities of Brahms and his all-powerful press clique. This is the only symphony of his he was never to hear performed. The special problems of its style, so different from that of the preceding six symphonies, have been discussed elsewhere.[1] The great refinement and growing complexity of its contrapuntal technique, as also certain features of its formal structure, give the lie to the oft-repeated assertion that Bruckner as a symphonist shows no real development. With this work the composer, now in his early fifties, reached a standard of maturity comparable to the polyphonic virtuosity and thematic integration achieved by Wagner at approximately the same age in *Die Meistersinger*.

The fifth Symphony contains two features by which it particularly differs from the rest of the symphonies: the slow introductions to its two outer movements and the form of the finale, in which a synthesis of sonata and fugal treatment may be observed that has only two precedents in the history of the species: the finales of Mozart's 'Jupiter' Symphony and of Beethoven's ninth. The latter had, as we already know, served as a thematic catalyst for Symphonies 'O' and III. Now Bruckner adopts its technique of thematic reminiscence for the finale of Symphony V.[2] The close interdependence of the two middle movements, as also the high degree of thematic integration in the whole work, have already been discussed. It remains to state that in the present writer's opinion the special quality of Bruckner's organ improvisation as well as of his ecclesiastical fervour materialized nowhere so completely as in the passage of the finale where the chorale is introduced into the rugged exposition of themes.

The Symphony was composed between 14th February 1875 and 9th August 1877. There is no indication that Bruckner afterwards revised the work as a whole or in parts. The score remained for a

[1] See Chapter VIII.

[2] That device of serialized self-quotations from earlier movements in the finale had already played a part in the first version of the finale of Symphony III as well as in the final version of the finale of Symphony IV.

decade in the composer's desk. At long last Joseph Schalk gave a performance in his own arrangement for two pianos (with himself and Franz Zottmann as executants) in Vienna on 20th April 1887. This performance (which incidentally scored a veritable triumph for Bruckner) had almost been torpedoed by the wrathful and ever-suspicious composer, who had evidently resented its element of surprise. The next performance, the first and only orchestral one to happen during his lifetime, took place at Graz on 9th April 1894 under Franz Schalk's direction. Bruckner was too ill to risk the journey, and he gave Schalk a free hand with regard to the public presentation of the work. It was Schalk's idea to score the final chorale (finale, letter U, R.V.) for a separate brass band of trumpets, trombones, tuba and four horns, which was to play on an elevated rostrum at the back of the orchestra—a theatrical device quite alien to Bruckner's simple mind, but undoubtedly very impressive. Schalk later maintained that he had been specially authorized to carry out this emendation. The facsimile reproduction of that particular page of the autograph shows clearly that Bruckner intended the chorale to be played in the main orchestra by its own brass section—unless a marginal note in faint handwriting, 'NB Choral neu,' is to be inter-preted as an approval of Schalk's idea. In addition the facsimile of that page reveals that the parts for flutes and clarinets, with their decorative trills and runs *à la Götterdämmerung*, as well as the stave for percussion instruments (cymbals and triangle), are missing in the autograph. It is hardly conceivable that Bruckner could have acquiesced in these addenda; it is equally unlikely that he would have approved of the truly appalling cuts in the finale, amounting to no less than 122 bars. Finally, it is difficult to believe that he would have endorsed the complete reorchestration of the work, as discussed earlier in this book.

The Symphony was eventually published in 1896 under Franz Schalk's supervision, at a time when Bruckner was much too ill to take any active interest in the fate of his works at the hands of posterity. Bruckner's hope, expressed in a letter to F. Schalk dated 12th April 1894, to hear the Symphony under his direction in Vienna remained sadly unfulfilled. A performance took place two years after his death, under Ferdinand Löwe. It was Vienna's last rebuff to Bruckner.

The string Quintet in F major, Bruckner's sole mature contribution to chamber music, in which at that time Brahms reigned supreme, is really an occasional piece, for it was suggested in 1878 by Joseph Hellmesberger, who wanted new music for his excellent quartet. Bruckner apparently could not or would not write a string quartet, which proves that he instinctively felt the need of a richer texture to do justice to his instrumental style. Yet it is a gross exaggeration to call the work, as has been done, 'a symphony in disguise.' It is a genuine attempt to adjust Bruckner's symphonic style to the requirements of an uncongenial medium. This is borne out by a comparison between its four movements and the corresponding movements in his symphonies. The happiest balance is struck in the serenely beautiful *Adagio*, one of Bruckner's supreme inspirations. Here he manages to fuse convincingly the seraphic style of his 'Benedictus' movements with limpid part-writing for a string *ensemble*. To be sure, the grandeur of this mainly subdued movement becomes apparent at its *fff* climax, which transgresses the limitations of sonority imposed on chamber music and cries out for translation into majestic orchestral sound. A passage such as this clearly indicates that Bruckner could not keep for long within the boundaries of this restricted medium without unnatural restraint. That he was chafing under this restriction is shown even more clearly by the scherzo. This ferocious and dissonant piece, one of Bruckner's least graceful middle movements, shows an indisputable element of strain. Small wonder that this movement proved a temporary stumbling-block for Hellmesberger, who even suggested its elimination and replacement by a later *Intermezzo,* written in the same key of D minor, but of a more restrained, *Ländler*-like character. This piece, however, was discarded in the end in favour of the original movement. There is no question that passages such as the eight-bar pedal-point on D♭, like that of sixteen bars at the beginning of the finale (with its curiously intangible association with the Beckmesser motives of *Die Meistersinger*) would greatly improve in an orchestral setting. All in all, here is plenty of evidence for Bruckner's comparative failure to provide the chosen medium with a really satisfactory work of intimate sonorities.

The sixth Symphony, in A major, is an even greater problem-child than the Quintet. The rough passage it had, both in its own time and later, recalls the vicissitudes associated with the score of Symphony V. Even a brief inspection of the score easily explains why friend and foe alike felt bewildered by a work in which some typical features of Bruckner's music were missing altogether, while certain idiosyncrasies seemed excessively underscored and emphasized.

The Symphony's greatest asset is the rhythmic originality of its first movement. Its thematic subjects skilfully mask Bruckner's favourite quintuple rhythm in metrical complexities, distinguished by their predilection for almost Elgarian interval-skips, as may be seen in the following examples:

Ex. 23

Ex. 24

The Wagnerian origin of motive *x* (Ex. 24) is fairly obvious, but it is only in the 'fantastic' scherzo—utterly different from all the preceding and all but one of the following scherzos—that Bruckner's dependence on the models of Bayreuth becomes painfully evident. A motive such as the following:

Ex. 25

is a plain and scarcely concealed echo from the scene of the Rhine-maidens in *Götterdämmerung*. I do not believe for a moment that Bruckner intended this as a deliberate homage to Wagner, as in the case of the Wagner quotations in Symphony III. He simply fell in love with the sound of that motive and was fascinated by its harmonic possibilities. The slow movement is the emotional climax of the whole work. But even that movement's haunting beauty, with its soul-piercing plaint of the oboe (bars 5 ff.), cannot compensate for the unfortunate impression created by the patchy and inconclusive finale, which resorts more than any other movement of Bruckner's to material exploited by him to the full elsewhere.

The sixth Symphony took nearly two years to write: 24th September 1879 to 3rd September 1881. It was dedicated to Bruckner's kind landlord, Herr von Oelzelt, and received a first performance of its middle movements (the only ones ever heard by Bruckner) at a Philharmonic concert conducted by Mahler's predecessor, Wilhelm Jahn, on 11th February 1883. The whole Symphony had to wait a long time for its first performance. This took place on 26th February 1899 at a Philharmonic concert under Mahler, who apparently cut the work to the bone to secure its initial success. It was published in 1899 under the supervision of Bruckner's one-time pupil, Cyrill Hynais, with the result that its score differs from the autograph in many small details of phrasing and expression marks.

THE LATE SYMPHONIES, 1881–96. The impression—perhaps conveyed by the heading of this section—that Bruckner's creative urge was beginning to slow down in the final period of his life is quite unfounded. On the contrary, these last fifteen years were fraught with feverish productivity, and filled to capacity with new musical conceptions. The three late symphonies were composed alongside the final large-scale choral works, the *Te Deum* (1881–4) and Psalm CL (1892), as well as his most important secular choral pieces, *Helgoland* and *Das deutsche Lied* (1892–3). They moreover had to share their creator's time and energy expended on the complete revisions of Symphonies I, II and III (published 1890–2), which amount almost to new compositions. To these chief works a final

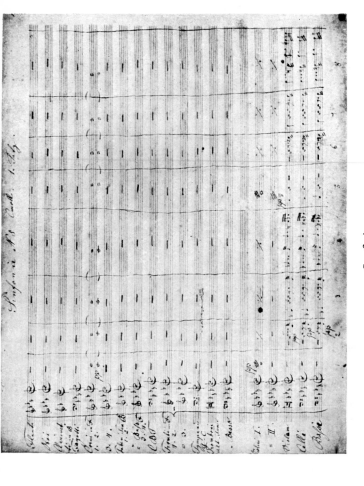

See facing page

(By courtesy of Bayerische Staatsbibliothek, Munich)

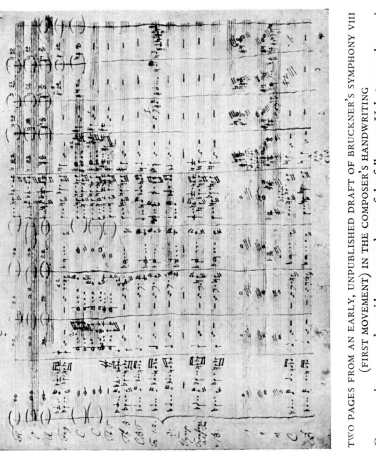

TWO PAGES FROM AN EARLY, UNPUBLISHED DRAFT OF BRUCKNER'S SYMPHONY VIII
(FIRST MOVEMENT) IN THE COMPOSER'S HANDWRITING

Compare sheets 1 and 4 with pp. 1 and 5–6 of the full score, Vol. 8, complete and
critical edition (ed. R. Haas), Wiesbaden, 1949. (*Bayerische Staatsbibliotbek, Munich*)

batch of some ten smaller religious compositions must be added, written mainly between 1879 and 1892.

The three late symphonies show so many likenesses of style and technique and differ so strongly from the preceding group that they really represent an ultimate phase in Bruckner's development, comparable to the style of Beethoven's last works, likewise written during the final decade of the composer's life. Features common to all three works include enormous length, even if compared with Bruckner's own earlier music, great extension of each single movement, a much wider range of orchestral sonorities, and finally strong thematic associations with Bruckner's religious music, abounding in quotations from the *Te Deum* as well as from the Mass in D minor.

As to length in general: Symphony VIII (O.V.) occupies eighty-seven minutes playing-time as compared with Symphony V, which takes eighty-one. The three famous *Adagio* movements of these late symphonies are probably the longest slow movements in the world's whole symphonic output. The orchestra has increased in number as well as in types. All three symphonies employ a quartet of Wagner tubas, well known from the score of *The Ring*, but used discriminately by Bruckner for the *Adagio* and finale only, thereby placing additional weight and emphasis on these movements.[1] Where the Wagner tubas are silent the group of horns is temporarily increased to six, or even to eight, since they can be used by the same players, and in addition percussion instruments and harp are used in the middle movements of Symphony VIII.[2]

The solemnity of all three works is expressed not only by the marked emphasis on the slow movements, the deliberate utilization of ecclesiastical matter, such as the 'Non confundar' melody from the *Te Deum*, and the length and rugged monumentality of their principal subjects, but also by the recipients of their dedications. Symphony VII is dedicated to King Ludwig II of Bavaria (though actually to

[1] The customary second place of Bruckner's *Adagio* shifts to the third in the last two symphonies, plainly because of the excessive length and monumentally slow pace of their first movements.

[2] Their inclusion in Symphony VII, however, is spurious, as is the use of the double bassoon in Löwe's edition of Symphony IX.

the memory of Wagner), Symphony VIII to the Emperor Francis Joseph I of Austria and Symphony IX 'dem lieben Gott.' This dedication of Bruckner's 'unfinished' Symphony is a clear pointer towards the conceptual core of all three. They aspire to God and attempt to describe the ecstasies of bliss and abysses of despair experienced by their creator on his journey to 'the blest courts of the Lord.' This transcendental artistic experience, no less than the melodic beauty and architectural magnitude of these works, links them to Beethoven's ninth Symphony, whose influence becomes noticeable especially in the *Adagio* of Symphony VII and the first movement of Symphony IX.

The seventh Symphony, in E major, composed in two years between September 1881 and 1883, is easily the most popular and surely the most strikingly beautiful of all Bruckner's symphonies. Quite deservedly it has also had the easiest passage, with its first performance taking place at Leipzig under Arthur Nikisch as early as 30th December 1884 and its score being published in the following year. The seraphic beauty of its first principal theme is the measure of the Symphony's rare height of inspiration. Here are the first seven bars of the long-drawn theme covering two octaves:

Ex. 26

It is matched by a consequent whose initial motive *x* forms the thematic base from which later on the majestic twenty-two-bar pedal-point on E emerges which introduces the first movement's coda (O.V., cue 390):

Ex. 27

This is nothing but an instrumentalized quotation from the 'Judicare' section in the 'Credo' of the D minor Mass, where the motive appears in the tenors:

Ex. 28

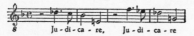

Ju - di - ca - re,   Ju - di - ca - re

The link with Bruckner's ecclesiastical world becomes strongest in the *Adagio,* whose two contrasting sections (the funereal 4–4 dirge in the tubas and the Viennese lilt of the *cantabile* theme in 3–4, on the model of the dual *Adagio* in Beethoven's ninth Symphony) finally coalesce in the incandescence of the 'Non confundar' motive from the *Te Deum* (O.V., letter T).

The scherzo of Symphony VII is unique in uniting rusticity and fantastic imagination. Its stubborn trumpet motive and the obstinacy of its rumbling accessory accompaniment in the strings have in-fluenced Mahler's conception (Symphony V). The golden sheen transfiguring the classical proportions and strangely elliptic modula-tions of its trio are as unearthly, remote and irrecoverable as the pictorial uniqueness of Hans von Marrées's contemporary painting 'The Golden Age.' Only a detailed analysis could do justice to the finale, whose chorale motive in the second-subject group revolves round the Neapolitan sixth, as did the chorale motive in Symphony V. Its principal subject is a clear derivation from Ex. 26.

The origin of the eighth Symphony, in C minor, which Bruckner believed to be his finest, presents the picture of a titanic struggle with its recalcitrant material, the scepticism of friends and foes and the increasing physical disabilities of oncoming old age. It is a work conceived on a heroic scale and the reflection of a truly heroic soul, undaunted by failures and disappointments. Haas is right in speak-ing of its 'Faustian disposition.' It scales celestial heights in the *Adagio* after having plumbed the depth of Dante's Inferno in the first movement, and it attempts a symphonic 'closing of the circle' in the finale by combining all the previous thematic matter in a final syn-thesis (at letter Z). A psychological exegesis on these lines surely does greater justice to this Symphony's sublimity than the composer's own incredibly naïve and inappropriate attempts at interpreting his visions *a posteriori*. In the letter to Weingartner of 27th January 1891, already quoted (Chapter VII, p. 41), he refers to the 'annunciation' of death in trumpets and horns at the end of the first movement as to one of the thematic main props of the whole symphonic edifice. He calls the Gargantuan scherzo 'Deutscher Michel,' evidently identifying himself with that symbolic figure of Teutonic uncouthness, and wants us to believe that the trio, with its melodic associations with the introductory song of Schubert's *Winter Journey*, expresses 'Michel's daydreams.' The gigantic if dangerously episodic finale is said by him to illustrate the meeting between the Austrian emperor and the Russian tsar at Olomouc, and he even identified the appoggiatura motive (strings, bar 1) permeating long stretches of this finale with the gallop of the Cossacks accompanying the tsar to the Moravian meeting-place. Fortunately the composer refrained from commenting on the meaning of the lovely *Adagio*, a movement of despair and loneliness, but also of ecstatic uplift, floating on the wings of syncopated triplets *à la Tristan* in the key of D flat, and growing out of the initial motive of Schubert's 'Wanderer' Fantasy, that dark hymn of lonely homesickness:

Ex. 29

Like its two sister-works, Symphony VIII can be appreciated only on the basis of a detailed analysis such as is outside the scope of this volume. Its melodic grandeurs are as apparent as its constructive weaknesses, especially in the finale, in which the 'military' and the 'ecclesiastic' elements threaten again and again to fall apart and to create intolerable *longueurs*.

Symphony VIII needed a long time to mature. Its earliest sketches go back to October 1884 and the finale (first draft) was completed on 10th August 1887. It was a period of halcyon happiness, inspired by the success of Symphony VII in Germany and by the first glimpses of more general recognition. Only two days after the completion of its first draft, work on Symphony IX began (12th August 1887). Hermann Levi's objections to the score of Symphony VIII in October of that year caused a nervous collapse (with thoughts of suicide), doubly painful in coming after the exultation of the previous years. The first sketch for Symphony IX occupied Bruckner wholly from now on until January 1889, when the revision of Symphony VIII (and of Symphonies I and III) began to cut across the natural growth of the ultimate symphony. The revision of Symphony VIII was carried out mainly between August 1889 and April 1890. The first performance took place, not at Munich under Levi, nor at Mannheim under Weingartner, but belatedly in Vienna, on 18th December 1892, under Richter. It met with a remarkable success which was even grudgingly acknowledged by Hanslick and his Brahms idolaters. Shortly before (1892) the score had been published in Berlin and Vienna simultaneously. The publication had been supervised by Max von Oberleithner, whose alterations play a part not dissimilar to those by F. Schalk and C. Hynais in the case of the other published scores. In spite of the excessive length of this Symphony, the episodic and sectional character of the finale and the dragging tempo of the *Adagio,* the published score of 1891 should not be condemned out of hand. Its suggestions for certain brief cuts will command attention, even if future interpreters will naturally prefer to base their study chiefly on the score of O.V. The case of this Symphony surely is a case for compromise between all the existing versions.

The ninth Symphony, in D minor, Bruckner's last and unfinished work, became the main occupation of the last nine years of his life (1887–96). It was conceived as a conscious sublimation of his whole preceding output, epitomizing the fruitful struggle for new symphonic proportions as well as the mystical solemnity of the great choral compositions. As in the early symphonies and also in Symphony VII a close thematic connection links this last Symphony with the Masses in B flat and D minor. The first movement represents, even thematically, the sum-total of Bruckner's D minor world of tragic expression. In subtlety of harmonization, exploitation of the relationship of the mediants, and also in the adventurous use of wide interval-skips (anticipatory of Mahler and Schoenberg), all three completed movements surpass anything previously written by Bruckner. Harmonic teasers such as the famous initial chord of the scherzo:

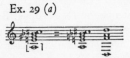

Ex. 29 (*a*)

the Neapolitan dissonance in the concluding bars of movement 1:

Ex. 30

and the ecstatic shout by the horns in the ambit of a ninth, in the *Adagio*:

Ex. 31

strongly affected the aural imagination of a whole generation of Austrian composers during the first quarter of this century. The proportions in all three movements outdo anything in Symphony VIII, and resemble Symphony VII in their conclusiveness. A special feature of the first as also of the planned fourth movement is the telescoping of development and recapitulation which leads to a remarkable tightening-up of Bruckner's too often sectional structure. The *Adagio*, similar in solemnity and length to the corresponding movements of the two preceding symphonies, again favours the ambivalence of two main groups of themes contrasted in mood and key, but not in rhythm, as in the *Adagio* of Symphony VII. Bruckner spoke of this favourite movement as of his 'farewell to life'—hence the numerous self-quotations towards the end ('Miserere' motive at letter T, *Adagio* of Symphony VIII quoted at letter X, *Adagio* of Symphony VII alluded to at letter Z).

The scherzo is one of Bruckner's most original inspirations: a miraculous synthesis of the rugged vernacular type and of a new element of elfin airiness, ushered in by the enigmatic chord of bar 1 with its quaint thematic contours, in *pizzicato* delineations, but really coming into its own in the fleeting vision of the F sharp major trio (rooted in a permanent pedal-point of F♯), with its syncopated gasps in the flute, set off by the ubiquitous silvery pattern in the plucked strings.

Bruckner had planned this Symphony as a work in four move-ments, conforming exactly to the structure of his preceding ten symphonies. He started work on it as early as 1887, as we have already seen. Movements 1 and 2 (scherzo) were finished in sketch by 1889, when work was interrupted by the revisions of Symphonies I and VIII and the composition of Psalm CL. It was taken up again early in 1891, and by February 1894 the first two movements were complete in full score. The third movement (*Adagio*) was the chief task of the year 1894, being completed at last on 30th November of that year. The remaining two years of Bruckner's life were devoted entirely to the finale, which exists in no fewer than six variants (in more or less full scoring) and was completed by him in full score up to the beginning of the coda. Far from being a transition leading up to the *Te Deum,* as has been assumed by earlier biographers, it is a purely instrumental finale of gigantic dimensions, in sonata form. The exposition begins with a characteristic theme of ambiguous tonality, in which the chord of the Neapolitan sixth of C minor acts as a harmonic astringent:

Ex. 32

The development section was first planned as a huge mirror reflection of the exposition, working with inversions of its principal subjects. This original idea was discarded at a later stage in favour of a develop-ment combining a fugue with a recapitulation of the second-subject group. This process of telescoping development and recapitulation is characteristic of late Bruckner. Its most obvious tendency is to split the whole movement into two main corresponding sections. Among the thematically important elements of the exposition proper are a 'Choralthema' (so labelled in the autograph) to which are attached the significant words 'Te Deum':

Ex. 33

This motive is a deliberate self-quotation from the *Te Deum,* and its reappearance here is of profound psychological and associative import. It is obviously not used as a pointer towards a final appear-ance of the *Te Deum* proper—although its sudden intrusion into this score may have led superficial observers to believe that such a trivial solution was actually planned by Bruckner—but as a reminiscence and an associative allusion to the idea of 'Te Deum laudamus,' which must have been uppermost in Bruckner's mind when nearing the end of this vast symphony. The chorale thus ultimately becomes fused with the *Te Deum* motive in a symbolic combination represent-ing the movement's last lap before the actual coda. It is here that the autograph actually uses the words 'Te Deum' when reintroducing the motive (which, however, had made a first appearance at a much earlier structural stage of the finale), and here it is that this 'Torso of Hercules' tantalizingly breaks off.

More than six years elapsed after Bruckner's death before Symphony IX was publicly performed, on 11th February 1903 under Ferdinand Löwe, who also issued the full score in the same year, acting as

Symphony IX: The Unfinished Finale

official editor. He also appended the *Te Deum* at that performance, to fill the place of the missing finale; allegedly in accordance with a wish of the dying composer, who is reported to have desired this link-up between the two works. That this is highly improbable has been shown in the foregoing. Since Löwe had arranged for the work to be issued as a fragment in three movements, the possible exist- ence of a finale was either openly discounted or tacitly ignored.[1] Only in 1934 did A. Orel publish the whole material in two critical editions simultaneously.[2] But even after Orel's publications and at a time when the Collected Edition was already well under way musicographers frequently persisted in asserting that Symphony IX simply 'lacked a finale'—as Alfred Einstein, for instance, did as late as 1947 in his *Music in the Romantic Era*. That this finale remained incomplete is the crowning tragedy in Bruckner's career as a composer. The stupendous originality of its design in itself deserves special praise. Orel has reduced the five versions of its full score to an arrange- ment on four staves only and thereby reconstructed the movement in its continuity (interrupted only by a few gaps) up to the transition from the recapitulation to the coda, thus enabling the student to appreciate the conception of the movement as a whole and to play it right through as far as it exists on paper. However, only an orchestral performance of this fragment (in itself almost complete in full score) could permit a deeper insight into the innermost recesses of Bruckner's creative mind, struggling to record faithfully its last artistic experience, undaunted even by approaching death.

[1] Although E. Decsey as early as 1919 (see Bibliography), p. 110 *et passim*, had related the fact that Löwe and Schalk had identified seventy-five sheets of full score among Bruckner's papers, representing the sketches for the finale of Symphony IX.

[2] One, containing Symphony IX in its O.V., i.e. in strict accordance with the autograph, the other, comprising sketches and drafts for all move- ments, including the contents of the seventy-five sheets of sketches for the finale.

MAHLER

CHAPTER I

CHILDHOOD AND ADOLESCENCE (1860–79)

GUSTAV MAHLER's life and achievement were an unceasing tug-of-war between the duties of one of Europe's most glamorous conductors and the increasing demands of a creative genius. This tragic dualism, which caused him lifelong suffering, and may have hastened his death, was conditioned by the peculiar circumstances of his birth.

Mahler was born into a family of poor Moravian Jews in the tottering Austrian Empire of Francis Joseph I. Jews settled in Bohemia and Moravia have played a remarkable part in the often dissonant concert of nations consisting of the many races living under Francis Joseph's rule. This is amply proved by men of international renown such as Sigmund Freud, the founder of modern psycho-analysis, Guido Adler, one of the principal figures in modern musicology, and Franz Kafka, the great novelist, all of whom hailed from that part of Austria. Although most of these Jews originally came from the easternmost recesses of the Austrian Empire, the provinces of Galicia and of Bukovina which to-day belong partly to Poland and partly to Russia and from time immemorial merged with Slavonic races such as Russians, Letts, Poles, Czechs and Slovaks, yet they retained a curious attachment to German culture and language, an attachment reflected by their idiomatic brogue of Yiddish and further emphasized by the significant fact that, in Bohemia and Moravia, they often acted as the main 'carriers' of German culture. Especially was this the case in German national 'islands' such as Iglau (Jihlava), the town in which Mahler spent most of his early years.

Mahler himself described his preordained, Ahasuerus-like position in life with sombre brevity in words related by his wife:[1] 'I am a thrice homeless man: as a Bohemian among Austrians, as

[1] ER (see Bibliography, p. 288), p. 135.

an Austrian among Germans and as a Jew among the peoples of the whole world. . . .' The tragic restlessness imposed on him as a member of his race, coupled with the poverty of his family and an urge to become absorbed into the hostile world of Gentiles, account for those traits in Mahler's character which have received so much censorious comment from unsympathetic critics: his will to dominate, his lack of consideration for others as well as for himself, his nervous tension and the dual nature of his artistic gifts. He remained to the last conscious of his origin, and throughout his life endeavoured to obliterate his emergence from poverty and Judaism by assimilation. He became a Roman Catholic in 1897, shortly before taking up his post in Vienna, and five years later married a girl of Gentile blood. Yet he never glossed over the fact that he came of Jewish stock, and remained closely attached to the surviving members of his father's family, whose care had become an onerous duty for the struggling conductor. In the comparatively liberal cultural climate of Francis Joseph's Austria it was possible for Jews not only to attain fame and wealth, but even to wield great administrative power. Yet in many respects they were condemned to remain outsiders, and their position became increasingly precarious. Mahler's path to fame and greatness was therefore thorny and only negotiable by ruthless zeal and fanatical energy. He was endowed with both in addition to musical genius, but tragically denied physical health. The relentless struggle of his powerful mind with his frail body was clearly the result of the oppressive conditions suffered by Jews throughout the north-eastern part of old Austria, bred as they were in often deplorable hygienic and social surroundings and perpetuating their race by weak and sometimes even degenerate offspring of surprisingly keen intelligence.

Mahler was born on 7th July 1860 [1] at Kališt, on the Bohemian side of the Moravian frontier, the second child of a union which was

[1] The date is not beyond doubt: Mahler's parents believed it to be 1st July. The official birth certificate is lost. See P. Stefan (Bibliography), p. 22. D. Mitchell (see Bibliography), opposite p. 124 shows the facsimile of an extract from the 'Birth Register of the Council of Jewish Religious Congregations in Prague', dated 26th November 1953, in which the date 7th July 1860 is confirmed.

eventually blessed with twelve children. Both parents came from the border country between the two crown-lands. The father was Bernhard Mahler, born at Kališt on 2nd August 1827, died at Jihlava on 18th February 1889; the mother, Marie,[1] born on 3rd March 1837 at Ledeč as the daughter of a soap manufacturer in comfortable circumstances. It was not a love-match, and both partners suffered under the incompatibility of their temperaments. Marie Mahler was frail, limping and subject to heart trouble from her early days, an ailment which she evidently bequeathed to her famous son, and to which she finally succumbed at Jihlava on 25th October 1889. The father, a passionate and somewhat irascible character, started as a coachman, but developed later into a kind of semi-intellectual. He owned a distillery of spirits which he transferred to Jihlava in December 1864, when the restrictions on the migration of Jews were lifted throughout Austria. The poverty of Mahler's child-hood (he was born in a house without window-panes), was to some extent mitigated after this transfer of the father's business, but his paternal grandmother continued as a street pedlar until her eightieth year.

Gustav, though born second, was in fact the eldest surviving off-spring of the family, an older brother, Isidor (b. 1858), having met with an accidental death in infancy. Of these twelve children no less than five succumbed to diphtheria at an early age, while a sixth—Mahler's youngest and favourite brother, Ernst—died at the age of thirteen of the heart complaint which seems to have been endemic to the family. Two brothers (Alois, b. 1867, and Otto, b. 1873) and two sisters (Justine, b. 1868, and Emma, b. 1875) were destined to play a greater part in Mahler's life; a third sister (Leopoldine, b. 1863) died as a young married woman of a malignant tumour of the brain as early as 1889. Otto, a musician of great promise, committed suicide in 1896, while Alois eventually extricated himself from the clutches of his creditors by escaping to America. Justine and Emma were able to replace the early loss of the beloved mother to a certain extent. Both shared Mahler's life for many years, and Justine

[1] G. Adler gives the mother's maiden name as 'Hermann' (see Biblio-graphy), p. 95. That name appears also on the official document, mentioned in footnote p. 110.

especially became an object of Mahler's frustrated mother fixation [1] and simultaneously an emotional barrier against marriage. Both sisters became so much part of Mahler's professional life that they married musicians, the brothers Arnold and Eduard Rosé. The constant care for his younger brothers and sisters, and the duty to provide for their education and keep after the premature and almost simultaneous death of the parents in 1889, determined Mahler's whole professional career until about the turn of the century.

In his early years Mahler must have suffered from the discordant relationship between his parents and the intermittent neglect into which he fell owing to his father's irritable temper and his mother's permanent ill health, which steadily deteriorated with the mounting number of confinements. But his unusual musical faculties asserted

---

[1] ER, p. 214, where Freud's own diagnosis of Mahler's mother-fixation, expressed in 1910, is quoted. Theodor Reik, in his book *The Haunting Melody* (New York, 1953, pp. 342 ff.), confirms that a meeting between Mahler and Sigmund Freud took place at Leyden on 26th or 27th August 1910, Mahler having three times before made and broken an appointment with the psycho-analyst, whom he wished to consult and a meeting with whom he seemed to dread at the same time. Ernest Jones, Freud's biographer, recently discovered the latter's analysis of Mahler, which he has kindly placed at my disposal. Its revelations concerning a mother-fixation in Mahler and difficulties in his married life elicited by Freud, though interesting biographically, even if they were not controversial, would hardly be matter for a small book on the composer, and they throw light on his music only indirectly, if at all. On the other hand an incident of Mahler's youth is worth reporting as giving a clear explanation for the first time of the intrusion of commonplace tunes into his works at the very moments where he expresses the most profound emotions. Mahler's father, who appears to have been a brutal person, often ill-treated his wife, and on one occasion, when Mahler as a child witnessed a painful scene between them and rushed out of the house, he ran into an organ-grinder playing the popular Viennese ditty of O *du lieber Augustin*. It was Mahler's own opinion that this clash of a tragic experience with a cheap and frivolous tune influenced his inspiration at moments of emotional tension for the rest of his life, and that it was this which prevented him from achieving the highest rank as a composer. I am indebted to Donald Mitchell for kindly making contact between Ernest Jones and myself.

themselves at an early date. Songs and military music from the nearby barracks in Litoměřice, besides nearly two hundred folk-tunes caught from the lips of Slavonic servant girls, were duly repro-duced on an accordion which as a boy of four he first learned to master. On an old piano, discovered in an attic of his grandparents' house, little Gustav taught himself the rudiments of piano playing. At the age of eight he was able to give piano lessons to a boy of seven, and he became a subscriber to a music lending library. Bernhard Mahler seems to have decided at an early date to develop Gustav into a professional musician. For a short time (winter 1870–1) the boy settled in Prague, where he studied at the 'Gymnasium' and lived as a boarder and piano pupil in the house of the parents of Alfred and Heinrich Grünfeld. Here he seems to have been brutally treated and shamefully neglected.[1] He was quickly transferred to Jihlava again, where he continued at the local 'Gymnasium' until 1875. By 1866 he had already received temporary music lessons from the operatic conductor Viktorin, as well as from a piano tutor named Brosch. This tuition cannot have amounted to much. Mahler's dreamy disposition, his lack of concentration, his obsession with as yet intangible musical experiences, made him appear a difficult pupil and a problem-child in the eyes of provincial educationists. How-ever, his real vocation never seems to have been doubted. When he was hardly fifteen his father went with him to Vienna and asked Professor Julius Epstein for a verdict on Gustav's artistic future. Epstein was so deeply impressed with Mahler's piano playing and with his personality that he accepted him at once as a pupil at the Conservatory of the Vienna Gesellschaft der Musikfreunde in the autumn of 1875. Mahler had, in fact—as in a dream—stepped on the bottom rung of the ladder to success.

The amount of work he was expected to get through for the next few years was prodigious and might have proved fatal to a talent of lesser fibre. Mahler's teachers at the Conservatory were Julius Epstein (piano), who befriended the lonely youth, and even appointed him piano tutor to his own son Richard, probably for humanitarian

---

[1] ER, p. 15.

as well as professional reasons; Robert Fuchs, composer of very popular serenades and symphonies (harmony); and finally Franz Krenn, a rather pedantic teacher of counterpoint and composition. Mahler seems to have been exempted by his director, Joseph Hellmesberger, from the counterpoint class on account of the high standard of his compositions at that time. Simultaneously he continued privately with his school work, which was successfully terminated by matriculation at the Jihlava 'Gynasium' in the autumn of 1878.[1] Fuchs is reported to have said much later: 'Mahler always stayed away from classes, yet knew everything.' As so young a student he was fortunate to win prizes at the annual competitions at the Conservatory, two for piano playing (1875–6 and 1876–7) and one for composition (first movement of a piano Quartet) in 1876–7. After a successful final examination at the end of his three-year course the scherzo of his piano Quartet was performed in public, at a concert arranged by the Conservatory (11th July 1878). Mahler left with a diploma. In his spare time he gave piano lessons to increase his pitifully slender means; he read and studied voraciously and generally led the bohemian life in which promising music students in the easy-going Vienna of those days frequently indulged.

Among Mahler's special friends and colleagues three may be singled out, because they continued to play a part in his adult life: Hugo Wolf, Anton Krisper and Hans Rott. The most interesting is undoubtedly Wolf, who studied at the Conservatory until his forcible exclusion in March 1877. Wolf and Mahler joined at the same time, and soon became intimate friends with the bond of mutual poverty, so much so that they shared lodgings and at times even one bed.[2] They frequently lived on cheese-parings, and when Wolf was completely out of funds Mahler paid for the hire of his

---

[1] A letter from Mahler, dated *c.* 1876, and preserved in the archives of the Gesellschaft der Musikfreunde, contains an apology for his rash decision to leave the Conservatory. Another (probably of a slightly earlier date) asks for exemption from school fees on account of his father's poverty. The latter document was initialled by J. Epstein. Mahler was eventually retained as a pupil at half the fee.

[2] F. Walker (see Bibliography), pp. 82 ff.

piano. At times they even shared their room with Rudolf Krzyzanowski, who together with his brother Heinrich was among the
intimate friends of Mahler's youth. It was presumably then that
Mahler composed a movement of his piano Quartet while Wolf and
Rudolf Krzyzanowski slept on benches on the Ringstrasse.[1] It has
been recorded that Wolf at that time tended to rate Mahler's songs
higher than his own efforts. The intimacy of poverty and artistic
struggles did not lead to a friendship based on mutual tolerance and
understanding. When Mahler and Wolf resumed their contacts
after a lapse of about sixteen years early in 1897 they had become
virtual strangers and potential antagonists. The ultimate tragedy of
Wolf's life is closely connected with this fatal revival of their early
friendship under utterly different social circumstances. That exalta-
tion bordering on hysteria and insanity were rampant in Mahler's
youthful circles is borne out by the fact that not only Hugo Wolf
and Hans Rott died insane, but that the third companion of
Mahler's early days, Anton Krisper, was also threatened by a similar
fate. All this seems like a sombre portent of the distressed mental
condition in which Mahler himself composed his last Symphony (in
the summer of 1910), whose autograph bears many traces of grave
mental disturbances. The tragic failure and anti-social defiance
already noticeable in Hugo Wolf, whose expulsion from the Conservatory must have been witnessed by Mahler, came to a catastrophic
climax in the pitifully short life of Mahler's colleague Hans Rott, to
whom he seems to have been linked by a deep identity of mind and
character.

Rott is of some interest to the biographer of Mahler, who continued
to feel a profound affinity with him. He had been Bruckner's declared
favourite by 1877, as may be gathered from an informative letter from
Bruckner to Ignaz Traumihler, the chorus-master of St Florian, in
which Bruckner recommends his pupil as a candidate for the post of
organist there. Fate chose Brahms as an instrument to crush Rott's
promising life—Brahms, who played an equally sinister part in the

[1] Walker gives the date as late as 1879, but as the two prize-winning
movements were performed in the summer of 1876 and 1878 respectively,
the latter date seems more likely. By 1879 Mahler had left the Conservatory.

early struggles of Wolf and Mahler. Brahms's hostility to the Vienna Conservatory in general and Bruckner in particular [1] is what mainly accounts for his malevolent attitude towards the three gifted young musicians whose chief crimes were that they had studied there and that Bruckner patronized them. The similarity of his attitude towards Rott, Wolf and Mahler is indeed striking, the more so as their contacts with him must have been made at about the same time, i.e. between 1879 and 1880. The first to approach Brahms was Rott, only to be advised to give up music altogether, since he was devoid of talent.[2] The blow was too much for Rott's undermined constitution: he went insane and died shortly afterwards.[3] It is a fair guess that Rott's meeting with Brahms took place in 1879, at about the time Hugo Wolf called on Brahms with equally negative results, but with the added advice to take lessons from Nottebohm. Wolf's almost maniacal hatred of Brahms dates from that unfortunate episode.[4] Mahler proceeded more cautiously, probably warned by the disastrous experiences of his friends; but he too was made to feel the icy blast of Brahms's spite. It is generally assumed [5] that he sent in *Das klagende Lied* for the competition for the Beethoven Prize sponsored by the Gesellschaft der Musikfreunde since 1875 and open to all present and former pupils of the Vienna Conservatory. Fate willed it that Brahms and Hanslick should head the jury for the prize

[1] *Briefwechsel Brahms-Herzogenberg*, Vol. I, No. 59, pp. 96 ff., dated 29th April 1879, contains a very critical appraisal of the merits of the Conservatory. In the same letter Brahms expressly mentions Nottebohm, to whom he sends all who come to him for advice. It was early in 1879 that —according to Walker (see Bibliography), p. 83—Wolf visited Brahms and that—according to Kalbeck—Brahms referred him to Nottebohm. It seems clear that the ' pupils of the Conservatory ' referred to in Brahms's letter were Wolf and Rott.

[2] See Dika Newlin (see Bibliography), pp. 210-11.

[3] Brahms and Bruckner (and probably Wolf and Mahler) were present at the funeral and the tension between the two factions seems to have been stretched to breaking-point.

[4] For more details see Walker (see Bibliography), pp. 83 ff.

[5] Dika Newlin (see Bibliography), p. 108, and N. Bauer-Lechner (see Bibliography), p. 104.

of 1881: Mahler's composition was rejected.[1] It is not easy to determine with certainty when Mahler actually competed for the prize. It cannot have been before 1st November 1880, and it is significant that no prize seems to have been awarded at all for the competition of 1880.[2] It seems likely that Brahms's verdict against Mahler's work was pronounced in the winter of 1880-1, just after his encounters with Hugo Wolf and Hans Rott.

The relations between Bruckner and Mahler may have considerably influenced Brahms's unfortunate opinion of the latter—an opinion very much modified by the cordial relationship that was to develop between Brahms and Mahler in the later 1890s. As the official Bruckner biographers have consistently played down this relationship,[3] facts will here be given to cover the whole of Mahler's life.

Mahler and Bruckner must have become very friendly as early as 1877-8. On 16th December 1877 Bruckner's third Symphony was performed in its second version (of 1876-7) by the Vienna Philharmonic Orchestra at one of its so-called 'Gesellschaftskonzerte' under the composer's direction. This ill-starred *première* turned out an unqualified disaster. Among the friends and admirers surrounding the broken-hearted composer after his defeat was Mahler, who with Rudolf Krzyzanowski soon afterwards undertook a piano-duet arrangement of the Symphony under Bruckner's and J. Epstein's supervision, which was published together with the full score and parts in the following year, 1878, by Rättig of Vienna, who had offered Bruckner a contract on the very night of the unlucky concert. Bruckner was delighted with Mahler's arrangement and presented him later on with the manuscript score of the Symphony (second

---

[1] According to Bauer-Lechner that rejection was made responsible by Mahler for all the subsequent drudgery of his conductor's career throughout the 1880s. Brahms's attitude was in its practical results no less damaging for Mahler than it had been for Wolf and Rott.

[2] According to information from Donald Mitchell the jury sat on 6th December 1880, i.e. a month after the completion of *Das klagende Lied*.

[3] A. Orel, in *Bruckner Brevier* (Vienna, 1953), for instance, all but suppressed Mahler's name.

ᵛversion) as a token of appreciation.[1]   Although Mahler never received
any tuition from Bruckner, he remained an admiring if discriminating
disciple.   This is reflected in his enthusiastic letters written to Bruckner in 1891 from Hamburg.   On the very eve of his new appointment
there, 31st March 1891, he conducted Bruckner's Mass in D minor
in the Municipal Theatre.   Later performances for his Hamburg
audiences were those of the *Te Deum* (of which he was particularly
fond) in 1892 and 1893 and of the fourth Symphony in 1895.   They
had a sensational success.   Mahler continued to fight for recognition
of Bruckner, especially during the first years of his directorship in
Vienna, when he conducted Symphonies VI, IV and V between
1899 and 1901.   After this last date, under the impact of his own
tempestuous creative development, a reaction seems to have set in,
and Bruckner began to come in for much criticism—along with
Brahms,[2] Wolf and Richard Strauss.   Yet we know that Mahler
performed all the Bruckner symphonies serially in New York (1908)
and that in 1910 for many a year to come he generously forfeited all
royalties accruing from his own Symphonies I–IV in order to help
the Universal Edition with the publication of and propaganda for
Bruckner's work.   This uncertain attitude towards Bruckner is
characteristic of Mahler's complicated reactions to most of his great
contemporaries.   Although his relations with Brahms became very
cordial early in 1891 (after Brahms had heard him conduct Mozart's
Don Giovanni in Budapest) and continued to improve, his opinion of
Brahms's music, as of Schumann's, inclined to fluctuate between
enthusiasm and revulsion.   It was much the same in the case of his
greatest contemporary, Richard Strauss, whose early symphonic

[1] This score remained in the possession of Mahler's widow until 1948,
when it was acquired by the Austrian State.   It is incomplete, the finale
missing and the scherzo differing from the published version.   See Auction
Catalogue L'Art Ancien, G.A., Zürich, 17th November 1948; also
facsimile of the first page of this manuscript score, published in ER,
facing p. 320.

[2] See his letter to Alma, dated 1904, extolling Beethoven and Wagner
at the expense of 'mediocrities' (*Mittelmass-Menschen*) like Brahms and
Bruckner (ER, pp. 302 ff.).

poems and *Salome* attracted and repulsed him in equal measure. His total inability to enter into the spirit of a great contemporary musician —a strange handicap for so great a conductor—is poignantly reflected in his harsh condemnation of Hugo Wolf, his lack of appreciation of Max Reger, his strange underestimation of Puccini and his total indifference to the French impressionists. These serious shortcomings are but partly redeemed by his later friendship with Schoenberg, whom he encouraged, admittedly without fully understanding his artistic aims.

CHAPTER II

THE YOUNG KAPELLMEISTER (1880-97)

MAHLER'S poverty during the years of his musical apprenticeship was chronic with him, as well as endemic in the circle of his friends. It was shared to the full by Hugo Wolf, Hans Rott, Hermann Bahr, Guido Adler, the brothers Krzyzanowski and others befriending him during those years. Work as a composer seemed to hold out but little prospect of material success after the rebuff suffered at the hands of the jury for the Beethoven Prize, and employment as piano tutor in Vienna, Jihlava and occasionally in Hungary found but meagre reward. Reluctantly Mahler decided for the career of operatic conductor, mainly for financial reasons, since he was probably quite unaware of his rare, almost uncanny talents in that direction.

His conducting career, begun at the age of twenty, which was to lead him within seven years to the very top of the profession, started inauspiciously enough in the summer of 1880 at Hall (Upper Austria), where he was engaged on Epstein's recommendation to conduct musical farces and comedies, to tidy up the orchestra pit after performances and occasionally even to push the perambulator containing his director's infant. In his spare time he continued to work furiously on the much-revised score of *Das klagende Lied* and on his operatic projects. The short season at Hall was followed, after a prolonged Viennese interlude, by a long season at Laibach (Ljubljana), where conditions were no less ludicrous. However, his genius as a conductor began to assert itself at the Landestheater of the crown-land of Carniola. He even managed to get through a performance of Gounod's *Faust* with a single male chorister, but was truly glad to get back to Vienna again, whence he departed for the third time to a conductor's post at the theatre of Olmütz (Olomouc) in Moravia, where he started work in a wellnigh hopeless mood in January 1883. Although this theatre too seems to have been in rather a poor condition, its director's ambition led to Mahler's conducting operas by

Gustav Mahler
Dezember 1892

MAHLER IN HAMBURG (AT THE AGE OF 32)
(*By courtesy of Universal Edition, Vienna-London*)

Meyerbeer and Verdi, and even to a production of Bizet's comparatively new *Carmen* under his direction. It must have been at Olmütz
that Mahler himself became aware of his conducting ability. He
disdained to conduct Mozart and Wagner in this Augean stable of
music, but produced Méhul's *Joseph in Egypt* with startling success.
Carmen at Olmütz had stirred an interest in young Mahler in the first
conductor of the Cassel Opera, who happened to attend a brilliant
performance of Flotow's *Martha*, conducted for the first time and from
memory. This secured Mahler the post of second conductor in the
Royal Prussian Court Theatre of Cassel at the age of twenty-three
(June 1883). Choirmaster's duties for an Italian season at the Carl
Theatre in Vienna and a visit to Bayreuth, where he heard the first
Parsifal performances since Wagner's death, tided him over until the
Cassel season re-opened in the autumn of that year.

The Cassel appointment was undoubtedly the first rung on the
ladder to fame and success; yet Mahler continued to feel deeply
dissatisfied, as may be gathered from a letter written to Hans von
Bülow, whose personality and conducting technique played such an
important part in the development of Mahler, as of Richard Strauss.
In that letter, penned in early January 1884, Mahler implored Bülow
to accept him as personal assistant and pupil. Although Bülow's
reactions seem to have been negative at that time (the letter was even
returned to Mahler's immediate superior, Kapellmeister Treiber), he
must soon have formed a favourable opinion of Mahler's powers,
to which he was later to pay so generous a tribute at Hamburg.
Although still prevented by the pedantic Treiber from conducting
the classics and confined to Meyerbeer and comic opera, Mahler's
demoniacal personality, his brilliant coaching and conducting, his
grasp of all the technical problems of an opera-house, his inspiring
enthusiasm for spiritual values in art and life, took philistinism by
storm. At the end of his Cassel appointment, during which he
managed to visit Dresden and to hear a first *Tristan* under Ernst von
Schuch, he was asked to conduct a musical festival at Cassel (29th
June–1st July 1885), culminating in stirring performances of Beethoven's ninth Symphony and Mendelssohn's *St Paul*. This was the
first spectacular success to bring Mahler tangible rewards such as a

golden repeater watch, a diamond ring, a laurel-wreath and other tokens of regard. But his personal situation was still so precarious that on the very day of his success his old watch had to be pawned. A violent love-affair with Johanne Richter, the success of his incidental music for a stage version of Scheffel's *Trompeter von Säckingen* and, more important, the composition of the song-cycle *Lieder eines fahrenden Gesellen* (completed on 1st January 1885) hastened Mahler's maturity. Theatre directors began to show marked interest in the young fanatic. F. Eckstein [1] draws the following characteristic thumbnail sketch of Mahler, based on impressions from the early 1880s:

. . . Gustav Mahler, of small stature; already in the curiously wagging manner of his gait [2] his unusual irritability manifested itself. His tense and intellectual face, thin and extremely mobile, was framed by a full brown beard; [3] his speech was pointed, with a strongly Austrian intonation. He invariably carried a parcel of books and music under his arm, and discussion with him proceeded by fits and starts. . . .

In the summer of 1885, having left Cassel for good on 1st July, Mahler succeeded in obtaining simultaneous engagements at two prominent opera-houses: the Municipal Theatre of Leipzig and the Deutsches Landestheater in Prague. At the former he was finally appointed, after a month's trial, in July 1885 for the season of 1886–7, as second-in-command. Meanwhile he accepted a short-term appointment to Prague, where he had successfully introduced himself with Cherubini's *Les Deux Journées* (August 1885). There too he was appointed second conductor (next to Kapellmeister Slansky), with the Wagner pioneer Angelo Neumann as director. It was under the latter's benevolent rule that Mahler was at last given a chance to conduct Wagner (*Lohengrin, Rheingold, Walküre, Rienzi*), Gluck (*Iphigenia in Aulis* in Wagner's arrangement) and *Fidelio*. In August

[1] *Alte, unnennbare Tage.*

[2] A residue of the St Vitus's dance from which Mahler suffered in early childhood.

[3] See portraits of *c.* 1885 in Carl Moll, *Gustav Mahler in Bildern.* The beard was eventually reduced to a moustache in February 1886 and from the autumn of 1887 onwards (Leipzig) Mahler was clean-shaven.

1886 he left Prague for Leipzig, where he started under director Staegemann as the younger colleague of the celebrated Arthur Nikisch, with whom relations soon became cool and strained, especially after Mahler had triumphantly asserted himself as Nikisch's equal during the latter's prolonged absence through illness. Mahler's Wagner performances in particular, although sometimes attacked in the press, became the rage of the city. A passionate love-affair with Frau von Weber, a woman much older than Mahler, wife of Weber's grandson, Hauptmann von Weber, with whom he completed and adapted Weber's operatic fragment *Die drei Pintos*, stimulated him to composition. He composed the first *Wunderhorn* songs from a copy of Arnim and Brentano's famous collection owned by the Weber children. He also wrote the first draft of Symphony I. How contagious his enthusiasm could be in those days is reflected by a letter to Hans von Bülow written by the young Richard Strauss, who made Mahler's acquaintance in the autumn of 1887 and fell in love with the *Drei Pintos* score, only to be severely reprimanded by Bülow for his rashness.[1]

The first performance of the *Drei Pintos* at Leipzig on 20th January 1888, followed by performances at Hamburg, Dresden and Vienna (1889), became a landmark in Mahler's career as conductor-composer. Very soon afterwards, in March 1888, the full score of the first Symphony was completed. Indirectly it caused the friction between Mahler and Staegemann which was eventually to lead to the former's resignation from Leipzig (17th May 1888) by temporarily undermining his conducting energies. All the conflicting claims on him conspired in causing a first serious breakdown in his health. The crisis became manifest when an intestinal operation had to be undergone by him in the summer of 1888.

[1] See R. Strauss's letter to H. von Bülow, dated Munich, 29th October 1887. According to this Strauss met Mahler in the middle of October at Leipzig, where he conducted his Symphony in F minor. See also Bülow's critical reply of 23rd March 1888 and Strauss's chastened rejoinder of 7th April 1888, in which he points out certain elementary mistakes in Mahler's scoring. Is it possible that Mahler at the age of twenty-seven still had so little experience in orchestration?

After Mahler's letter of resignation from Leipzig he started frantically to negotiate with other opera-houses—even with New York.
When these negotiations seemed doomed to failure Mahler's pessimism
found ample food in the unpromising situation during the summer of
1888. His mood of despondency was but little relieved by intermittent distractions such as Bayreuth and Vienna offered. Worry
over the health of his ailing parents, worry over the future of his
sisters and a crisis in his relations with Frau von Weber, who at one
moment seems to have contemplated elopement with him, contributed
in equal measure to his mounting cares. A turn of fortune, however,
was close at hand. Franz von Beniczky, intendant of the royal court
theatres of Budapest, had already started negotiations, with David
Popper and Guido Adler as intermediaries. Thanks to their sympathy for Mahler he was at last able to obtain, at the age of twenty-
eight, a ten years' contract as artistic director of the Royal Opera in
Budapest with a salary of 10,000 fl., to come into force early in
October 1888.

It was in the Hungarian capital that Mahler first proved his mettle
as administrator, reorganizer, opera producer and fascinating conductor, and that he laid the foundation to his subsequent world fame
as one of the great forces in contemporary music. It was here that
Mahler's production of *Don Giovanni* won him the heart of crusty
Brahms (January 1891) and that his first uncut performances of
Wagner's *Ring* in Hungarian were universally hailed as model performances comparable with those at Bayreuth. Mahler's difficulties
in training an undisciplined crowd of singers and players, and welding
them into a pliable instrument of his own, were aggravated by the
language barrier. He had to carry on with the help of an interpreter,
but he was intent on creating a national Hungarian opera with
indigenous artists, and in the end he miraculously succeeded by
sheer will-power in the short span of three years.

Meanwhile Mahler's parents had both died within a year: his
father on 18th February 1889, his mother on 11th October of the
same year. His younger brothers and sisters were thus left wholly in
his care. In the spring of 1889 his sister Justine became his housekeeper for many years to come. Later on she was joined by her

younger sister Emma, who eventually shared their household. On 20th November 1889 Mahler conducted his first Symphony (under the title of *Titan*) in Budapest before a bewildered audience and increasingly hostile critics. The constant care for his younger brothers and sisters began to act as a heavy drag on his vitality. His health broke down in the spring of 1890 and necessitated an operation and a recuperative journey to Italy (May 1890) in the company of Justine. On that first visit to Italy he studiously avoided picture galleries and other sightseeing attractions of the conventional tourist. However, he enjoyed the radiance of an Italian spring to the full. When Beniczky retired in January 1891 to make way for his successor, the rabid nationalist Count Géza Zichy, Mahler knew at once that his time in Budapest was up. The increasing xenophobia of the Hungarian press fanned the flames of intrigue. After a violent quarrel with Zichy, who interfered more and more with Mahler's operatic duties, the latter found himself locked out of his own office. He then insisted on a cash settlement, as his ten years' contract had clearly been violated by the high-handed action of the Hungarian authorities. When eventually the indemnifying sum of 25,000 fl. was paid, Mahler had already succeeded in obtaining a contract as first conductor of the Municipal Theatre at Hamburg from its shrewd director, Pollini, with whom he had conducted protracted negotiations ever since his position in Budapest had been threatened by Beniczky's resignation. Mahler resigned formally from Budapest on 14th March 1891 and, appointed by telegram to Hamburg, took up his post there a fortnight later, on 1st April 1891. This Hamburg appointment was to last for six years, a period in which he reached maturity as a conductor of European reputation, besides becoming a symphonist of the greatest promise.

Although in some respects the change from a directorship at the Royal Opera in Budapest to a first conductorship at Hamburg at a smaller salary and under the dictatorial rule of Hofrat Bernhard Pollini might be considered a retrograde step, Mahler started here for the first time in charge of first-rate singers and a first-class orchestra. As long as his relations with the wily Pollini remained cordial, he was given a free hand in the choice of operas as well as singers, and could therefore build up a company on long-term planning. It was at Hamburg that he met and befriended some of the future stars of his later company in Vienna, among them Bruno Walter as chorus-master, Anna Bahr-Mildenburg, one of his staunchest admirers and the finest executant of his own music, and Bertha Förster-Lauterer, whose husband, the Czech composer J. B. Förster, became one of Mahler's confidential friends during the Hamburg period and one of the most sympathetic analysts of his second Symphony.

It was at Hamburg that Mahler was at last able to perform signifi-cant new operas, destined to become corner-stones of the future repertory, such as Puccini's *Manon Lescaut,* Humperdinck's *Hänsel und Gretel*, the operas of Smetana, Tchaikovsky's *Eugene Onegin*, Verdi's *Falstaff*, Bizet's *Djamileh* and Rubinstein's *Demon*—one of Mahler's less easily justifiable favourites. However, Mozart, Beet-hoven and Wagner remained the backbone of his policy, and nothing reveals his eminence as an interpreter of Wagner better, even as early as 1891, than a letter from Bülow, who was destined to act in the very last period of his ebbing life as a kind of psychological catalyst for Mahler's genius and whose fluctuating relations with his much younger rival recall those with the youthful Richard Strauss eight years earlier. In a letter to his daughter Daniela, dated 24th April 1891, Bülow describes his impressions of a performance of *Siegfried*, conducted by Mahler without an orchestral rehearsal in the very first weeks of his appointment, in a vivid sketch of the man and artist:

. . . Hamburg has now acquired a simply first-rate opera conductor in Mr Gustav Mahler (serious, energetic—Jew from Budapest), who in my opinion equals the very best conductors (Mottl, Richter, etc.). Recently I heard *Siegfried* under his direction . . . sincere admiration has filled me for him, when without an orchestral rehearsal he compelled the musical rabble to whistle according to his dance. . . .

Bülow was demonstrative in showing his high regard for Mahler as a conductor whenever the latter attended his own symphony concerts. He even once sent him a laurel wreath with the inscription 'To the Pygmalion of the Hamburg Opera. . . .' When increasing ill health compelled him to abstain from further regular conducting at Hamburg, he asked Mahler to act as his deputy. Mahler conducted the fifth concert on 12th December 1892 in Bülow's absence, and eventually took over the concerts in the season of 1894-5, after Bülow's tragic end in Cairo (12th February 1894). Yet a fundamental lack of sympathy for Mahler as a composer, so stingingly expressed in his letters to Strauss about *Die drei Pintos*, remained with Bülow to the end. He flatly rejected Mahler's *Totenfeier* (i.e. the first movement of the later Symphony II), declaring that, compared with it, Wagner's *Tristan* was like a symphony by Haydn! He also stubbornly refused to conduct Mahler's *Humoresken* (i.e. some of the earlier *Wunderhorn* songs with orchestra) because they seemed to him 'much too strange.' It is interesting to note that Brahms reacted similarly, calling Mahler 'the king of revolutionaries' after studying the score of Symphony II. The cleavage between the two musical generations of 1830 (Bülow, Joachim, Brahms) and 1860 (Mahler, Strauss) could not be shown more clearly. Bülow's death and solemn funeral acted as a stimulus for Mahler, inspiring him to integrate Klopstock's hymn into the finale of Symphony II, which, together with Symphony III, was one of the main creative tasks of these Hamburg years.

This period at Hamburg was punctuated by the terrors of two cholera epidemics, by long vacations at Steinbach-am-Attersee in the Austrian Salzkammergut, where in 1893-6 Symphonies II and III matured alongside many of the *Wunderhorn* songs, and by frequent business journeys. The longest of these was Mahler's visit to London in the summer of 1892, as conductor of a travelling opera company consisting of members of the Hamburg Opera and performing Wagner and Beethoven under his baton at Drury Lane. During these Hamburg years, too, the first signs of public recognition for Mahler as a composer may be detected. Conspicuously placed if not always enthusiastically received performances of Symphonies I (Weimar, 1894; Berlin, 1896) and II (Berlin, 1895 under Richard Strauss, three movements only; later in the year complete under Mahler's own direction) continued to draw attention to a new personality in the musical life of the post-Wagnerian era.

When Mahler completed the full score of Symphony III at Steinbach in the summer of 1896, secret negotiations between himself and the administration of the Vienna Opera had already been carried on for almost a year. They were continued for nearly another year until they reached a critical phase. Meanwhile Mahler's relations with Pollini had seriously deteriorated, although Mahler's success as the one and only conductor of the Hamburg Opera (especially after the sudden departure of his colleague Otto Lohse in 1895) was, if anything, increasing. In 1895–6 Mahler was literally conducting nearly every night of the week for long stretches at a time. Early in 1897 he asked to be released from his Hamburg contract. By that time he was already deeply committed by negotiations with Berlin, Dresden, Munich, Vienna and other operatic centres. However, nothing materialized. Everywhere Mahler's Jewish descent was a serious obstacle, despite Bülow's early sympathy and Brahms's increasing moral support, which continued to play a powerful part in the negotiations with Vienna, particularly in the very last year of Brahms's life (1896–7), during which Mahler repeatedly paid visits to Brahms at Ischl and Vienna. Probably under the persuasion of Anna BahrMildenburg Mahler at last decided to embrace the Christian faith. He was baptized and became a member of the Roman Catholic Church very shortly before leaving Hamburg, i.e. in the spring of 1897. Although deeply attracted by the mysticism of the Roman creed to which he was to pay so eloquent a tribute in the second part of Symphony VIII, his conversion was at that particular moment ot his life clearly dictated by expediency. Baptism was for him what it had been seventy odd years earlier for Heine: 'The admissionticket to European culture.' It certainly smoothed his path in the critical weeks and months lying ahead of him in Vienna. So little was Mahler convinced that he would succeed in becoming Wilhelm Jahn's and Hans Richter's successor that he seriously contemplated returning to Berlin for a time and, if he failed to obtain a satisfactory contract anywhere, to earn his livelihood temporarily by private lessons and coaching.

CHAPTER III

DIRECTOR OF THE VIENNA OPERA (1897–1907)

UNDER Mahler's immediate predecessor, Wilhelm Jahn, the artistic standard of the Vienna Opera had gradually deteriorated. Director since 1881 and loyally supported by Hans Richter, Jahn, an amiable man, and by no means a negligible musician, but increasingly impeded by ill health, had begun to let things drift. It is to the credit of Intendant von Bezecny to have energetically pursued the idea of appointing the ruthlessly industrious, fanatical and modernistic Mahler to get the Opera out of its rut. Mahler's attainment to a director's office was the less easy because Jahn, Richter and Nepomuk Fuchs, the second conductor, did all in their power to circumvent his appointment, rumour of which began to circulate in early April 1897. Only a few weeks earlier Mahler had conducted concerts in Moscow with sensational success. On 1st May his engagement as *Kapellmeister* in Vienna was announced. On 11th May he conducted at the Opera for the first time, 'on trial' (*Lohengrin*). The success of this improvised performance was phenomenal: by 21st July he had been created a deputy director next to Jahn. Finally, on 8th October 1897, he was definitely appointed artistic director for life, with practically dictatorial powers, at a salary of 24,000 k. plus gratuities and a pension, in succession to Jahn, who was pensioned off as from the end of the current year. For ten years Mahler was to remain in that exalted position, which turned him into one of the most powerful and influential figures in the musical life of the Continent. On 13th October 1903 he received the Order of the Iron Cross of the third class from the Emperor Francis Joseph I, who throughout Mahler's tenure of office did not stint him of generous appreciation of his administrative and artistic achievements. This was sometimes conveyed him by the chamberlain, Prince Montenuovo, who was equally appreciative of Mahler and remained on exceptionally good terms with him until early in 1907, when a gradual estrangement between the two men set in.

Mahler's activity as director-general and principal conductor of the Vienna Opera at the turn of the century had had a determining influence on the modern approach to interpretative problems of opera production in general, comparable to the operatic reforms of Lully, Gluck and Wagner, and simultaneous with Max Reinhardt's revolution of the German drama during the first two decades of the new century. It was Mahler who, on the basis of Hermann Levi's valuable preparatory work in Munich, started to produce Mozart's operas in a stylish way, endeavouring to re-create the conditions of the original production, restoring the recitatives and the harpsichord, banishing realism from the stage and achieving complete co-ordina-tion between stage and orchestra. It was Mahler who at long last produced Wagner without cuts and in close accordance with the stylistic principles of Bayreuth, yet outside Bayreuth in a repertory opera-house which was expected to cater for various tastes. In his struggle for a simplified operatic scene and for a change-over from the romantic realism of the nineteenth century to the expressionist sym-bolism of the early twentieth, he found an enthusiastic supporter in the brilliant painter Alfred Roller, whose much-debated 'Roller towers' (a permanent revolving set) became especially popular in Mahler's Mozart productions and started a new epoch in the history of operatic design. Mahler's desire to elevate the performances of classical operas to the level of Wagner's *Festspiel* ideal was not con-fined to Mozart only. Weber, whose *Euryanthe* he produced with a new libretto of his own in 1904 and whose *Oberon* he adapted to a new libretto (in an arrangement not produced in Vienna and only published in a vocal score as late as 1919), Hermann Goetz, whose *Taming of the Shrew* was given in 1906, Offenbach, whose *Contes d'Hoffmann* achieved their long-delayed world success only under Mahler in 1901, Gluck, whose *Iphigenia in Aulis* was Mahler's last new production in Vienna on 18th March 1907, and many more 'classics' benefited by his reformatory zeal as much as contemporary opera composers, for some of whom Mahler became a veritable champion.

It was by the irony of fate that *Der Corregidor*, the only completed opera by Hugo Wolf, should be produced by Mahler posthumously as late as 10th March 1904 (in the restored original version).[1] This performance came as a belated consolatory finale after a tragic rupture of an old friendship. Early in June 1897 Wolf had received a vague promise from Mahler [2] for a later performance of his opera in Vienna. However, shortly before 20th September 1897 (i.e. three weeks before Mahler's definite appointment) a violent clash of opinion on the subject of *Der Corregidor* as well as on the merits of Rubinstein's *Demon* occurred between Wolf and Mahler.[3] This accelerated the outbreak of Wolf's mental disease, which is inextricably connected with the appointment of Mahler,[4] whom Wolf in his delirous ravings replaced as director of the Vienna Opera. Mahler's posthumous *Corregidor* performance of 1904 tried to make amends for the tragic events of 1897.

Other contemporaries fared much better at Mahler's hands. Among them should be mentioned Humperdinck's pupil, Siegfried Wagner, whose *Bärenhäuter* was successfully given in 1899, and Hans Pfitzner, whose second opera, *Die Rose vom Liebesgarten*, received a magnificent performance under Mahler's direction (6th April 1905). Despite initial misgivings Mahler gradually became more and more attracted by this work and championed the cause of the future composer of *Palestrina*. Other notable first nights at the Vienna Opera while Mahler held office included Rezniček's *Donna Diana*, Zemlinsky's *Es war einmal*, Thuille's *Lobetanz*, Richard Strauss's *Feuersnot*, Charpentier's *Louise*, Leo Blech's *Das war ich*, Eugen d'Albert's *Die Abreise*, Ermanno Wolf-Ferrari's *Le donne curiose* and the middle-period operas of Puccini.

---

[1] The opera had already been given on 18th February 1904 in a revision of Wolf's with which Mahler did not entirely agree.

[2] Letter of 4th June 1897, cf. F. Walker (see Bibliography), p. 415.

[3] See the unpublished letter of Hugo Wolf to Victor Boller, of 20th September 1897, in which Wolf actually announces the dismissal of Mahler for the very next day. The letter obviously indicates the outbreak of Wolf's insanity.

[4] See Walker (see Bibliography), pp. 421 ff.

In his arduous task Mahler was splendidly supported by younger conductors of remarkable qualities such as Franz Schalk and Bruno Walter (both of whom later on became musical directors of the Vienna Opera in their own right), as well as by a host of glamorous singers many of whom owed their discovery to Mahler's sharply discerning eye and ear. Among them were Leo Slezak, Marie Gutheil-Schoder, Richard Mayr, Erik Schmedes and Friedrich Weidemann.

A truly lasting improvement (noticeable in its beneficent after-effects right up to 1938 when Hitler's racial laws destroyed its time-honoured cohesion) was effected in the organization of the orchestra, which was for many decades led by Arnold Rosé, Mahler's brother-in-law since 1902, in a manner worthy of its lofty traditions.

The orchestra's Philharmonic concerts were conducted by Mahler only from 26th September 1898 until April 1901. He was decidedly unsuccessful in his association with the orchestra as far as these concerts were concerned. The players' suppressed but persistent antagonism to his exacting, ruthless and uncomfortable methods of rehearsal tended to flare up in the less constrained atmosphere of the concert-hall. However, while Mahler's temporary conductorship lasted, the programmes continued to contain works of extraordinary interest, such as Bruckner's fifth and sixth Symphonies, Dvořák's *Wood Pigeon* and *Song of a Hero*, Strauss's *Aus Italien*, besides Mahler's own Symphonies I and II and the *Lieder eines fahrenden Gesellen*. In 1900 Mahler accompanied the orchestra on its visit to the World Exhibition in Paris; but the concerts, although patronized by Princess Metternich herself, who forty years earlier had done so much for Wagner's *Tannhäuser* in the French capital, received but scant recognition from the public and the press, a fact which seemed to contribute to Mahler's growing unpopularity with the orchestra. Matters came to a head when, grossly overworked and emotionally over-wrought, he suffered a haemorrhage in early spring 1901, in consequence of which he had to undergo several painful operations. While he was temporarily incapacitated, taking a cure at Abbazia on the Adriatic coast, the orchestra elected as his successor a musical nonentity: Joseph Hellmesberger junior, ballet conductor of the

Opera. Not till he was informed of this act of treachery did Mahler send in his letter of resignation, dated April 1901.[1] This unfortunate rift revealed, as in a flash, the latent possibilities of Mahler's ultimate downfall. Needless to say, Hellmesberger's tenure of the conductorship was a complete failure and Mahler was repeatedly invited by the orchestra to appear as guest-conductor for his own symphonies.

It was Mahler the composer ('der Sommerkomponist,' as he called himself ruefully with reference to the short holiday weeks into which he had to compress all his creative work) who suffered most under the rigours of Mahler the conductor. Within the ten years of his Vienna appointment no less than five symphonies were composed, published and performed, to which should be added for good measure the later *Wunderhorn* songs and all the Rückert songs, as well as the revisions of *Das klagende Lied*, of *Die Lieder eines fahrenden Gesellen* and numerous editorial arrangements of classical operas and symphonies, necessitated by Mahler's unusual conception of them. Those which particularly aroused animated controversy in the Viennese press were his revisions of the orchestration of Beethoven's and Schumann's symphonies and performances of the former's string quartets (particularly Opp. 95 and 131) with a full string orchestra.

In spite of this perpetual tug-of-war between the rival claims of conductor and composer (a dualism in life and work which would have killed a man of lesser fibre and which laid even him low with alarming frequency) Mahler managed to live a full life of his own in his spare time. From 1899 until 1907 he continued to spend the summer weeks in a little house called Schwarzenfels at Maiernigg on the shore of the beautiful Carinthian Wörthersee, which had so often inspired Brahms and was to become Alban Berg's last and most beloved refuge. The only exception was the summer of 1898, when Mahler spent his holidays, after a painful operation, at Vahrns in the Southern Tyrol.

The year 1901 became in every respect a year of crisis for Mahler. It started auspiciously enough with the first performance of *Das*

[1] ER, p. 272. This letter, first published by Alma, was reproduced in facsimile by H. v. Kralik, Vienna 1952 (see Bibliography) pp. 180–1, and also reprinted by Christl Schönfeldt, Vienna 1956 (see Bibliography), p. 65.

klagende Lied (17th February) and with Bruno Walter's appointment
as second conductor at the Vienna Opera; but it continued disastrously with Mahler's haemorrhage and his subsequent resignation
from the conductorship of the Philharmonic concerts. After this
came the first performance of Symphony IV (Munich), the composition of the Rückert songs and the first sketch for Symphony V
at Maiernigg, and the year ended with Mahler's first meeting with
Alma Schindler (November 1901), the young, beautiful and high-
spirited daughter of the distinguished · Viennese painter Anton
Schindler. Alma, whose charming mother had married again after
Schindler's early death and whose stepfather, the landscape painter
Carl Moll, had been her own father's trusted friend and pupil, had
grown up in an atmosphere of artistic culture and intellectual fastidiousness. A brilliant pianist and gifted composer, and as such
a pupil of Alexander von Zemlinsky, she fascinated Mahler, the
inveterate bachelor, so deeply that he soon proposed to her and married
her after a passionate courtship of less than five months, on 9th March
1902, only twenty-four hours before his sister Justine became Arnold
Rosé's wife. There can be no doubt that Alma completely transformed Mahler's whole life. As an accurate copyist of his own scores,
a deeply understanding and sympathetic critic of his music, no less
than as a woman of rare physical beauty and originality of mind, she
was worthy to become the companion of the demoniacal, dualistic,
self-centred musician whose eccentric conducting no less than his
efficient ruthlessness as opera director had turned him into a kind
of legendary figure. Mahler's increasingly friendly relations with
younger composers of progressive or even revolutionary outlook such
as Pfitzner, Zemlinsky and Schoenberg and his disciples were greatly
stimulated by her advice and sympathy, while those with friends and
companions of his earlier years, among them the queer Nietzschean
philosopher Siegfried Lipiner, the musicologist Guido Adler, the
singer Anna Bahr-Mildenburg, the violinist Nathalie Bauer-Lechner,
as well as the female members of his own family, suffered in the long
run under the impact of her imperious personality. In the house of
her parents Mahler met many choice spirits, among them artists like
Klimt, Kolo Moser and Hoffmann, intercourse with whom made

him at last more eye-conscious and more open-minded to the beauties of painting and sculpture.

Two daughters were born of this union: Maria Anna (3rd November 1902), Mahler's favourite 'Putzi,' who died tragically of diphtheria and scarlet fever on 5th July 1907, and Anna Justina (15th July 1904), who became a gifted sculptor in her own right and was married in succession to the composer Ernst Křenek, the publisher Szolnay and the conductor Anatole Fistoulari. The first years of Mahler's marriage were brightened by the arrival and development of these two children as well as by his ever-increasing productivity. His directorial duties were frequently interrupted, not always to Prince Montenuovo's satisfaction, by numerous journeys to Germany, Holland or Italy, undertaken mainly to conduct his own symphonies. This strenuous yet happy way of life was rudely shattered by the hammer-blows of fate which fell on Mahler in 1907. In the spring of that year the intrigues worked up against him by a clique of artistic as well as personal enemies began at last to show results. After a disagreement with Montenuovo, who had already been vainly looking about for a worthy successor, Mahler tendered his resignation, which, after many ups and downs, was to take effect on 31st December 1907. As there was apparently no suitable post for him in all Germany, he quickly concluded in early July an agreement with Conried, the director of the Metropolitan Opera in New York, who secured his services for four months in the coming season of 1907–8.

On 5th July his elder child died at Maiernigg. Alma collapsed and fell gravely ill. Ten days later Dr Blumenthal, the family's doctor at Maiernigg, after a call on his wife, diagnosed a grave heart complaint in Mahler, a diagnosis fully confirmed by Professor Kovacs in Vienna (mid July 1907). Mahler was given to understand that he would have to change his whole mode of life and that his favourite long walks in mountainous country would have to be given up. In the autumn of that year, profoundly dejected by the death of his child, undermined in health and sick at heart at the prospect of having to relinquish his powerful position, he returned to Vienna in order to wind up his directorial affairs. He found time to conduct a series of concerts in Moscow and Helsinki (where he met Sibelius, whom he liked personally as much as he detested his music). His last opera performance in Vienna, badly attended because of a campaign of vitriolic hate, was *Fidelio* on 15th October 1907, his last concert there a performance of his second Symphony in November. It was his last concert with the Vienna Philharmonic Orchestra. His official letter of farewell, addressed to all the members of the opera-house, was dated 7th December 1907. It was found torn to shreds the day after it had been pinned on the news-board.

Mahler's departure from Europe has been called 'a cultural tragedy. It was more: it marked the passing of an age, of the epoch of more than a century of supremacy in Austro-German musical classicism. Mahler himself never had a real successor in Vienna. Even the years of uneasy compromise between Richard Strauss and Franz Schalk (1919–24) were no more than a faintly glowing sunset after the glorious day of Mahler's achievement. Meanwhile European music ceased to receive its decisive stimuli from Vienna and Berlin. Two world wars, intervening between our time and Mahler's passing, have succeeded in segregating his decade of artistic glory from the world of to-day and to-morrow. Mahler's Vienna belongs to past history as surely as Goethe's Weimar and Wagner's Bayreuth.

MAHLER IN 1902 (AFTER THE ETCHING BY ORLIK)
(*By courtesy of Universal Edition, Vienna-London*)

CHAPTER IV

LAST YEARS (1908–11)

MAHLER's decision to continue for a while in the burdensome profession of operatic conducting was, in a roundabout way, a concession to his creative genius. He was determined to retire as a conductor after his fiftieth birthday and to dedicate the rest of his life to composition alone. From the proceeds of his American engagements he purchased a plot of land on the Semmering, south of Vienna, and he eventually started to build a house there which he was destined never to inhabit. Four years of intermittent drudgery as a guest conductor in the United States seemed but a small sacrifice for security to be enjoyed ever after. But the sands were swiftly running out. Undermined in health, with a badly damaged heart, deeply affected by the tragic events of the past months and smarting under the callous indifference of the Viennese public to his departure, he started for the new world with his wife and surviving daughter on 9th December 1907. At the Metropolitan Opera he conducted mainly German works until May 1908 with spectacular success and repeated that feat in the season of 1908–9.[1] In 1909 a newly founded Philharmonic Society in New York enabled Mahler to give up opera conducting at the Metropolitan, which had become irksome to him despite isolated moments of artistic satisfaction, as in the case of Smetana's *Bartered Bride* in 1910. He confined himself mainly to concerts, of which he conducted no less than forty-six in the season of 1909–10. In his last American winter (1910–11) he managed to conduct forty-eight out of a total of sixty-five concerts contracted for, some of them in far-off cities. Friction with the orchestra as well as with the

[1] About Mahler's difficulties with Conried, his vain attempt to secure an appointment for Roller to the 'Met' and about his unstable position in America in general, see his letters to Alfred Roller, written from America in 1908–10. BR , Nos. 391–400.

committee of the society became a new source of worry early in 1911, and the long, strenuous journeys did their share in undermining Mahler's indifferent health, which had already given more than usual trouble during the final preparations for the first performance of Symphony VIII at Munich in the late summer of 1910. Mahler conducted his last concert in the U.S.A., and indeed anywhere, on 21st February 1911, running a high temperature. A few days later it was clear that he was mortally ill.

In the spring and summer months of 1908–10, between his American engagements, Mahler not only composed his final works (Symphonies IX and X, and *Das Lied von der Erde*) but also reappeared in Europe as conductor of works of his own (Symphony VII: Prague and Munich, 1908; Amsterdam, 1909. Symphony I: Wiesbaden, 1908. Symphony II: Paris, 1910. Symphony VIII: Munich, 12th and 13th September 1910—his last concert in Europe).

These last creative summer weeks, full of joys in creation experienced against the emotional undercurrent of a passionate reattachment to Alma, have been amply described by her and are reflected with almost painful clarity in Mahler's last letters to her as well as in the marginal jottings accompanying the first sketch of Symphony X, over which the shadow of impending death seems to creep. Death never let go of Mahler after the feverish attack of late February 1911. A pernicious auto-intoxication of his blood by streptococci, diagnosed by Fraenkel of New York and later confirmed by Calmette of Paris, spelt doom to a man with a seriously weakened heart and generally undermined physical constitution. Practically in a dying condition Mahler sailed for Europe in April 1911, accompanied by his wife, his daughter and well-beloved mother-in-law, in the vain hope that a serum cure in Paris might save him. Professor Chvostek of Vienna was summoned to his sick-bed, and although he too could hold out no hope, he agreed with Mahler's wife that a return to the accustomed surroundings might relieve the patient's mind. In the middle of May he was transferred to Vienna, where he was installed in Löw's sanatorium.

Mahler's return occasioned fulsome expressions of love and sympathy, often coming from those who had done their utmost in the past to turn him into a voluntary exile. Public tributes in the press as well as from many artistic organizations may have given some pleasure to the dying man, who accepted his fate with stoic calm, passing the time reading philosophical books—always a habit of his —and expressing his love and gratitude to his distraught wife and her mother. The end came quickly on 18th May 1911, not long before midnight. Mahler was still six weeks short of his fifty-first birthday when he died, without having heard a note of his last works, which were posthumously performed in 1911, 1912 and 1924. His funeral —watched at a roadside by the writer of this book—took place a few days later. The burial in the little suburban cemetery of Grinzing turned into a demonstration of loyalty quite comparable with the impressive funerals Vienna had granted its musical heroes in the past. However, there was also a sense of irreparable loss, of silent despair, and at the same time of mystic exultation, felt by many but understood by but a few at the historic moment of Gustav Mahler's passing, for ever embodied, it would seem, in the musical echo of Arnold Schoenberg's *Klavierstück*, Op. 19, No. 6, conceived in that very hour and evoking the strange serenity of that rainy May day, which had started so sombrely, only to end consolingly in sunshine and with the jubilant song of the nightingale.

CHAPTER V

ROMANTIC ANCESTRY

IF Nietzsche's estimation of music's function as that of the swan-song of its age is justified, then the importance of Mahler's music to a deeper insight into the intellectual subsoil and the psychological premises of his own epoch is not easily overrated. Like Hugo Wolf—his exact contemporary and the companion of his early days of musical apprenticeship in Vienna—Mahler is a late comer to the scene of the romantic movement. Again like Wolf—who (as an almost exclusive composer of *Lieder* systematically exploring the highways and byways of German lyrical poetry from Goethe to Gottfried Keller) continued where Schubert's and Schumann's romantic song-cycles had left off, and eventually discovered the last romantic poet of the century, Eduard Mörike—Mahler appears to be subject to the artistic stimuli of that romantic movement as it was heading towards its emotional and artistic climax in Wagner's music-drama and in Liszt's symphonic poem at the very time of Mahler's birth. Among those stimuli the one which continued to exercise a paramount influence on central European composers of various creeds and nationalities was a desire to re-create a style of popular lyrical expression (*Volkstümlichkeit*). Ever since J. A. P. Schulz's *Lieder im Volkston* (1782–1790), J. A. Hiller's *Lieder für Kinder* (1769) and Herder's *Briefwechsel über Ossian und die Lieder alter Völker* (1773) (eventually growing into his internationally conceived anthology of folk poetry, *Stimmen der Völker in Liedern*) German composers had striven to create a music complementary to the folk-tune-inspired avalanche of singable poetry from the pens of Goethe, Hölty, Matthisson, the rest of the 'Hainbündler' and the early poets of the romantic movement. The very climax of this struggle to gain musically the simplicity and directness of German folksong—itself emerging from the medieval carol and the Protestant chorale—was reached in such musical gems as the bridal song in Weber's *Freischütz*, Schubert's *Lindenbaum* (*Winter Journey*) and various songs and piano pieces by Schumann headed *Im Volkston*. Between about 1770 and 1880 poets and composers in Central Europe vied with each other in issuing collections of folk-songs and folk tunes. These semi-scholarly, often intensely national-istic collections of Zuccalmaglio, Ziska-Schottky, Erk, Boehme and many others stirred the imagination of the great musical creators of the time. When Brahms's last collection of *Volkslieder* was issued in December 1893 the literary and antiquarian urge of the movement seemed to have spent itself, only to be revived by modern composers who by that time had achieved a complete integration of the German folksong into their musical idiom and were thus able to write music of a *volkstümlich* bent without forfeiting the technical achievements of their day. Shortly before Brahms's final collection Humperdinck's fairy-tale opera *Hänsel und Gretel* was first performed at Weimar, the only dramatic work which succeeded in reconciling folkloristic melody with Wagnerian harmony and orchestration. It is seen in retrospect as the culmination of Weber's, Schubert's and Lortzing's earlier efforts to write popular music on a large scale for the stage without condescending self-consciousness. Humperdinck's unique operatic achievement, immediately hailed as the greatest event in German opera since Wagner's death (to the intense chagrin of Hugo Wolf, to whom genuine *volkstümlich* expression was to remain for ever a closed book), was matched by Mahler's exploits in the fields of song and symphony of a much earlier date. Some of these early songs of Mahler lead up to the chief work among his 'juvenilia' which became the starting-point of his career as a composer: Symphony I, in whose third movement the second trio is based on this melody ('very simple and plain, like a folk tune'):

Ex. 1

It is a piece of self-quotation characteristic of Mahler the symphonist who, like Schubert before him, acquired the habit of using his songs as material for larger conceptions, and it is taken from the fourth song of his early song-cycle *Lieder eines fahrenden Gesellen*. When Mahler wrote the words and music of this work (December 1883–January 1885) he had not yet discovered the treasure-trove of the anthology *Des Knaben Wunderhorn* that was to become the igniting spark for his creative imagination and the inexhaustible reservoir of tone-poetical subject-matter for his songs and symphonies. This famous collection of German poems, folksongs and carols, dating from about 1539 to 1807, had been assembled by the poets Achim von Arnim and Clemens Brentano in the early years of the nineteenth century and issued in two volumes in 1806–8. It is hard to understand that this glorious anthology should have remained neglected by most German composers [1] until a young Moravian Jew discovered its qualities in the 1880s. From the *Wunderhorn* Mahler received the double stimulus to evolve a folk-tune-like style of music and to seek inspiration from subjects of a spookish and nightmarish character; and it is Arnim's and Brentano's literary bent and style of verse that led him eventually to the minor romantic poet Friedrich Rückert, whose songs, though not always of great distinction, retain in their best moments something of the directness and aphoristic quality of a *Volkslied*.

In strange contrast to the deliberate simplicity of these lyrical compositions stands Mahler's life-long ambition to become a symphonist in the royal line of succession to Schubert and Bruckner. But the romantic ancestry of the symphonist in him offers a clue to a closer understanding of his peculiar type of symphony. The Mahlerian symphony, although outwardly conforming to the classical type, is in more than one sense symphony with a programme, more often than not partly concealed, for which the song-cycles are, as it were, preliminary essays, as certain songs by Schubert are for some of his instrumental works (e.g. the *Death and the Maiden* Quartet), Berlioz's early romance *Estelle et Némorin* for the *Symphonie fantastique* or Wagner's Wesendonk songs for the score of *Tristan*. The intrusion of actual songs and of choral movements into some of these symphonies acts as a further means of programmatic elucidation—quite

---

[1] J. Thibaut (Heidelberg, 1810) was an exception.

apart from the elaborate drafts of programmes, some of which were actually issued in the programme-books at the first performances of the symphonies, only to be withdrawn by the composer later on and to be completely suppressed in the first issues of the full scores. The autobiographical character of Mahler's symphony—clearly borne out by that possibly apocryphal assertion of his: 'Symphony means to me the building of an imaginary world with the aid of every resource of musical technique . . .[1] but also emerging from his *a posteriori* programmatic explanation of his second Symphony [2]—reveals a link with its historical archetype, Berlioz the arch-romantic's *Fantastic Symphony*. On the other hand its admittedly literary and philosophically conceived plan, with its operatic and oratorio-like connotations (especially in works of a mixed style such as Symphonies II, III and VIII and the early dramatic cantata *Das klagende Lied*), establishes a clear evolutionary connection with oratorio-symphonies such as Beethoven's ninth, Spohr's *Die Weihe der Töne*, Berlioz's *Roméo et Juliette* and Liszt's *Faust*—all of them typical expressions of the fundamental urge of early theoretical romanticism:[3] to fuse and merge the arts into a total work of art, i.e. Wagner's *Gesamtkunstwerk*. The fact that most of Mahler's symphonies are literary conceptions as much as musical structures proves the overpowering weight of Wagnerian influence from which he could best free himself by avoiding music-drama altogether [4] and by concentrating on a type of music held in but little favour by Wagner and many of his followers: the classical Viennese symphony and the romantic song-cycle.

If Bruckner showed Mahler that symphonies could still be written

---

[1] See R. Specht (see Bibliography), p. 228.

[2] See BR (ed. Alma Mahler, 1924), p. 188, letter No. 178. Cf. for complete quotation Chapter XI, p. 187.

[3] See Jean Paul's *Vorschule der Aesthetik* (1820), E. T. A. Hoffmann's leading articles on music, and especially his dialogue *Der Dichter und der Komponist* (*Serapionsbrüder*). Both authors were lifelong favourites of Mahler's, whose likeness to Hoffmann's scurrilous 'Kapellmeister Kreisler' has often been commented upon.

[4] Similarly Hugo Wolf tried to escape Wagner's overpowering influence by concentrating on an opera-comedy of a Mediterranean type.

in the four-movement form perfected by Beethoven and Schubert, with the addition of stylistic peculiarities in the Wagner-Liszt idiom,[1] Berlioz, and to a lesser extent Liszt and Wagner, had anticipated him in his most characteristic vein—the orchestral song-cycle, which is itself a typically romantic creation. Mahler's song-cycles are true successors to Beethoven's, Schubert's and Schumann's earlier *Lieder-kreise* with piano accompaniment in that they too revolve around the pivotal figure of the experiencing ego, who is either a wayfarer or a poet, or both, or even a poetically inclined journeyman, a more sophisticated type of poet (*Kindertotenlieder*) or a fusion of several Chinese poets merging into the super-ego of *Das Lied von der Erde*. The overmastering solipsism of these egocentric song-cycles, fore-shadowed as it is in Wilhelm Müller's and Schubert's profound melancholy, is as typically romantic as Mahler's actual choice of poetic subjects, ranging from his discarded 'juvenilia' down to the lofty conceptions of the last summer of his life.

Mahler's early operatic and symphonic plans already show such romantic predilections. The opera project of *Die Argonauten* may have been a belated echo of Grillparzer's trilogy *Das goldene Vliess*; Rübezahl, the hero of another unfinished opera of Mahler's, is also the hero of an incomplete early opera of Weber's, from which the *Beherrscher der Geister* overture alone survives; a *Nordic Symphony* may or may not have been prompted by Ossian and Percy's *Reliques*, which exercised a dominating influence on German minds for nearly a century; Herzog Ernst von Schwaben, the hero of an opera, had been singled out for dramatic treatment by Uhland long before Mahler; in *Das klagende Lied*, originally conceived as a fairy-play in three acts, of which only a concert version in two parts has survived, the gruesome legend of the 'singing bone' plays an integral part. This last work, the only large conception of Mahler's youth that has at least partly survived, is the first to express Mahler's leanings towards the mysterious and spookish side in the relationship between man and nature, the happy hunting-ground of early romantics like

[1] A popular misconception of Bruckner which was exploded only when his earlier church music was at last brought into organic relationship with his later symphonies.

A FACSIMILE PAGE FROM THE FIRST DRAFT OF MAHLER'S
'DAS KLAGENDE LIED' (1880)
(*By courtesy of Mr Donald Mitchell*)

Weber (*Freischütz*), Marschner (*Hans Heiling*), Grillparzer (*Die Ahn-frau*) and the lesser poets of the so-called *Schiksalstragödie*. Mahler's romantic interest in the 'night side of nature'[1] is strongly borne out by his *Wunderhorn* songs (originally called *Humoresken*, although their humour is rather on the macabre side), with their enchanted world of medieval soldiery, tramping to the rhythm of half-forgotten march melodies and with their unique utilization of parody, irony and satire for the characterization of their nocturnal and legendary events. Mahler finds inspiration of a quite peculiar kind in the midnight return of the dead soldier to his sweetheart (*Wo die schönen Trompeten blasen*), in the roll-call of an army of ghosts (*Revelge*), in the seductive apparition of night fairies trying to lure the solitary sentinel from the path of duty (*Der Schildwache Nachtlied*), in the hallucinations of a sweetheart yearning outside the prison-gate for the solitary prisoner (*Lied des Verfolgten im Turm*). But he also chooses almost Freudian moods of a nightmarish quality, such as the thoughts of military deserters shortly before their execution (*Tamboursg'sell, Zu Strassburg auf der Schanz*) or the spectre of famine slowly emerging from the heart-rending cry of a starving child (*Das irdische Leben*), for his songs, some of which were later to be transformed into symphonic movements. Mahler's lifelong love of military music of every conceivable type, very probably resulting from his earliest aural experiences near the barracks of Jihlava, was fanned by the subject-matter of this romantic anthology. It remained with him for life, re-echoing in the thud of remote footsteps which seem to accompany the last of his many funeral marches in Symphonies IX and X, at a time when the poetic symbols of the *Wunderhorn* had faded into limbo. A romantic's choice, too, is the final scene of Goethe's *Faust*, Part II, with its hierarchy of ecclesiastical figures ranging upwards to the remote splendour of the Mater Gloriosa. This second part of Symphony VIII is the nearest Mahler ever came to an operatic stylization of music whose inter-planetary connection with *Parsifal* and Liszt's operatic oratorios

[1] See D. Schubart's book, also Novalis's *Hymnen an die Nacht*, which Mahler loved, and which in turn had inspired the nocturnal part of the second act of Wagner's *Tristan*. Their literary ancestor was Young's *Night Thoughts*.

becomes especially apparent.   Only in the works of Mahler's very last years did the ties with the romantic movement loosen: it was in those works—Symphonies IX and X and the *Lied von der Erde*—which he was never to hear in performance—that he came nearest to the music of the future, by now the music of the half-century, so far removed from the world of romanticism and 'beyond good and evil' in the Nietzschean sense.

CHAPTER VI

MELODY, HARMONY AND COUNTERPOINT

ALTHOUGH Mahler's music in general shows a surprisingly steep upward trend of development, leading from a kind of neo-primitive simplicity and strict tonal diatonicism to the chromatically refined subtlety and rarefied atmosphere of the last symphonies, a number of static features of style are noticeable which seem to permeate his music up to the very end of his life. Their sum-total amounts to a specific personal idiom enabling the composer to turn even more clearly derivative melodies and eclectic harmonies into something intensely 'Mahlerian.'

The peculiar position of Mahler as a melodist whose eclectic allegiance to the Viennese classics in the widest sense (i.e. including Brahms and Bruckner) was never in doubt, and whose inclination towards *Volkstümlichkeit* may strike the observer of to-day as almost quixotic, is best explained by a morphological analysis of two typical symphonic subjects and an investigation of their stylistic ancestry. Both these melodies stand for an elemental side in Mahler's musical personality, the first representing, as it were, the Hungaric-Slavonic side of his artistic character, the other being a decidedly German type of *Volksweise* with manifold undertones and associations with other melodies, stored up in the subconscious memory of every German listener. Here is an example of the first type:

Ex. 2

a savagely melancholy tune that forms an episode in the third move-ment of Symphony I. It foreshadows a deliberately vulgar and blatantly scored melody, 'Mit Parodie' (see Ex. 3), with a csárdás flavour, a cheap guitar-like *pizzicato* accompaniment and obstinately

147

repeated motives hovering on the brink of triviality from which it is saved only by the pungent counterpoint in the trumpets. All this must have scandalized audiences in the later 1880s by its departure from the idiom of musical respectability as displayed in the symphonies of Brahms, Raff and Volkmann; yet, carefully analysed, the tune reveals its respectable pedigree, for it clearly derives from the second subject in the finale of Schubert's great C major Symphony. Both melodies are repetitive down to the smallest motif-particle, both achieve a cheap 'folky' atmosphere by being doubled in thirds, in both cases the self-assertive obstinacy of repetitions (x) is followed by a weak falling-off at the tail-end (y) and both tunes display a peculiar mixture of vulgar jauntiness, with an undertone of weariness; finally both are played against a background of primitive accompaniment in the strings. It is Schubert who first made such deliberately 'popular' tunes eligible for serious symphonic treatment, chiefly because of the psychologically complex connotations aroused by some of them.[1]   Just as Schubert's theme is a relaxation from the symphonic rigours of other parts of his finale, it becomes the subtle purpose of Mahler's to act as a weary foil for its parodistic afterthought:

Ex. 3

Here in a flash all its features are turned into a frightening grimace. The guitar accompaniment of the strings is changed into the spectral crackling of the wooden *col legno* effect; the rhythmic background of the *pizzicato* is savagely underlined by the vulgar 'oompa' rhythm of cymbals and bass drum, served by a single player in a manner reminiscent of the booths at a fair, and the melody itself is deliberately vulgarized by alcoholic skips, culminating in a vile *glissando* slide (z). The whole intentional vulgarization and the psychological subtlety in

---

[1] It was after all Schubert who inserted into the third movement of his *Wanderer* Fantasy, Op. 15, a reminiscence from Wenzel Müller's fashionable operetta *Aline*.

utilizing trivial tunes of the fair-ground type for the purposes of an escapist anticlimax (coming after the funereal 'Frère Jacques' canon with which the movement begins and ends) is a tremendous achieve-ment of Mahler's even if it took its cue from the vulgarizing trans-formation of the original *idée fixe* in the Witches' Sabbath of Berlioz's *Fantastique*.[1]

The second archetype of Mahler's symphonic melody may be exemplified by the main subject of Symphony III: an unaccompanied horn-call, not unlike the initial theme of Schubert's great C major Symphony, with which it seems associated also by virtue of the peculiar order of its motivic cells. However, other associations obtrude themselves even more inescapably and show, so to speak, the point at which Mahler and the Viennese classical tradition converge:

Ex. 4

For this theme is even more strikingly similar to the very familiar principal strain in the finale of Brahms's first Symphony, and therefore also to a development of that in the last movement of Beethoven's choral Symphony, the resemblance of which to his tune Brahms irritably said 'any fool' could see. Moreover, there is a clear affinity with one of the students' songs used by Brahms in the *Academic Festival* overture.

Such similarities and sometimes irritating resemblances are apt to occur frequently in the case of Mahler's popular tunes, barnacled, as it were, with the accretions of manifold melodic experiences. It is safe to assume that he used these melodies because of their associative values rather than despite of them. This is part of a technique as evolved slowly but eventually brought to the highest pitch of virtu-osity by Stravinsky,[2] a technique sometimes stigmatized as *pastiche*,

[1] See Eulenburg pocket score, p. 170, Allegro 6–8, solo for E flat clarinet.
[2] e.g. Stravinsky's ballets, operas, masses, etc., composed since 1923 based on Pergolesi, Lully, Weber, Tchaikovsky and Dufay.

especially when it is used to re-create a certain historic atmosphere. Mahler showed a masterly understanding of its implications in the early case of the 'Lutheran' chorale tune prefacing the contralto's solo, *Urlicht*, in Symphony II and anticipating there and then the later *a cappella* chorus of the finale. This is the kind of ecclesiastical tune which Mahler, following in the footsteps of Bruckner, was fond of calling *Choral* and liked to insert at emotional climaxes of his symphonies (e.g. Symphony V, II; Symphony VI, IV; Symphony VIII, etc.):

Ex. 5

This superb imitation of style is in its way as successful a *tour de force* as Wagner's introductory chorale tune 'Da zu dir der Heiland kam' at the beginning of *Die Meistersinger*.

The subtle art of spiritualizing a hymn-tune by throwing it into a certain perspective of harmonies may occasionally lead to temporary abdication of clear-cut melody in favour of dominating modulatory energies, swamping the thematic development by their elemental vigour. This may be observed in the juxtaposition of two chorale tunes from Symphonies II and VIII, standing in a kind of corroborative relationship to one another and disclosing thereby the deep-seated affinity between the only great choral finales composed by Mahler, at the outset and towards the close of his career:

Ex. 6

Ex. 7

Al - les Ver - gäng - li - che   ist nur ein Gleich - nis.

In both instances a chromatically descending bass paves the way for an expressionist suspension (*x*) which in the latter case leads to an enharmonic change with a bias towards the sharp keys. In both quotations it is the pivotal chord of the added sixth (*y*) which sets the modulatory train in motion and all but obliterates the original melodic trend.

Pastiche effects are not confined to the ecclesiastical orbit. They are even more frequently found in the sphere of music inspired by military signals—undoubtedly one of Mahler's most easily recognizable 'fingerprints.' They range from the imitation of actual army signals (e.g. the 'Abblasen' motif of the former Imperial Austrian army, in the third movement of Symphony III):

Ex. 8

to the stylized melody of a sentimental 'Biedermeier' posthorn. Here the continuation of the coachman's melody ('wie nachhorchend'—as if listening on) results in the almost comical identity with a melody of Liszt's *Rapsodie espagnole*:

Ex. 9

which may or may not have been based on Spanish folk tunes.

Far removed from stylization and clearly emerging from a stratum of primordial experiences are those 'nature motifs' which Mahler

often asks to be produced 'wie ein Naturlaut' (like a natural sound).
They again range from amorphous acoustic symbols, such as the
unforgettable luminous harmonics of the high-pitched A with
which Symphony I starts, conjuring up the infinite Slavonic plain of
Moravia in which Mahler grew up, to primitive intervallic steps like
the first recognizable motif of the same Symphony, with its falling
fourths—again one of Mahler's most characteristic traits:

Ex. 10

out of which the cuckoo-call as well as the watchmen's distant
trumpet-call in the exposition of that movement grow.

The motivic stylization of repetitive bird-cries:

Ex. 11

Ex. 12

(herunterziehen)

inexpressibly lonely and remote, seems to symbolize the infinity of
nature—in contrast to the neatly fashioned bird motifs in Beethoven's
'Pastoral' Symphony. These bird-cries are a persistent feature in
Mahler's musical idiom from beginning to end. In their immobility
and complete refusal to submit to traditional methods of symphonic
treatment they represent the other extreme in Mahler's world of

melodies. They inhabit the misty region of indistinct noises and amorphous sound-patterns of which Mahler was so fond and which make him seem like an early forerunner of the Alban Berg of the *Three Orchestral Pieces*, Op. 6, and of the latest French *bruitistes*. Ex. 11 is the essence of a Mahlerian sound-picture of midnight in the sense of Nietzsche's and Rückert's visionary dreams. Motif *x* permeates Mahler's music from the early *Klagende Lied* to the autumnal pages of *Der Abschied* in *Das Lied von der Erde*. It signifies the eternity of motion in nature—rippling of the brook, rustling of leaves—and it is set rigidly against the pliant curve of lonely and harmonically vague melodies, like the following in *Das Lied von der Erde*:

Ex. 13

This is very different from similar incidents in earlier works because here Mahler temporarily abandoned diatonicism for the pentatonic scale. But this brings us to the subject of Mahler's orientalisms, which it would stretch this chapter beyond endurance to deal with here.

To discuss Mahler as a harmonist seems in a sense contradictory, for he was a composer who throughout his life clung stoutly to the principle of two-part counterpoint and deliberately avoided the concept of primary harmony, so prevalent in the opulent days of his youth. It is characteristic of him to think of music, generally speaking, in terms of thematic antithesis rather than as melody supported by an undercurrent of ever-changing harmony. Conjointly with this goes an inclination towards the intervals of the fourth and fifth in faburden-like pedal-point effects. This odd employment of bare intervals, which may sometimes strike the casual listener as a revival of the medieval practice of organum, eventually leads to a gradual emancipation of the fourth and fifth in Mahler's work, paving the way for a conception of music almost wholly based on combinations of these two intervals and to a codification of their chordal possibilities in works like Schoenberg's *Kammersymphonie* No. 1, Op. 9 (1906), and Alban Berg's piano Sonata, Op. 1 (1908). Mahler's essentially negative position regarding problems of harmony may be exemplified by two cases which also indicate the peculiar function allotted to bare fifths and fourths in his musical procedures:

Ex. 14

Ex. 15

In the second example figure *a* is immediately presented in canon at the octave at a bar's distance, while *b* is simultaneously played as a melodic continuation of *a* and in an augmentation (*b* 1) in the bass clarinet. In both examples harmony appears as a result of clashing contrapuntal entities rather than as a primary conception—except for the faburden fifths at *x* in the first example.

In later years Mahler liked to dispose of supporting pedal-points like the persistent one at *y*, Ex. 14, and to present his music as all sinews and no fat at all. This process of 'slimming' also heralds the approach to a different concept of tonality, as may be seen in the following two examples of his later music:

Ex. 16

Here the two contrapuntal parts are completely independent and capable of separate development. The resultant harmonies—with prevailing bare fifths and fourths—are accidental. This peculiar technique, pursued to its limits, leads Mahler less than ten years later to two-part combinations almost devoid of any traditional feeling of tonality:

Ex. 17

Even where he brings primary harmony (i.e. fifths and fourths in chordal arrangement) into play for some special effect, it still appears as if it were intervallic motion, suddenly congealed in the very act of enunciation and still incapable of bringing about a modulatory shift of key (*Wo die schönen Trompeten blasen; Wunderhorn*):

Ex. 18

This eventually leads to a bold emancipation of those intervals and to a temporary suspension of the traditional structure in thirds of the fundamental concept of harmony, as in the extreme case of Symphony VII and its progressions in fourths:

Ex. 19

This 'atonal verticalization' of progression in fourths may occasionally be harnessed to a scheme of tonal modulation, with startling results, as in the finale of Symphony I.

Modulation in the traditional sense was conspicuously absent even from Mahler's early works, where he did not hesitate, for instance, to use primitive key progressions in consecutive fifths in song and symphony dating from before 1900. Later on his increasing tendency to present thematic expositions in the kind of dualistic bareness shown in Exs. 16 and 17 was capable of leading to actual polytonality, to combinations of unrelated harmonies such as Darius Milhaud's experiments in polytonal procedures accustomed us to at a later period. Mahler's boldest harmonic adventures result either from a stubborn clinging to pedal-points or from a truly amazing integration of the whole-tone and the pentatonic scale, into his musical resources. His employment of the pentatonic scale, rare in his later works apart from Symphony V and *Das Lied von der Erde*, though it sometimes produces no more than casual exoticisms, can lend itself to constructive purposes. Where, as in the latter work, his task was to reshape his musical idiom in order to evoke a far-eastern atmosphere, he found himself for once confronted with the necessity of working with a type of preconceived note-series. This led to one of his most ingenious inventions: the application of the five-note scale to the final but inconclusive chord of the work (C major with added sixth), which is nothing more than a verticalization of the basic series (A, G, E, D, C) which opens the work and fertilizes most of its thematic features. The fourth note (D) of this basic series is insisted on in the *ostinato* reiteration by the voice of the word 'ewig,' fading away one bar before that final chord.

The impressionistic use of consecutive sevenths, probably used by Mahler years before Erik Satie tried similar experiments in 1887, may in fact be observed in one of his earliest compositions, the song *Erinnerung (Lieder und Gesänge aus der Jugendzeit*, Vol. I), in a passage which may be compared with Verdi's bold progressions in the magical postlude to the first scene of Act III of *Falstaff* (1893).

Chromatic progressions are very rare in Mahler's earlier works, which in fact derive much of their independent individuality from their absence; but in his later music the general weakening of key-feeling, combined with a tendency towards acrid sonorities, leads to a more frequent use of such progressions and thus to a certain approach to Bruckner's processes of harmonization. The following extracts, from the *Adagio* of Bruckner's seventh Symphony:

Ex. 20

and from the *Urlicht* movement in Mahler's second:

Ex. 21

show a kind of harmonic emotionalism which reveals Mahler as a whole-hearted and eclectic adherent to the somewhat Parsifalesque pathos of Bruckner's Symphony. These examples, incidentally, give the lie to the oft-repeated assertion that no bond of style existed between Bruckner and Mahler, whose close spiritual affinity is after all one of the chief topics of this book.

CHAPTER VII

FORM, TEXTURE AND ORCHESTRATION

THE forms of Mahler's music undergo a gradual process of refinement and increasing complexity without ever entirely giving up their basic simplicity. A case in point are the songs. The simple strophic *Lied* (with interpolated contrasting sections) remains the model for many of his earlier songs; later on a subtle change towards a more symphonic structure takes effect, still within the narrow limits of the romantic song; last of all his songs are planned on a more ambitious scale.

A similar gradual development is noticeable in his textures as the diatonic homophony and two-part counterpoint of the earlier songs and symphonies changes almost imperceptibly to the more poly-phonic manner of the middle symphonies. It is quite possible that Mahler's increasing interest in Bach led to the adoption of polyphonic technique in the symphonies of his maturity; but it should not be forgotten that Mahler was a born contrapuntist and that writing in canonically intertwined parts came quite easily to him (see Ex. 15). I for one believe that his growing predilection for strict polyphony had something to do with his tendency to avoid excessive chromaticism and the over-seasoned harmony of the late romantics. It is a fact worth noting that fugal writing crops up for the first time in his work in the finale of Symphony V and that great variety of texture is pro-vided by the only sets of variations Mahler ever composed: the *Adagio* of Symphony IV and the two somewhat similarly planned rondo-finales of Symphonies V and VII. The climax of these tendencies was surely reached in the colossal double fugue in the first part of Symphony VIII ('Ductore praevio') and also by the fugal sections of the 'Rondo-Burleske' in Symphony IX. Mahler's astonishing mastery of strict fugal writing helped him to exercise the vitality of his creative faculties, but it was as little an end in itself as was Bruckner's rarely displayed skill in the writing of choral fugues. Both were consciously following Beethoven in their application of fugal technique to climactic parts of their works which needed an additional tightening-up of texture to avoid slipping into the chaos of uncontrolled expression.

The augmented sonata form used in nearly all Mahler's larger compositions—discerned by some of his analysts even in so unorthodox a structure as Symphony VIII in two parts and the vocal 'symphony' of the *Lied von der Erde* in six song-movements—obviously hails as much from Beethoven's late string quartets as from Berlioz's sym- phonies (five movements in the *Fantastique* as well as in *Harold en Italie*) and finally from Liszt's tableaux-sections in his *Faust* and *Dante* symphonies. The number and character of Mahler's movements as well as the extent of their deviation from classical form depend on the psychological programme of each of his symphonies. How that programme and especially its condensation into a lyrical or choral text affects his whole conception becomes evident from a frank con- fession addressed to Arthur Seidl in connection with Symphony II: [1]

> ... When I conceive a great musical organism I invariably arrive at a point where I feel compelled to call in the aid of words as a carrier of my musical idea. ... In the case of the last movement of my second Symphony this went so far that I had to search through the whole world-literature, down to the Holy Bible, in order to find the appropriate words. ...

If a surprising variety of types seems to result from the intrusion of vocal movements into a majority of the symphonies, the purely instru- mental movements nevertheless revert again and again to certain fundamental archetypes significant of Mahler's obsession with a *volkstümlich* type of music. Nearly all these movements are based on a type of march (or funeral march), dance (waltz or *Ländler*) or elab- orations on a song-like theme (this last especially in *adagio* movements). The march type occurs in nearly all the symphonies, sometimes con- ceived as a lusty military band tune, more often as a sombre funeral march of gigantic proportions. Such funeral marches either start the symphony (e.g. II, V, VI and VII) or occur at some climactic point (Symphony I, third movement). These march and dance

---

[1] Letter of 17th February 1897, BR, No. 209. See translation of parts of this letter in Chapter XI, p. 186.

elements are inseparably bound up with fierce insistence on rhythm in its more brutal aspects and often emphasized by a highly specialized use of percussion—features of style which must have struck audiences as very strange at the end of the nineteenth century, when sharp contours of rhythm had become blurred in the luscious sonorities of the Wagnerian orchestra.

The dance scherzo of the *Ländler* type occurs in all the symphonies except the third and eighth, and the *Lied* character of the few genuine *adagio* movements Mahler wrote is marked by their reliance on variation technique (Symphony IV) or by their employment of a primitive binary form (*Adagietto* of Symphony V). Only in the ultra-emotional, meandering and complex slow movements of the last two symphonies does Mahler at last attain to an *adagio* of Brucknerian dimensions, and it is deeply significant that he should there revert to something like Bruckner's idiom in those solemn, hymn-like tunes introducing his two 'farewell' movements, which owe so much to Bruckner's own valediction to life—the *Adagio* of his unfinished ninth Symphony.

To the uninitiated Mahler's symphony movements in sonata form appear bewilderingly complex because of the increased number of thematic groups he presents with as much deliberation as Bruckner and with less rapidity than Beethoven, whose 'Eroica' first introduced agglomerative thematic matter on a large scale into the symphonic process. The inordinate length of some of Mahler's movements is easily explained by the fact that they sometimes contain two development sections (e.g. first movement of Symphony III; finale of Symphony VI; in both cases Beethoven's idea of a symphonically augmented coda is responsible for such structural inflation) and that their very long introductions are granted a complete or even extended recapitulation (e.g. first movement of Symphony III, cues 55–62; finale of Symphony VI, cues 143–50).[1] Mahler usually succeeds in holding these straggling movements together, not only by thematic workmanship and the psychological implications of his programmes, but also with the aid of certain *Leitmotiv* symbols which act as

---

[1] These two movements are singled out here as probably the longest written by any symphonist at any time.

landmarks in a boiling sea of developing thematic matter. These are usually of a primitive, almost primeval character and convey messages from the region of the subconscious.[1] *Urmotive* or *Leitrhythmen* of this kind appear as interplanetary entities, as it were, in most of the symphonies. One of them darkens the atmosphere from a major tonic to its minor key: the symbol of day turning to night, order reverting to chaos. Here is its most impressive appearance as a 'Fate' motif in Symphony VI, with a sinister thematic rhythm in the kettledrums underpinning it with a suggestion of inexorable finality:

Ex. 22

The same motif plays an integral part in Symphony II, in the *Nacht-musiken* of Symphony VII and also in songs of a lugubrious character such as *Tamboursg'sell* and *Um Mitternacht*. In a telling abbreviation it indicates the ambivalent instability of Mahler's musical idiom, at the same time heralding the twentieth-century weakening of the key-sense.

A similar *Leitmotiv* function is generally assigned to chorale motifs, sometimes shaped in deliberate allusion to the plainsong melody of 'Dies irae,' as in the case of the chorale tune which permeates the whole fabric of Symphony II, only to reveal its cosmic message at the climax of the finale:

Ex. 23

Mahler's art of orchestration is the one aspect of his work which

[1] The dark realm of *Die Mütter*: cf. Goethe's *Faust*, Part II, where such primeval figures are used as a poetical symbol for the remote region where thought and dream, action intended and action carried out, are not yet separated.

received unstinted praise from the very start of his creative career. Even those among his critics who remained unconvinced of his inventive originality admitted the revolutionizing novelty of his orchestral technique. His orchestral *pleinairisme*, his predilection for primary colours, his liking for exposed passages in woodwinds and trumpets and his discovery of the expressive qualities of the percussion section represented a startling contrast to Wagner's principle of blended sonorities as well as to Bruckner's terraced orchestral layout, learnt from the organ. In his approach to the problem of establishing an orchestra free of blurred contours and superabundant pedals (Wagner's horn parts), and convincing by sobriety of colour and economical terseness rather than lush sensuousness, Mahler stood alone in his lifetime. Only to-day is it possible at last to see that his principles were to bear fruit in the orchestral designs of Schoenberg and Alban Berg as well as in the stark and economical scoring of young and highly skilled craftsmen such as Shostakovich and Britten.

Certain features of Mahler's scoring have been widely discussed and have come in for some censorious comment. Chief among them is his undeniable preference for an outsize orchestra, which went to extravagant lengths in Symphony VIII, the notorious 'symphony of a thousand,' lampooned by a scurrilous poem in the *Meggendorfer Blätter* at the time of its first performance (1910).[1] The exaggerations of its doggerel need not be refuted, but the fact that mammoth orchestras such as that employed for this symphony became the subject of satirical comment about 1910 clearly indicates that the period of orchestral aggrandizement was coming to an end. Yet Mahler's monster apparatus seems wholly justified by the cosmic grandeur of his chosen subjects, the early Christian hymn *Veni Creator* and the final scene from Part II of Goethe's *Faust*. His original vision, which in his view dictated the choice of a super orchestra and a super chorus, is cogently expressed in a letter to Willem Mengelberg of 18th August 1906:

... I have just now completed my Eighth ... it is the biggest thing I have done so far. ... Imagine that the universe begins to vibrate and to sound. These are no longer human voices, but planets and suns rotating....

[1] Quoted in full on page 214.

This cosmic aspect of the Symphony led Mahler to conceive motifs, so to speak, more than life size and of long-range power. They were intended to be used as projectiles capable of piercing the hearts of the most distant listeners and of being effectively reproduced by a multitude of sound-media. They were conceived as tone vehicles of 'community-building qualities,' to borrow Paul Bekker's phrase explaining the strange effect of Mahler's music on post-1914 audiences, breaking down any lingering resistance in their minds by the hectoring force of their striding and strident intervals:

Ex. 24

adaptable even to the ultimate outsize augmentation of their root-motif *z* in the last bar of the 'distant brass orchestra, placed in an isolated spot' and enunciating the eternal message of Christian love through the parabolic mists of the *Faust* finale. In the light of these Michelangelesque visions it is easier to-day to become reconciled to the host of strange and unusual instruments (church bells, celesta, pianoforte, harmonium, organ, mandolines) discriminately used to depict Goethe's 'mount of anchorites' in sound. It is also easier now to understand the famous *crescendo* of the percussion section, occurring in the finale of Symphony II (before cue 14), where it precedes the eerie 'March of the Dead' in an attempt to express the happenings on the day of the Last Judgment. This *crescendo*—a forerunner of a similar orchestral climax in Berg's *Wozzeck,* Act III, shortly before scene iii —gives an indication of Mahler's originality in the use of amorphous sounds and their dramatic possibilities.

Mahler's imaginative powers seem never more admirable than when he attempts to translate a metaphysical experience into terms of realistic sound. In such passages as the distant tramping of feet in the first movement of Symphony III or the inexorable hammer-blows in the finale of Symphony VI he seems to anticipate not only the beginning of Alban Berg's *Drei Orchesterstücke*, Op. 6, but even the recent *bruitisme* of French *musique concrète*. Mahler's peculiar use of percussion gives the lie to allegations of his noisiness, and proves the high degree of his sense of aural differentiation and perfect functioning of a creatively observant ear, enabling him to produce a dazzling variety of sound from the allegedly soulless medium of the orchestral 'kitchen department.' His fastidiousness in scoring, evidenced by the minuteness of his expression marks alone, becomes even more evident in episodes of uncanny, grotesque or evanescent atmospherics of sound, as in the parodistic march of the third movement of Symphony I, which peters out in the shuffling and slurring sounds of violins, bowed *col legno*: [1]

Ex. 25

The Hoffmann-like 'puppet' scherzo of Symphony VI uses xylophone, strings and woodwind in a stupendous combination of sound equally suggestive of the rattling of bones by skeletons *à la danse macabre* and of the metallic laughter of the devil himself:

Ex. 26

---

[1] The score bears the following: 'Note for the conductor: No mistake! To be bowed with the wood of the bow.'

The gossamer texture of the late Rückert song *Ich atmet' einen linden Duft*, in contrast to the foregoing quotations, is produced with a minimum of instrumental means—a clear pointer towards the chamber-orchestra combinations in the *Lied von der Erde* with its piercing clear melodic contours, as in the plaintive oboe melody,[1] sung against monotonously reiterated scale passages in the violins, with which No. 2 (*Der Einsame im Herbst*) opens.

Mahler's expressionist art of scoring can perhaps best be studied in passages of almost violent expression, as in the final bars of No. 1 (*Das Trinklied vom Jammer der Erde*), where the faint and yet piercing sound of the trumpet is set off against the plaintive shriek of the flutes and clarinets, while the opaque thud of trombones, bassoons and harps adds to it a sense of hopeless finality, as if the door of life were shut for all eternity:

Ex. 27

The many new instruments introduced by Mahler into the post-classical symphony orchestra for special purposes of symbolism and poetical characterization come from very different sources. Some, like the tenor horn which adds its poignant edge to the sombre introduction of Symphony VII, the 'biedermeierish' cornet (in Symphony III), the bass drum with firmly attached cymbals and the side-drum, undeniably hail from the department of military music (with imperial Austrian connotations) which exercised a lifelong charm on Mahler. Others, like the hammer (finale, Symphony VI), the cowbells (Symphonies VI and VII [2]), the mandoline (*Lied von der Erde*) and

[1] See Ex. 43, p. 224.

[2] Mahler himself explained the cowbells as symbolic of the last terrestial sounds, penetrating into the remote solitude of mountain peaks. See Edgar Istel, *Mahler's Symphonien* (1910), p. 13.

Mahler

also distant orchestras 'in the wings,' humming choirs without words, organ and pianoforte, may have suggested themselves to the great conductor living and working in the acoustic conditions of an opera-house. An element of theatricalism introduced into a symphony concert is inseparable from any 'stage effect' such as distant orchestras, signals from the organ-loft, etc.; yet the application of these exceptional sonorities for purposes of expressing strange, even unique poetical experiences gives the measure of Mahler's instinct for their hitherto untapped possibilities. The exuberance of the *corno obbligato* in the scherzo of Symphony V gives way to the impressionistic treatment of the whole group of horns in unique echo effects, suggesting deep ravines and far-off valleys in an alpine setting, thoroughly established by the initial yodel motif.[1] The intimate colour of the mandoline turns into the symbol of a mournful poet's solitude in the final portion of *Der Abschied* (*Lied von der Erde*), mingling as it does with the tender sounds of harp and flute:

Ex. 28

It would be a grave mistake to assume that this subtle art of orchestration was only a matter of Mahler's infallible instinct. On the contrary, his scores attained their high standard of clarity and mastery of intricate sonorities only after trial and error and as the result of frequent redrafting. We have already seen that Bruckner had similar difficulties in the final scoring of his symphonies. Egon Wellesz has related [2] his first-hand experiences in rehearsals of new Mahler symphonies under the composer's direction and testified to the prodigious amount of revision they were subjected to at a time when Mahler was undoubtedly at the height of his fame and powers. The early second

[1] See Ex. 37, p. 200.
[2] In the *Musical Quarterly*, July 1938, article on Bruckner and Mahler.

Symphony is a case in point: Mahler revised its score as late as 1910. Richard Specht [1] published the facsimile of a page from the finale of that Symphony, showing extensive additions and emendations in Mahler's hand. The present writer remembers having seen a score of Symphony III (belonging to the Vienna Gesellschaft der Musik-freunde) and a similar one of Symphony V—obviously the score to which recurrent letters of Mahler refer from 1907 onwards—into which the composer had written in red ink his innumerable corrections of scoring and dynamics. In both cases the corrected scores differ so widely from the published ones that their publication as original versions is at least as desirable as in the similar case of Bruckner. In the case of Symphony V we know from Alma that Mahler began to rescore it even before the first performance, and she says she persuaded him to cut down the lavish parts allotted to the percussion section in the original draft. In one of his last letters Mahler confessed to Georg Göhler that Symphony V had to be completely reorchestrated, and that only then (i.e. seven years after the first publication and the first performance of 1904) was the score ready for performance, adding in savage self-criticism: 'I fail to comprehend how I could then have blundered so like a greenhorn. . . .' Similarly the preserved juvenilia —*Das klagende Lied* and *Lieder eines fahrenden Gesellen*—appeared only at the turn of the century in a revised orchestral garb.

Mahler's acute aural perception and his almost fanatical striving for clarity are mainly responsible for the application of his special faculties to the improvement of the orchestral scores of Beethoven and Schumann. His systematic rescoring of the latter's symphonies in particular has to-day achieved a remarkable degree of popularity among conductors and audiences alike. Mahler's skill in the solution of problems of orchestral sonority underwent the sternest test in his encounters with the great ancestral figures of the past.

[1] (See Bibliography) App., p. 51.

CHAPTER VIII

GRADUALLY, as the years went by, composition became for Mahler a concurrent antithesis to his conducting, a deliberately romantic make-believe, an escapist's nostalgic dream, consciously excluding all the features of the 'wicked' world of opera in which as a successful star-conductor he was condemned to live a glamorous but haunted existence. His creative personality stresses those elements which are so conspicuously missing in the atmosphere of the stage; pantheistic worship of nature, a child's heaven with its innocent spiritualization of the animal world, Jacob's wrestling with the Angel ('Ich bin von Gott und will wieder zu Gott . . .'). Occasionally it indulges in homely, mock-medieval romanticism, mysteriously emanating from ancient townships and wonderfully coming to life in the paintings of Spitzweg. Only once does it shed an introspective light into the recesses of its creator's tortured soul, in a gruesome anticipation of future private grief (*Kindertotenlieder*). It exults ecstatically in the patristic hymn music for the final scene of Goethe's *Faust.* Finally it fades away into the blue eternity of ancient Chinese poetry.

Into this world Mahler plunged regularly during short holiday weeks or when he happened to be without a conductor's post. His own music could never grow up organically as the central factor of his artistic existence; up to the very end it was doomed to an uneasy co-existence with Mahler's conducting and remained a 'side-line.' Mahler died at the very moment of general recognition, only a year after he had signed the first exclusive contract with a publisher—the Universal Edition—and before he had himself tried out and heard the works of his maturity (*Lied von der Erde*, Symphonies IX and X). The simple truth is that his music was left in a state of precarious incompleteness owing to the fact that fate had denied it finality of shape after various and often inconclusive revisions.[1] This is the more tragic because Mahler strove throughout his life—more desperately even than Bruckner—for perfection of utterance and unequivocal clarity of the musical formula. It is his fanatical, never satisfied self-criticism that has deprived posterity of nearly all the compositions of his youth, just as it is his loyalty to his own vision which has turned works developed at haphazard into an organic unity of design and purpose. Perhaps the most amazing thing about Mahler's symphonies and songs, scattered as they are over a period of feverish professional life, is their interdependence and a spiritual as well as a thematic kinship that assigns nearly every song or melodic unit a definite place in his creative world. Certain groups of interconnected song-cycles and symphonies may be easily detected. Their relationship gives to his work as a whole the firm outline of a definite creative purpose, though widely separated dates of composition, first performance and publication often make it difficult to perceive.

Mahler's music did not at once show that duality of song-cycle and symphony which was to become so conspicuous after the *Lieder eines fahrenden Gesellen* and their symphonic corollary, Symphony I, had appeared (1885–8). Up to the date of completion of that latter work, i.e. up to his twenty-ninth year, his music struck out almost frantically in different directions, testing subjects and media of sound, as though in search of its own congenial tone-poetical atmosphere. The three lost or destroyed operas, the vanished or discarded chamber music, the incidental music for plays and even the published score of his version of Weber's opera fragment *Die drei Pintos* were in the nature of experiments. The only large conception of these early years he permitted to survive in part, *Das klagende Lied*, already contains the seeds from which future symphonies and song-cycles were to spring, just as his early choice of eclectic poetry anticipates the romantic 'blue flower' of the later *Wunderhorn* world. It was about 1886 that Mahler fell under the spell of the Arnim-Brentano anthology. Symphonies II, III and IV, utilizing *Wunderhorn* songs, are inspired by it. They are flanked by a rich harvest of songs based on *Wunderhorn* poems, yet

[1] See BR, Nos. 409 and 420 on the final revisions (1910) of Symphonies IV and V only.

169

by no means always thematically associated with them. These songs (originally called *Humoresken*) were published at intervals spread over more than twenty years. The dates of composition of the very first and the last *Wunderhorn* songs lie far apart, the earliest of them about 1888 (second book of *Lieder und Gesänge aus der Jugendzeit*), the last (*Revelge* and *Tamboursg'sell*) 1899 and 1901 respectively (published in 1905 as part of *Letzte Lieder*). The *Wunderhorn* epoch of about 1888–1900 is followed by the three middle symphonies without words (Nos. V, VI and VII). They reveal, despite their marked emphasis on instrumental design and their adherence to classical symphonic processes, certain thematic connections with the Rückert songs of that period. These appear in two separate song-cycles, composed between 1901 and 1904 as lyrical interludes to the middle symphonies, themselves composed between 1901 and 1905. The climax of Mahler's striving towards a complete integration of vocal elements into a symphonic structure is reached at last with the tremendous effort of Symphony VIII, composed in 1906 but not published and first performed till 1910. After the shattering disclosure of Mahler's heart trouble, the much-lamented death of his elder child, the nerve-racking resignation from the director's post at the Vienna Opera—all of them events of the sinister summer of 1907—the moving epilogue to his creative work, undertaken in the scanty intervals between his professional visits to America, opens with the symphonic song-cycle *Das Lied von der Erde* (1908), whose novel idiom, with its pentatonic colour-scheme, its general atmosphere of far-eastern contemplation and its febrile outbursts of *joie de vivre*, alternating with sombre anticipations of death, becomes even more eloquent in the two last symphonies composed in 1909–10, but only posthumously performed and published. They are carried along on the same emotional wave which had thrown up the *Lied* from the very depths of Mahler's life-weary soul.

CHAPTER IX

JUVENILIA

VERY little of Mahler's early music has survived the holocaust he made of it in later years; and as long as the present lack of a truly critical edition of his preserved works persists it will be difficult to form an adequate opinion of the extent of his creative activities, especially during the years of his adolescence and musical apprenticeship (1876–88). That he must have been a prolific composer at times, and one with a gift of naturally flowing melody, may be deduced from the fact that he was nicknamed 'Schubert' by his fellow students and that his crony Hugo Wolf praised his songs and attached greater importance to them than to his own.[1] Although there are good reasons for believing that some at least of Mahler's juvenilia are still in existence and in the possession of members of his family, none seems to be known except by name. Natalie Bauer-Lechner mentions more titles than any other biographer, including a Quartet for piano and strings (the autograph of which was lost on a journey to Russia),[2] a Quintet for piano and strings, two early symphonies (one of them in A minor, of which three movements are said to have existed as late as 1896) and the prelude to the planned opera *Die Argonauten*. Of the piano Quartet two movements, the first and a scherzo, were performed in 1876 and 1878 respectively on the occasion of a prize competition at the Vienna Conservatory and awarded a first prize each.[3] A Sonata for violin and piano is also mentioned. Of

[1] See E. Decsey, 'Stunden mit Mahler' (*Die Musik*, June–August 1911).
[2] It has been rediscovered lately.
[3] See R. Specht, *Thematische Analyse der VIII Symphonie* (Universal Edition, No. 3399), pp. 46 ff.

numerous songs written in those days Mahler later had but a poor opinion.[1] However, his main creative energies were expended on opera, very probably under the stimulus of Wagner, whose music created such a stir among the music students of Vienna in the years between the first Bayreuth production of the *Ring* and the first per-formance of *Parsifal* (1876–82). Mahler worked at no less than four operatic projects during these years. The somewhat old-fashioned choice of their ultra-romantic subjects may be explained by his Moravian provincialism as well as by the fact that as a Jew striving frantically for integration and indeed absorption into the Gentile world he was anxious to assimilate older traditions of German cultural heritage. The subject of his opera *Herzog Ernst von Schwaben* (probably inspired by Uhland's verse-drama of that name), like that of *Die Argonauten* (probably based on Grillparzer's dramatic trilogy *Das goldene Vliess*, of which *Die Argonauten* forms the middle portion), is rooted in early German romanticism. The same is true of his 'Märchenspiel' *Rübezahl*, whose protagonist is the mythical mountain spirit of the Silesian Riesengebirge, often alluded to in E. T. A. Hoff-mann's writings, and hero of one of Grimms' fairy tales. This phase is musically represented by Weber and Marschner rather than by the more sophisticated Wagner, whose influence on Mahler can nevertheless be detected in the significant fact that the latter himself wrote the words for all these operas with the exception of the very first.[2] Nothing has so far been discovered of these three youthful operatic projects except a few unreliable biographical data. *Herzog Ernst* seems to have been planned and sketched in parts during the years 1878–9. The *Argonauten* was evidently planned in 1880 while Mahler was conducting musical comedies and farces at Hall. The libretto is said to have been written in alliterative verse, which suggests that Mahler must already have been fairly familiar with the libretto of Wagner's *Ring* at that time. On *Rübezahl*, a subject which may

[1] N. Bauer-Lechner (see Bibliography).

[2] The libretto of *Herzog Ernst von Schwaben* was provided by his early friend Josef Steiner in 1878–9.

have been suggested to him by Wolf,[1] he was engaged during his appointment at Lljubljana in 1881-2 and Olomouc, up to the very time he became 'Königlicher Musikdirektor' at Cassel (June 1883). Nothing has survived of this latter work, although as late as May 1896 Mahler actually sent the autograph of the libretto to Max Marschalk, suggesting that he should compose new music for it.[2] A *Nordic Symphony* seems to have been planned and composed at Olomouc—without leaving any trace.

Only one of these ambitious projects met with a kinder fate: *Das klagende Lied*, of which Mahler himself said in a letter to Marschalk of December 1896:

> . . . The first of my works in which I found myself again as 'Mahler' is a fairy-tale for chorus, soloists and orchestra, *Das klagende Lied*. This work I designated as my Op. 1. . . .

Das klagende Lied was originally planned and composed as a fairy-tale opera in three parts labelled:

1. *Waldmärchen* (Woodland Legend).
2. *Der Spielmann* (The Minstrel).
3. *Hochzeitsstück* (Wedding Piece).[3]

Work on this operatic version had started in the autumn of 1879 in Vienna, and the score was completed there on 1st November 1880. Mahler's avowed intention to secure an early performance of this true 'child of his sorrows' came to nought.[4] In a subsequent first

---

[1] See ER, pp. 81 and 177. The libretto still existed in 1908 in possession of Mahler's sister Justine Rosé. Alma Mahler's account does not clearly show whether Mahler actually destroyed it after that date.

[2] See BR, No. 183, where Mahler says that he feels he has quite outgrown 'poor *Rübezahl*.' Where are score and libretto now?

[3] See Hans Hollaender, 'Unbekannte Jugendbriefe Mahlers' (*Die Musik*, XX/11, 1928).

[4] See Mahler's letter to Emil Freund, 1st November 1880, BR, No. 4. On the question of *Das klagende Lied* and Mahler's competition for the Vienna Beethoven prize, see Chapter I, p. 116.

revision, undertaken in 1888, Part I was eliminated and the whole work turned into a cantata in two sections. After that it seems to have been dismissed from Mahler's mind until the time of his correspondence with Marschalk (1896). Soon afterwards it was revised a second time.[1] It was eventually published in 1900 (or 1899), after some revision of its orchestration, and finally performed for the first time—more than twenty years after the completion of its operatic version—under the composer's direction at a Philharmonic concert in Vienna on 17th February 1901. The autograph of the eliminated Part I remained in the possession of Mahler's sister Justine Rosé, and suddenly turned up again, soon after her death, at a broadcast from Czechoslovakia in 1934, conducted by the composer's nephew Alfred Rosé, in whose possession it now is. Mahler's poem, inspired by fairytales by Bechstein and Grimm and foreshadowed in an earlier lyrical draft called *Ballade vom blonden und braunen Reitersmann*,[2] is based on the old German legend of two hostile brothers fighting for the love of the same woman. The victim of this fratricidal strife lies secretly buried in the depths of a forest while the murderer celebrates his wedding. A wandering minstrel by chance picks up a bone from the gruesome place of murder and cuts a pipe from it. The 'singing bone' reveals the ghastly secret of the lonely woodland grave, and when the defiant bridegroom puts the pipe to his own lips during the wedding banquet, he himself uncovers his crime to all and sundry.

[1] A collation of Part II (Part I of the printed version) with a photostat copy of its original draft of 1880 (*Spielmann*, short score completed 20th March 1880, full score completed 1st November 1880, now preserved in the Vienna City Library) surprisingly confirms Mahler's orchestration of 1880, which already shows all the fingerprints of the mature artist. The revision of 1898 was concerned for the most part merely with the dotting of i's and crossing of t's, and the addition of a profusion of expression marks to what was already a perfectly organized score. I am indebted to Donald Mitchell for the opportunity to study the photostat of the score at close quarters.

[2] This was first published in H. Hollaender's article mentioned above, which also reproduces Mahler's letters to his early friend, Anton Krisper.

Mahler's naïve doggerel rhymes keep close to the literary tradition of Heine and Eichendorff with their slightly affected folksong simplicity and artificial medieval diction. But the music shows an altogether surprising degree of originality, which manages to break through the outworn gestures of operatic tradition. All the characteristic traits of Mahler's later symphonic manner are assembled in the terse orchestral prelude with its stubborn insistence on march rhythm (cf. Ex. 14), on contrapuntal antithesis rather than on conventional underpinning by lush harmonies, with the chorale-like 'Dies irae' allusion in the trombones and the Slavonic lilt of the minstrel motif (cue 6). With great skill the music manages to integrate cross-influences such as Wagner's *Ring*, Bruckner's earlier symphonies and the operatic gesture of Weber and Marschner, whose music re-echoes here and later in Mahler's work. Very effective, if clearly in an eclectic way, is the connection managed between the dramatic declamation of the soloists and the more detached contemplation by the chorus. The wedding feast (Part II) employs, in somewhat naïve theatricalism, a 'distant orchestra' (posted in the wings) of winds and percussion which dexterously sets off the ceremonious happenings from the sombre 'inner drama.' The ghostly music of the 'singing bone,' the motives of the wandering minstrel, as well as the music for the wedding celebration are treated in the manner of operatic reminiscence. Musically perhaps the most original page is the very last, accompanying the extinguishing lights in the royal hall, achieved by means of an eerie three-part contrapuntal combination of strings over fifty bars of pedal-point on E. Its spectral contours, bereft of any supporting harmony, anticipate the lean and ascetic part-writing of the mature Mahler, and obliterate in the listener's mind the numerous passages of conventional operatic emotion in which this immature work too frequently indulges. The revision of 1898, with its almost slick efficiency, its virtuosic handling of winds and percussion and its elaborate expression marks, forms a curious contrast to the intrinsic simplicity of the music, conceived by an adolescent of nineteen. A cruder method of scoring would no doubt have been better suited to this fairy-tale, in which so much of the later Mahlerian *Wanderlust*, so much woodland romanticism, but also a Freudian complex of fratricidal conflict as a contrast between outward glamour and inward misery of the soul seem anticipated, even if still presented in the threadbare costumes of obsolescent romantic conventions.

The only other extant work of Mahler's early years is the collection of *Lieder und Gesänge aus der Jugendzeit*. Three parts were published in two instalments in 1885 and 1892. The first book (1885) contains songs composed in and before 1883, while Books II and III (1892) are based entirely on poems from the *Wunderhorn*, some of which play a great part as thematic quarry for the three subsequent *Wunderhorn* symphonies, and therefore invite a discussion alongside the rest of Mahler's *Wunderhorn* compositions. The poems of Book I are taken from the minor romantic poet Richard Leander, from a German translation of Tirso de Molina's Don Juan drama and from a *Volks-lied* text for which the composer himself was responsible. This rather odd choice of poetry hints at a similar immaturity in the music, in which only very occasionally some flashes of originality may be found. The amiable water-colour sketch of *Frühlingsmorgen*, as well as *Erinnerung*, which are the only songs Mahler originally conceived with piano accompaniment, already anticipate No. 2 of the *Lieder eines fahrenden Gesellen* as well as *Das klagende Lied*. The passage in 6–8 time, 'Die Bienen summen und Käfer . . .' reflects the melody of the trio in the scherzo of Bruckner's third Symphony, which Mahler arranged for piano duet in 1878. It is therefore a fair guess to assume that this song was written in 1879–80 at the latest. The initial melody of *Erinnerung* reminds the hearer of to-day of Brahms's clarinet Quintet (composed nearly ten years later), whereas an obstinately recurrent motif in the folksong-like *Hans und Grete* is a clear pointer towards Symphony I (second movement). Despite its conventionality of rhythm and harmony, the yodel type of its melody (bars 3–6) clearly foreshadows the manner of Mahler's later *Ländler* scherzo (still camouflaged here under the direction 'Gemächliches Walzertempo'). The somewhat orchestral aspect of the piano part of *Hans und Grete* leads in the two Tirso de Molina songs to admittedly orchestral designs. *Serenade* should be accompanied by wind instru-ments (although a full score seems never to have been published) and for the accompaniment of *Phantasie* a harp is recommended. Both these songs, though effective in an eclectic sort of way, seem to hover between Mendelssohn and Brahms. The poverty of their rhythmic impulse, the insipid regularity of their bar-accents, the threadbare conventionality of their melodic patterns form a startling contrast to the complete originality of style and rhythm so strikingly displayed in the *Lieder eines fahrenden Gesellen*, which must have been composed almost immediately after.

CHAPTER X

'SONGS OF THE WAYFARER' AND SYMPHONY I

IN 1897 Mahler confessed to the friendly critic Arthur Seidl: '. . . Only when I experience do I act as a tone-poet—only when I act as a tone-poet do I undergo an experience. . . .' His first song-cycle and his first symphonic essay, closely interdependent as they are, confirm this self-appraisal. Both works vividly reflect youthful passions and the first collision with the traditional inertia of the 'world of yesterday'; both are autobiographical and programmatic in the sense of the above quotation; both create a new musical idiom out of the elements of discarded romantic conventions; both are inspired by a new conception of folky tunefulness. Each work is unique in that nothing of the kind was being composed by anybody between 1883 and 1888, dates which indicate the beginning of work on the cycle and the completion of the Symphony. The songs were composed between December 1883 and 1st January 1885, while Mahler was opera conductor at Cassel. They re-echo the unhappy love-affair with the actress Johanne Richter, as may be guessed from Mahler's words to his friend Löhr:

I have written a cycle of songs, six for the present, all of which are dedicated to her . . . the songs are conceived to suggest a wayfarer who has met with adversity, setting out into the world and wandering on in solitude. . . .

The cycle in the revised version of its first issue of 1897 consists of four songs only.[1] The poems were written by Mahler himself, and he later confessed that he had suppressed his authorship for fear of being ridiculed for their somewhat naïve simplicity. Mahler's 'Fahrender Gesell' is a near relation of Wilhelm Müller's melancholy hero in *Die Winterreise*. In both cases the unhappy lover is being jilted by his sweetheart, whose marriage to another man plunges him

[1] Perhaps the wistful little poem, *Vergessene Liebe*, of 1880 is a forerunner to the whole cycle (cf. Hans Hollaender, *Die Musik*, XX/11, 1928).

into despair and whose 'blue eyes' send him out on the road.   The
third song has a suicidal ring:

> I wish they laid me upon my bier,
> My eyelids never to open hereafter. . . .

And in the fourth and last song he begins his wanderings to the
rhythm of the kind of funeral march that is soon to become a feature
of Mahler's music in general.   But in the end 'all was well again. . . .
Gone were love and grief and dream . . .' when he finds a haven of
peace under the branches of a lime-tree by the wayside.

Two songs (Nos. 2 and 4) later became integrated into the first and
third movements of Symphony I, providing a programmatic background for the complicated psychological implications of that work.
The music of the cycle displays all the characteristics of Mahler's
mature lyric-symphonic style: the fundamentally orchestral conception of the accompaniment, the folktune-like lilt of its elongated
melodies (especially in No. 2), the masterly economy of means in the
use of thematic matter as well as in the disposition of instruments, the
rugged diatonicism of the whole tonal atmosphere, the more remarkable in the very year of Wagner's *Parsifal*.   The startling novelty of
these songs becomes evident on closer inspection and by comparison
with contemporary lyricism, as for instance the songs of Brahms, who
never invented singable melodies of such symphonic adaptability nor
ever conceived songs in the manner of extended instrumental movements, as Mahler plainly does in No. 4, whose dotted funereal rhythm
and the clangour of bells (alternating basses in tonic and dominant)
almost entirely permeate the song.   Surely one of the most remarkable
passages of No. 2 (and one which does not reappear in the respective
movement of the Symphony) is the delightful tone-painting reflecting
the wayfarer's fleeting pleasure on passing through a meadow sparkling with the dewdrops of early morning:

Ex. 29

with the characteristic fourths (marked with brackets) that were to become Mahler's favourite interval. Equally original in its striving for thematic unity between ritornel and verse is the thematic alignment of both in the simple strophic No. 1, with the Slavonic wistfulness of its falling fourth, partaking equally of the *lassu* and *friss* type of prelude and verse:

Ex. 30

Wenn mein Schatz Hoch-zeit macht

Another revolutionary feature of the cycle is its unorthodox approach to tonality. The *Songs of a Wayfarer*, for all their folky simplicity, start out in D minor, only to fade away in F minor by way of passing through F sharp minor, B major and E minor. This disregard of the logic of the traditional key-relationships is character-istically shown in No. 3, which starts in D minor, but on reaching E flat minor in the colossal orchestral wrench leading to the outburst 'I wish they laid me upon my bier,' it remains in the latter key to the end of the song. Mahler's habit of juxtaposing keys in this rugged manner and his avoidance of the leading-note give his music the disarming guilelessness of expression which becomes a feature of the later *Wunderhorn* music. His curious method of switching from one key to another first becomes noticeable in No. 4, where the circum-vention of the leading-note D♯ in bar 3 results in a kind of fictitious D major ambience.

Although the *Lieder eines fahrenden Gesellen* were completed by January 1885, their first performance took place as late as 1896, in Berlin, and the score appeared in the following year. Even a super-ficial comparison of the vocal and orchestral scores (published almost simultaneously by V. Weinberger of Vienna) shows that the former is based on an earlier version and that the latter embodies, as so often with Mahler, the result of a later revision. This is the first of many instances which make the lack of a truly critical edition of Mahler's works so acutely felt. Nothing less than collation of both versions and a fusion of them in an authoritative practical edition is fit to meet the demands of scrupulous performers.[1]

The remarkable first Symphony was composed, with interruptions, between 1884 and 1888, begun at Cassel, with the *Wayfarer* songs still on the stocks, and completed at Leipzig, where Mahler had become enmeshed in a passionate love-affair with Frau von Weber. To this Mahler applied similarly unorthodox methods of composition. Although outwardly conforming to the classical type with its four instrumental movements, the work is obviously vocally inspired by the two *Wayfarer* songs it incorporates, and also programmatically conceived. In the Hungarian programme book of its first performance (Budapest, 20th November 1889) it was called a 'symphonic poem in two parts,' and furnished with an elaborate programme in the manner of Berlioz's *Symphonie fantastique*. This was discarded later on in favour of the misleading title of 'Titan,' which nearly everybody associated with the rebels against the Olympian gods and nobody with a half-forgotten sentimental novel by Jean Paul. This subtitle was eventually dropped and an *Andante* middle movement was replaced by the now famous funeral march of the third movement, which Mahler himself associated with the naïve romantic painting 'The Huntsman's Funeral.' This too is misleading, as Mahler himself discovered when he said:

... However, here it is quite irrelevant to know what is being described—it is important only to grasp the mood which is being expressed and from which the fourth movement springs precipitately, like the flash of lightning from a sombre cloud. It is simply the cry of a deeply wounded heart which is preceded by the uncannily oppressive and ironically close atmosphere of the funeral march. . . . Ironical, that is to say, in the sense of the *eironeia* of Aristotle. . . .

The programme of the Symphony is easy to reconstruct on the basis of its affinity to the songs. It is a wayfarer's experience again, with the delightful, expectant open-air feeling of early dawn (introduction

[1] Cf. the foreword to my new edition of the *Songs of a Wayfarer* (see Appendices B and D).

to the first movement which should be 'like a sound of nature') merging into the exultant joy of the symphonically extended *Wayfarer* song, No. 2; the contrasting scherzo movement, based on the obstinate bass motif of *Hans und Grete* and displaying for the first time all the features of Mahler's typically Austrian yodel-inspired peasant dance with its distinctly alpine climate, its rusticity *à la* Bruckner and its Jewish-Slavonic ferocity; the psychological collapse in the eerie, self-lacerating third movement; and a finale in which the conflicts of the preceding movements are fought out to the last—interrupted by reminiscences of the first movement—until the Symphony's hero scores his ultimate triumph. This programme has a convincing ring because of the close unity of thematic matter and because the hero's fate is fully reflected in the musical events of the main themes. The passage from somnolent dawn to bright daylight is musically symbolized by this transformation:

Ex. 31

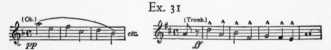

from a dreamy 'Naturlaut' to the triumphant chorale at the very end of the Symphony. This also emphasizes the thematic kinship between the two outer movements which is even more poignantly expressed by the sinister intrusion of the following F minor motif (*a*) into the morning brightness of the first movement. This in turn becomes the thematic cells for the *allegro* theme of the finale (*b*):

Ex. 32

The first movement can easily dispense with the customary second subject because its introduction ('Wie ein Naturlaut . . .') is treated like a legitimate first exposition of themes, recurring in an intensified and thematically enriched version during the development section and thereby acting, with its dreamlike cuckoo-call, its distant trumpet signals and its morning haze, symbolized by an all-pervading high-pitched pedal on A, as a contrast to the naïve exuberance of the symphonic commentary on 'Ging heut' morgens übers Feld. . . .' This 'before dawn' section of the first movement leads to further delightful structural unorthodoxy in the finale: the almost cine-matographically conceived 'flash-back' to the first movement at cue 38. This dramatically interrupts the second premature mock-anticipation of the final 'triumphal' section in D major (Ex. 31), which had already been preceded by an even more fictitious antici-pation of its triumphal coda at cue 26 (in 'unreal' C major). The return to the 'dream of youth' at the very climax of the struggle for attainment of the ultimate goal is significant of Mahler the romanticist, who headed a motif in his last completed Symphony (No. 9) with the words 'O vanished days of youth: O scattered love!' It is also proof of the often disputed fact that the structure of Mahler's sym-phonies depends on his tone-poetical experience and on the psycholo-gical condition of their creator. The intrusion of the 'before dawn' episode into the development section of the finale, whose lyrical, almost italianate contrast theme (cue 16) in itself forms an antithesis to the fierce fighting-spirit of Ex. 32 (*b*), as well as the integration of vocally conceived melodic complexes into movements 1 and 3, constitute highly original accretions to the traditional symphonic scheme. No less original is the symphonically extended waltz-*Ländler* of the second movement. Finally, the introduction of the 'Frère Jacques' melody as a perpetual canon into the spookish atmo-sphere of the 'Huntsman's Funeral' is a master-stroke, setting the seal of romantic eccentricity on a work named after a novel of Jean Paul's but conceived in the rebellious spirit of E. T. A. Hoffmann's Kapell-meister Kreisler, the patron saint of all true romantics from Schumann and Brahms to Hugo Wolf and Mahler.

Mahler's first Symphony, although produced on 20th November 1889, in Budapest, where it met with a rather chilly reception, was not published till 1898, by Weinberger of Vienna. Its engraving was made possible only by the support of the Gesellschaft zur

Förderung deutscher Wissenschaft, Kunst und Literatur in Böhmen, accorded to the composer at the suggestion of Guido Adler. Even in Vienna, where Mahler performed it several times at the turn of the century, the Symphony made but slow headway and elicited hostile and jeering comments in richer profusion than its later companions, Symphonies II, III and IV.

CHAPTER XI

THE 'WUNDERHORN' SYMPHONIES AND SONGS

MAHLER's Symphonies II, III and IV represent a symphonic trilogy reflecting the composer's struggle for a lasting religious belief and ultimate finding of it in the victory of love and forgiveness over doubt and fear. These works stand in the closest relationship to each other, not only because they share the same philosophical outlook, expressed by similar musical means, but also because in every one of them a poem from *Des Knaben Wunderhorn* occupies a central position, determining the emotional and religious approach and expressing Mahler's faith in resurrection and eternal life through the power of all-conquering love. In Symphony II this message emanates from the simple words of an ancient song, *Urlicht* (*Primeval Light*), and a devotional hymn by Klopstock. In Symphony III it is the cheerful message of a multitude of angelic voices ('Es sungen drei Engel einen süssen Gesang') dispelling the introspective gloom of the contralto's solo to words from Nietzsche's *Zarathustra* and announcing to repentant sinners the childlike glories of the celestial city of eternal forgiveness. This childlike dream of plenty and of eternal rejoicing should originally have formed the seventh movement of Symphony III in its first draft. It was eventually replaced by the final *Adagio*—now the Symphony's sixth movement, a purely instrumental piece—and transferred to Symphony IV, where it now forms the fourth and last movement (the soprano solo 'Wir geniessen die himmlischen Freuden'). This interdependence, especially between Symphonies III and IV, becomes evident from the fact that they share thematic material to a considerable extent. The motives used for the 'celestial joys' in the finale of Symphony IV are anticipated in the angels' song (fifth movement) of Symphony III and occur already in the second movement (*tempo di minuetto*) at cue 5.

Each work in this symphonic trilogy culminates in a devotional song from the *Wunderhorn*. In addition, Symphonies II and III contain an instrumental movement based on a *Wunderhorn* song and

extending its lyricism according to the structural demands of a symphony movement in a manner reminiscent of Symphony I and its
lyrical companion (*Songs of a Wayfarer*). In both cases the subject is
taken from the animal world, but contains a homiletic lesson for the
human listener. In Symphony II it is *St Anthony's Sermon to the
Fishes* (from Mahler's *Wunderhorn* songs) which is transformed into a
symphonic scherzo of gigantic proportions (movement 3). In Symphony III it is the early *Wunderhorn* song *Ablösung im Sommer* which
becomes the animal scherzo (movement 3) with the famous cornet solo.

It will by now have become evident that the *Wunderhorn* trilogy
shows strong programmatic leanings. Actually all three symphonies
are based on elaborate programmes which were issued at their first
performances, only to be withdrawn immediately afterwards and to
be entirely suppressed in the published scores. These curious facts
indicate the latent ambiguity in Mahler's lifelong attitude towards the
vexed problem of programme music. He loathed these programmes
aesthetically, but needed them intellectually. Although as a symphonist he felt ashamed of the need of a supporting programme, in
oral and written explanations later on he was unable to avoid reference
to the tone-poetical foundations on which his symphonic structures
were built. This dualistic attitude is best demonstrated in two
quotations from his letters, of which the first especially deals with the
programmatic aspect of Symphony II:

... Just as it seems trivial to me to invent music to a preconceived programme, I find it unsatisfactory and sterile to add one to an existing musical
composition; notwithstanding the fact that the creative urge for a musical
organism certainly springs from an experience of its author, i.e. from a fact,
after all, which should be positive enough to be expressible in words. ...

... After all no objections need be levelled against a programme. ...
Only, a musician must thus express himself, and not a man of letters, a
philosopher, a painter (they are all integrated in the musician). ...

Perhaps a less inconclusive self-explanation may be found in
another letter (of 1897), addressed to Arthur Seidl, in which he
agrees with Seidl's dictum that 'my music arrives at a programme as
its last clarification, whereas in the case of Richard Strauss the programme already exists as a given task. ...' Mahler then goes on to

describe the creative process of conceiving a symphony in all its component parts, with particular application to Symphony II. His commentary establishes a link with Beethoven's ninth Symphony, whose quest for the 'redeeming word' he compares with his own search for the proper vocal finale of Symphony II. The programme for that Symphony is here condensed from two authentic sources [1] in the composer's own words:

Movement 1. I have called the first movement 'funeral rites' . . . it is the hero from my Symphony in D major [Symphony I] whom I am here laying in his grave, and whose life I reflect in a pure mirror, as it were, from an elevated position. At the same time it expresses the great question: To what purpose have you lived? . . . Whosoever has heard this question must give an answer, and this answer I give in the last movement.

Movement 2. Remembering the past. . . . A ray of sunshine, pure and unspoiled, from the hero's past life.

Movement 3. When you awaken from the wistful dream of movement 2, to return into the turmoil of life again, it may easily happen to you that the ceaseless flow of life strikes you with horror—like the swaying of dancers in a brightly lit ballroom into which you happen to gaze from the outer darkness, and from such a distance that its music remains inaudible. . . . Life appears senseless to you and like a dreadful nightmare from which you may start up with a cry of disgust. . . .

Movement 4. The stirring voice of simple faith reaches our ear: I am of God and will go back to God. . . .

Movement 5. The voice in the desert sounds: the end of all life has come —doomsday is approaching. . . . The earth trembles, the graves are opening, the dead rise and march past in endless procession. The great and the small of this earth—kings and beggars. . . . The 'great tattoo' is sounded—the trumpets of the Revelation call: then, in the midst of a horrible silence we seem to hear a distant nightingale, like a last trembling echo of earthly life. Softly a choir of saints and celestial beings sings: 'Resurrection, yea, Resurrection, will be granted you.' And the glory of God appears. A wonderful, soft light penetrates into the depth of our hearts—everything is silent and blissful. And lo and behold! there is no judgment—there is no sinner, no righteous, no great and no small—there is no punishment and no reward. . . . An all-powerful feeling of love transfigures us with blissful knowledge and being. . . .

---

[1] Cf. BR, No. 178 (1896); ER, p. 261.

When compared with some of Berlioz's and Strauss's programme notes, the difference of this kind of ideological programme (which Mahler once likened to an astronomical chart) becomes evident and his desire to be assessed as a symphonist pure and simple more understandable. The first three movements of Symphony II can dispense with any programme, as their musical content is largely self-explanatory. In the first movement the irreconcilable elements of a symphonically extended funeral march and of effusive lyricism at its most romantic form a violent contrast, emphasized by their conflicting tonalities.

The unorthodox choice of the key of E major in a symphony in C minor foreshadows the middle section of the second movement, which in turn exploits to the full the modulatory possibilities of an enharmonic change from E♭ to D♯. The double-barrelled development section throws up two chorale-like motives, of which the latter (cf. Ex. 23), with its affiliation to the plainsong 'Dies irae,' is destined to play an integral part in the apocalyptic march of the finale. The lengthy movement, with its nerve-shattering climaxes of militant oppression, collapses finally on a pale chord of C major, turning in dismay, as it were, into minor—the sinister symbol of symphonic tragedy.

The almost Schubertian *Ländler* character of the second movement provides a psychological contrast. Its more passionate middle section throws into relief the serene amiability and Austrian playfulness of the exposition with its two variations (cues 5 and 12 respectively), the latter being attractively elongated by an irregular period of one inter-calary bar. The idyllic mood is rudely destroyed by the sinister root-motif of Mahlerian thematic thought: the rising fourth, bursting from timpani and suggesting, as it were, the parable of life's futility as seen through St Anthony's temperament. This rondo-like symphonic movement, with its undercurrent of *Ländler* rhythm, extends the melodic elements of the *Wunderhorn* song. New melodic matter of lyrical contrast (trumpet *cantilena*, cue 40) is added, and the movement ultimately heads towards a tremendous outburst which in turn anti-cipates the beginning of the fifth movement.

The simple chorale strain of the contralto's *Urlicht* (fourth movement) stands in similar psychological and structural relationship to the preceding music as Beethoven's baritone solo 'Oh Freunde, nicht diese Töne' in the ninth Symphony. It determines the emotional and the musical climate of the finale, which breaks into the *fff* outcry borrowed from the third movement very much as the dissonant orchestral passage at the very beginning of Beethoven's finale obliterates the tenderness of the preceding *Adagio*. Like Beethoven's choral finale (which Mahler freely acknowledged as his model), Mahler's own finale can be divided into many sections linked to each other by apocalyptic fanfares the most important of which is the distant horn-signal evidently representing the voice in the desert calling on the day of judgment. A sinister march of the dead is preceded by a long, pot-pourri-like orchestral prelude in which not only the chorale but also a motif of plaintive yearning, backed by a nervous tremolo in the violins, plays an integral part. In the later stages of the march a second orchestra, playing in the distance, joins in with lusty military music, symbolizing the final clash of militant humanity, until after a terrific crash an unearthly silence falls with the 'last trump' re-echoing in the hollow vacuum of the empty earth, whose least message is expressed by lonely bird cries in the flute. The ghostly dialogue of flute and trumpet makes way for the 'mysterious' entry of the chorus, enunciating *a cappella* and in the manner of a Lutheran chorale Klopstock's resurrection hymn. The verses are punctuated by short, ecstatic ritornels in the orchestra. Soloists join in, and when chorus and soloists continue the hymn in Mahler's own words the music quotes the passionate appeal of the contralto in the fourth movement, 'Ich bin von Gott und will wieder zu Gott. . . .' In monumental *al fresco* style chorus, orchestra and organ join in proclaiming the message of eternal life while solemn fanfares in the mightily increased brass and the clangorous peal of church bells create a sonorous aura of strange luminosity.

The 'Resurrection' Symphony, as it was called by friend and foe, despite its theatrical crudities of style and the undeniable fact that its music is in its weaker moments plainly rhetorical while in its best achieving a high degree of thematic integration and originality of texture, won an early popular success where other symphonies by Mahler initially failed. The first and third movements were performed by Richard Strauss, one of the work's warmest admirers, in Berlin in March 1895; the whole work was first given there later in the same year (13th December) under Mahler's direction. Full score and arrangement for piano duet (by Bruno Walter) were issued in the winter of 1896-7. The composition took seven years (begun at Leipzig in 1887, completed on 29th June 1894 at Steinbach on the Attersee). The main portion was sketched at Hamburg, where the funeral service for Hans von Bülow inspired Mahler to integrate Klopstock's hymn into the fabric of the Symphony.

This Symphony of 'death and transfiguration' is followed by the Symphony invoking the 'great god Pan.' This third Symphony, planned on a similarly vast scale as the preceding one and scored for a similarly huge and differentiated orchestra, was conceived as a musical reflection of Mahler's experience of the physical world, in reactive contrast to the metaphysical bias of Symphony II. It was originally planned in seven movements, and Mahler was long undecided whether to call it *Pan* or (after Nietzsche) *The Gay Science* or even (not after Shakespeare, as he hastened to add in a humorous marginal note to an early draft) *A Midsummer Night's Dream*. There are at least five different drafts of the programme, from which I have selected the one that comes nearest to the Symphony as it stands to-day:

Symphony III

The Gay Science

A Summer-morning Dream

1. Summer marches in.
2. What the Flowers on the Meadow tell me.
3. What the Animals of the Forest tell me.
4. What Night tells me (alto solo).
5. What the Morning Bells tell me (women's choir and alto).
6. What Love tells me.
7. The Celestial Life (soprano solo, humorous).

It was this last movement which was eventually transferred to Symphony IV. In its final shape the Symphony is divided into two unequal parts: the first consisting of No. 1 only, the second comprising all the rest. This first movement is one of the longest in existence.

It consists of two sharply contrasted complexes: (*a*) a slow and brooding introduction (which at one stage was to have been given the title 'What the Rocks of the Mountains tell me'), with a martial motto theme (Ex. 4) that gives way to a mysterious sequence of chords in root position, shifting underneath the murmuring surface motif and with eloquent recitative passages in the double basses and the brass culminating in a signal of the trumpet, anticipatory of the later *Midnight Song*:

Ex. 33

(*b*) an orgiastic and corybantic march of gigantic proportions thematically determined by the motto in a march-like transformation as well as by a deliberately trivial tune whose associations with 'entertainment' music are here used to add pungency to a music of dionysiac self-abandonment. The ostensible commonness of this tune conceals chaotic forces breaking out tempestuously in exultant dissonance at the two elemental climaxes of the movement (near cues 29 and 74 respectively). Mahler wanted the movement to express summer's victory in the midst of the warring forces of nature, but Richard Strauss, the realist, could not rid himself of the image of thousands of socialist workers marching in demonstrative unity in the Prater to celebrate May Day. The aggressively proletarian strain of this march music is undeniable and has been more widely misunderstood than any other experiment of Mahler's in Aristotelian 'irony.'

The remainder is easier to follow, in so far as the Symphony conforms partly to traditional types of orchestral music. Mahler here consciously creates a world of romantic make-believe, with its nostalgic revival of obsolescent rhythm and melody in the rococo minuet of the *Blumenstück* (movement 2) as well as in the postilion's cornet tune, occasionally interrupted by military signals (movement 3). However, in the cobweb-like sonorities of the variations on his Schubertian minuet theme and in the symphonic extension of his cuckoo *Humoreske*, the Symphony proves his mettle as the future maker of more complicated textures. With the sombre *Midnight Song*, and the chiming, gay and sparkling, chorally extended *Wunderborn* song 'Es sungen drei Engel' the clarifying vocal element is again introduced into the elemental chaos of the Symphony's emotions. In both movements the orchestral sonorities are unusual. The hollow void between high-pitched violin harmonics and trombones in movement 4 no less than the tubular bells and bell imitations in the boys' chorus of movement 5 suggest vastness of space, preparing for the passionate beauty of the final instrumental *Adagio*. This is a chain of variations on two simple, hymn-like tunes, treated contrapuntally or canonically from their inception, in a manner typical of Mahler's maturing style. The unorthodox solution of ending a symphony of such length with an *Adagio* (even if anticipated by Tchaikovsky in the 'Pathétique' of 1893) is a welcome change after the choral exuberance of Symphony II. It sets a precedent for Mahler's ninth Symphony, the only other with a similarly ecstatic and polyphonically designed *Adagio*.

Again, as in the case of its predecessor, the chief difficulty for the listener of to-day lies in the fact that Symphony III progresses on different planes of style. Movements 2, 3 and 5, with their archaic flavour and their deliberate use of obsolete sonorities for the sake of illustrative associations, sometimes approximate to pastiche, while movements 1, 4 and 6 contain modernistic elements (unprepared dissonances anticipating polytonality, 'off stage' noises, parodistic vulgarity, etc.) which were not to bear fruit till long after Mahler's death. The Symphony was composed in the summer holidays of 1893-6 at Steinbach on the Attersee and published in 1898. Although the second movement (minuet) was performed by Nikisch and Weingartner late in 1896, the work had to wait for its first complete performance until June 1902, when Mahler conducted it himself at the Music Festival of the Allgemeine Deutsche Musikverein at Crefeld. The success was instantaneous and it at long last brought Mahler as a composer into the limelight of universal if by no means invariably benevolent attention.[1]

[1] Here, as in the similar case of Symphony II, scores which Mahler used later on in Vienna (1904 ff.), and which were seen by the present writer

The fourth Symphony grows out of the planned and later discarded seventh movement of Mahler's original draft for Symphony III. Yet, despite its affinity with the preceding *Wunderhorn* symphonies, it stands at the crossroads. If it still aims at expressing a quaint day-dream, its musical idiom already shows the first-fruits of a remarkably self-critical process of contrapuntal discipline and structural logic. Three of its four movements adhere more closely to the classical symphonic pattern than anything previously composed by Mahler. It is only when the third movement (*Poco adagio*) explodes fantastic-ally in the brilliant radiance of its coda (cue 12) that a musical effect seems contrived, not by means of musical logic, but by a somersault into the world of programme music. The least orthodox movement is the finale: a strophic song from *Des Knaben Wunderhorn*, far removed from the type of classical rondo finale and yet thematically the gener-ating cell of the whole Symphony. Its music, picturesquely tone-painting the realistic pleasures of this cloud-cuckoo heaven of a celestial Land of Cockaigne in a series of strophic tableaux, and especially its orchestral ritornel as well as its vocal refrain, represents a thematic link with movements 2 and 5 of Symphony III. The ubiquitous motive of this ritornel sets its seal on the initial bars of the Symphony, permeating the structure of the whole work with its insect-like semiquavers and the cackling sound of its quaver rhythm, reiterated in the flute and re-echoed in the tintinnabulation of the jingles. It is impossible to convey within the space of this book an adequate impression of the prodigious wealth of themes and motives cropping up ceaselessly in the first movement, only to become com-pletely transformed and often 'to be reshuffled like a pack of cards,' or to show, as Mahler himself pointed out, the close thematic connec-tions between the movements of his Symphony. The first movement, despite its manifold episodic bypaths, remains one of Mahler's most accessible compositions. It strictly adheres to its G major tonality (though the work actually begins in B minor), which also dominates

there in 1918, prove that he was not satisfied with its orchestration, despite its brilliant originality. A critical edition of Mahler's symphonies should embody his important revisions.

the *Adagio* as well as the greater part of the finale, only to be discarded at the very end of the Symphony (cue 12) for its submediant (E major), and even attempts to reconstitute the atmosphere of a Mozart or Haydn symphony in the sparkling sound of its light-weight orchestra (excluding trombones, tuba and heavy percussion). Its structural conciseness is matched by the scherzo, which is fantastic despite the *Ländler* character of its thematic material. A curious feeling of indefinite tonality is spread by its solo violin, which plays in a *scordatura* tuning of the strings a whole tone higher and is directed to sound 'like a fiddle,'[1] suggesting a Dance of Death as imagined by medieva German woodcutters. The macabre ferocity of its fiddling:

Ex. 34

throws into relief the luminosity of its *Länder*-like consequent with its inimitable sparkling accents on the harp. The typically Austrian joviality of its two trio sections, in the second of which (shortly before cue 11) the very end of the whole work is thematically anticipated, contrasts sharply to the scherzo's restless main part, which is repeated in two intersecting recapitulations.

The spell of its oppressive mood is broken by the serenity of the *Adagio*, in which sonata form and variation technique are made to co-operate in the most original manner. The thematic exposition of this movement proceeds in psychological ambivalence. Its serene musing is transformed at cue 2 into a plaintive theme, capable of self-lacerating despair. The first variation (cue 4), an almost Schubertian transformation, is followed by an intensified return of the main theme in the sombre key of C minor. A bridge-passage of magical modulations then leads to the remaining variations 2, 3 and 4. The third variation shows Mahler's ingenuity in transforming his thematic matter melodically as well as rhythmically. With the music suddenly veering round to E major (cue 12) the gates to the child's celestial

[1] Mahler's German term *Fiedel* refers to a medieval type of one of the forerunners of the modern violin.

dream-city are flung open and with it the descriptive, programmatic character of certain sections of the preceding symphony returns. This erratic intrusion of E major into the otherwise strictly observed tonality of G lends a fantastic hue to a finale oscillating between the Austriacism of its verse, the elfin character of its ritornels and the romantic organum-like archaism of its mock-naïve refrain:

Ex. 35

Die Eng-lein die ba - cken das Brot

This movement is the song 'Wir geniessen die himmlischen Freuden . . .' composed as early as 1892 and characteristic of Mahler's *Wunderhorn-Humoresken* in general, for it contains the three elements of that lyrical complement to the three symphonies: religious feeling, spookishness and drollery. Composition on these songs (the earliest of which may date from 1888, whereas the last two, *Revelge* and *Tamboursg'sell*, were written in 1899) spread over more than twelve years, while their publication, in three different collections, took even longer. There are twenty-four *Wunderhorn* songs in all, three of them appearing as songs in the symphonies, while two others co-exist as songs in their own right and as transformation into symphony movements. Nine are contained in Vols. 2 and 3 of the early collection *Lieder und Gesänge aus der Jugendzeit*. This early batch differs from all the later songs in that it exists only in a version for voice and piano. However, there are many indications that even these early *Wunderhorn* songs were conceived in the spirit of the orchestra. Thus in *Zu Strassburg auf der Schanz* the pianist is asked to play 'like a shawm' and again to imitate the sound of 'muffled side-drums'; and the sombre pedal-point in *Nicht-Wiederseh'n* is to be made to sound like 'a distant peal of bells from a churchyard.' They also contain a veritable melodic jewel in the dewdrop-fresh *Ich ging mit Lust durch einen grünen Wald*, where for once Mahler recreates the atmosphere of traditional German feeling for landscape and for the magic of the woodland without the slightest self-consciousness.

Among the twelve orchestrated *Wunderhorn* songs, published as late as 1905, although partly composed as early as 1888–90, i.e. shortly after the completion of Symphony I, those expressing eeriness of atmosphere and inspired by march rhythms show the highest degree of originality. Mahler's skill in transforming trivial military signals, drum-beats or sullen march tunes into something ghostlike and nightmarish achieves its greatest triumph in nocturns such as *Wo die schönen Trompeten blasen, Revelge, Tamboursg'sell* and *Der Schildwache Nachtlied*. This last, a ghostly dialogue between a lonely sentry and a female apparition, ceaselessly taunting him with a little triplet figure, is somewhat reminiscent of a similar turn in Othello's monologue in Verdi's opera of 1887 (Act III, 'Dio mi potevi scagliar. . .'). The song (composed about 1888, while Mahler was still at Leipzig, i.e. very shortly after Verdi's masterpiece had been given to the world), in which intricate chromaticism becomes for once insistent, fades away in a unique and typically Mahlerian melodic unfolding of a short motif. It ends—not unlike Chopin's Prelude in F (No. 23)—on the unresolved chord of the dominant ninth. Effects foreshadowing the appearance of ambiguous tonality and polytonality as frequently used in the later symphonies—and yet at the same time expressive of the archaic quaintness of the tone-poetical atmosphere of the *Wunderhorn*, are especially noticeable in the two latest songs, *Revelge* and *Tamboursg'sell*, published in 1905 in the collection *Sieben letzte Lieder*, together with five Rückert songs. The neo-primitive ring of tonic and dominant sounding simultaneously in *Revelge* leads later on to polytonal combinations in Symphony VI, anticipated in the ambiguous tonality of *Tamboursg'sell*. Whereas *Ländler*-like songs like the charming *Rheinlegendchen* (originally called *Tanzlegendchen*), with its unmistakable Schubert fingerprint in the horn's pedal-point, the brilliant *Wer hat dies Liedel erdacht?* and the naïve drollery of the dialogue *Verlorene Müh'* seem to look back to the simplicity of early Mahler, the Jacques Callot-like humour of a satiric parable such as the 'Tierstück' *Lob des hohen Verstandes* (composed 21st June 1896) foreshadows the contrapuntal ingenuities of the Mahler of Symphony V, in whose finale it is 'quoted' (cf. rondo finale, bassoon, bars 4 ff.).

The fourth Symphony, composed in the summer weeks of 1899

and 1900 at Aussee (Styria) and Maiernigg/Wörthersee (Carinthia) (except for its vocal finale dating back to 1892) and revised in the winter 1900–1 in Vienna, was first performed at Munich on 25th November 1901 by the Kaim Orchestra under Mahler's direction. It was published in 1901 by Waldheim-Eberle, a firm which later became part of Universal Edition, Mahler's later publishers. The Symphony at first fell on stony ground, as we know from Alma Mahler's own confession of her initial difficulties to enter into its enchanted world. In a letter to Julius Buths (1903) Mahler called it 'a persecuted stepchild.' In 1903 he already started to revise it, and these revisions went on until the very last version of the Symphony (not published so far), dated 11th October 1910.

Less than ten years separate the date of the first performance of Symphony IV from the day of Mahler's death. The mature and the late Mahler are, as it were, telescoped in the febrile creative development of that final decade. Between his forty-first and his fifty-first years Mahler composed no less than six symphonies, among them the colossus of Symphony VIII and the fragment of the tenth. In addition he wrote all the songs to words by Rückert and the symphonic song-cycle *Das Lied von der Erde*. All these works were conceived and written during the scanty holidays between his exacting operatic work. The latest compositions emerged in the shadow of illness and approaching death. Whereas up to 1900 one could still assess Mahler as a great conductor who occasionally indulged in composition, this was impossible after the eruptive appearance of the middle symphonies during the first semi-decade of the new century. That Mahler was quickly becoming one of the greatest and most consequential forces in contemporary music began to dawn on audiences privileged to attend the first performances of his later symphonies, in which his creative ego underwent an amazing transformation.

CHAPTER XII

SYMPHONIES V, VI, VII AND RÜCKERT SONGS

MAHLER's three middle symphonies, composed in the short time between 1901 and 1905, and all purely instrumental, again represent a closely interrelated group. They seem so utterly different from the preceding *Wunderhorn* trilogy that it is possible to speak of a funda-mental change of style. They are not associated with any kind of programme, they show a common tendency to link up with the traditions of the Viennese classical symphony, and by excluding the human voice they achieve greater structural cohesion. They also contain fewer movements. Their neo-classical tendencies are em-phasized by the fact that two of them close with a highly organized rondo-finale applying the variation technique to a very extensive sonata scheme. In Symphony V, for the first time, fugal technique is employed for the purpose of thematic exposition, a turning towards the processes of polyphony that was going to play an important part in Symphonies VIII and IX. Still, in spite of the complete absence of the human voice, these middle symphonies are by no means totally devoid of vocal connotations. While a note-for-note quotation from the first *Kindertotenlied* crops up in the first movement of Sym-phony V (11 bars before cue 2), both that Symphony and the seventh clearly display the fertilizing influence of the last two *Wunderhorn* songs (*Revelge* and *Tamboursg'sell*) in the former's Funeral March and the latter's first 'Nachtmusik'. Symphonies VI and VII are further linked by Mahler's favourite symbol of tragedy darkening the world: the major triad turning into the minor with the effect of a solar eclipse.[1] This symbol (foreshadowed in the Funeral March of Beethoven's 'Eroica,' twenty bars before the end, and used by Mahler at the end of the first movement in Symphony II, and again in the song *Tam-boursg'sell*) dominates the whole structure of Symphony VI, only to

[1] See Ex. 22.

make an eerie reappearance in the first 'Nachtmusik' of Symphony VII. The two 'Nachtmusiken' of Symphony VII, with their deliberate approximation to the types of romance and serenade, as well as the *Adagio* of Symphony VI and the trio sections in the scherzo of Symphony V, contain an undeniable element of landscape pictorialism. Even if their alleged connection with poems by Eichendorff, with Rembrandt's 'Night Watch' and other extra-musical subjects is disregarded as unproven, a residue of tone-poetical colouring remains, irrepressibly expressed by exotic instrumental media such as guitar and mandolin ('Nachtmusik' 2, Symphony VII), cow-bells (Symphony VI) and the sinister symbol of the hammer whose 'three strokes of fate' ultimately exterminate that symphony's 'hero.' The orchestral medium of the three works is numerically as extravagant as that of Symphonies II and III, but the tendency to create great contrasts in sonority here leads to the chamber-musical design of the *Adagietto* for strings (with harp) in Symphony V. However, by far the greatest evolutionary change is noticeable in the increased wealth of thematic material and in its complex treatment within the framework of the classical symphony.

Symphonies V and VII may perhaps be discussed together because of the similarities of their design. Both begin with an introductory funeral march and culminate in a vast rondo-finale tending to variation form. Both lack a slow movement proper, which is replaced by serenade-like, decidedly romantic intermezzi. In both cases a fantastic scherzo acts as a great contrast to the extended canvases of the outer movements. Further, in both symphonies elements of the military atmosphere of the *Wunderhorn* are re-echoed in their march movements. Finally both symphonies show a steeply rising emotional temperature. They start in the gloomy depth of funereal processions, only to end in the glory of jubilant, hymn-like harmony, as it were in the blaze of fierce midday sunlight. By emphasizing a clamorously 'happy ending' they establish the strongest possible contrast to Symphony VI, Mahler's tragic symphony *par excellence*.

In the fifth Symphony the traditional first movement appears split up into two separate halves: an introductory and, as it were, thematically expository funeral march and a second section ('Stürmisch bewegt') which in turn represents an extended development of the thematic groups of the march, all of which (except for the introductory trumpet fanfare) recur in it as extended reminiscences. So close is the thematic affinity between the two sections that accompanying motives of the former may become the germinal cells of new thematic matter. Mahler's uncanny ability to create a trivial tune with an undercurrent of tragedy by using obsolescent devices of accompaniment for the purposes of satirical pastiche can nowhere be studied to greater advantage than in the march parody of this movement. The dual movement oscillates between funereal gloom and almost hysterical excitement. Sequential climaxes of great power are driven towards ultimate exultation, only to be halted four times by a chord of the diminished seventh (cues 9 and 11, section 2), until at last these heights are scaled with the brassy enunciation of a chorale tune which represents the thematic cell of the third and most important theme of the rondo finale:

Ex. 36

The end is inconclusive, with fragments of the main motives at last dissolving in the haze of mysterious distances. In the colossal scherzo the *concertante* brilliance of its *corno obbligato* and the dreamy *Ländler* tunes of its two trios bring about a complete change of atmosphere. With the dissonant ruggedness of its contrasting motives in the strings, the organ-like orchestration of its development, its Schubertian overall design of combined sonata movement (scherzo, trio and variation form), and lastly with the distinctly alpine character of its yodel:

Ex. 37

this is perhaps the most strikingly Austrian movement in Mahler's symphonies.

Probably the most singular is the diminutive *Adagietto*, a *romanza*-like mood picture in ternary form, to the superficial observer something like a belated offspring of Schumann's *Abendlied*. The somewhat precious austerity of its harmonies, occasionally flavoured by pungent chromatic changing-notes, and the retrospective romanticism of its melody deceptively conceal the kind of egocentric withdrawal which appears most clearly in the principal melody's allusion to the Rückert song *Ich bin der Welt abhanden gekommem*, which is perhaps the most perfect expression of Mahler's wishful thinking during the decade of his greatest external success and—together with that success —represents the ambivalence of feeling and creation which lies at the core of Mahler's dualistic personality:

Ex. 38

Ich bin ge-stor-ben dem Welt-ge-tüm-mel

By an ingenious use of the Neapolitan sixth (G♭ in F major) Mahler sails into a distant key only to give out a melody of tender charm, destined to become the rondo-finale's principal contrast episode (12 bars after cue 2). The wealth of thematic material in that movement cannot be fully discussed here. The rondo is remarkable for its achievements in thematic interrelationship, yet often curiously dependent on classical models. The wind instruments' good-humoured discussion of a principal theme seems to conjure up the shade of Beethoven, not only by adopting the process of thematic assembly as used in the finale of the choral Symphony, but also by choosing a rondo subject clearly hailing from the second-subject group of the finale of Beethoven's second Symphony.

Mahler's little joke of letting the bassoon intone the initial motif of the *Wunderhorn* song *Lob des hohen Verstandes* (bars 4 ff.) is a pointer towards the processes to which the principal thematic matter is going to be subjected. One has been quoted (Ex. 36) and the other mentioned a moment ago; the third proliferates from an introductory suggestion (bars 13 ff.) of ascending fourths by the horn. Only a detailed analysis could reveal the mastery of Mahler's handling of combined sonata-rondo form and variation technique as well as his occasional shortcomings (e.g. the unashamed allusion to the third movement of Tchaikovsky's 'Pathétique'). But the widening of the expressive range in Mahler's idiom particularly noticeable in this movement must at least be mentioned: the resourceful utilization of the chord of the Neapolitan sixth for purposes of continuous modulation and use made for the first time of the whole-tone scale for the obvious purpose of blurring the firm outlines of tonality (cf. scherzo, four bars before cue 4 and *passim*; finale, seven bars before the end).

Symphony V, composed in the summer months of 1901 and 1902 in Maiernigg on the Wörthersee, and copied out by Mahler's young wife in the following summer of 1903, was first performed at a Gürzenich concert at Cologne under the composer's direction on 18th October 1904. Although published already in the winter of 1904-5 by Peters of Leipzig, it was continuously and mercilessly revised for every single later performance until, shortly before his death, Mahler announced to Georg Göhler the completion of yet another version to replace the old one of 1904. Unfortunately that version is still largely unknown owing to the fact that the score seems to have remained unpublished so far, although Peters issued three different earlier versions. Mahler's unceasing self-criticism is reflected in the letter already quoted in Chapter VII, p. 167.

In the seventh Symphony, composed during the summer holidays of 1904 and 1905, an alarming thing becomes apparent for the first time in Mahler's career as a composer: the self-repetition which was destined to mar the last two symphonies and to weaken their artistic impact. Not only do the outer movements reveal striking similarities with the parallel movements of Symphony V, but the primeval ruggedness of the introductory tenor-horn solo re-echoes the solo trombone in the first movement of Symphony III. The first principal theme of the first movement is rhythmically all but identical with its opposite number in Symphony VI. The first 'Nachtmusik' works almost throughout with thematic matter already used in the last *Wunderborn* songs, utilizing the symbol of the chordal change from major to minor as a kind of join to bind the loose ends of romantic melodies together, some of which sound like an echo from Mahler's early years (cf. second movement, three bars before cue 79, cello melody). It seems likely that Mahler's continued preoccupation with *Wunderborn* moods, though he mentally outgrew them in his maturity, came to amount to an obsession. Even the second 'Nacht-musik,' one of his most delightfully scored musical *genre* paintings, suffers from his urge to create once more the vanishing world of medieval romanticism with its nocturnal fountain murmurings, moonlight serenades and the amorous strummings and retunings of guitar and mandolin. It also suffers—like so many thematic subjects of the Symphony—from unintended resemblances to other com-positions. A serenading horn theme recurs rondo-like and inter-rupted by several episodes, and there is a veritable trio section in B flat major. The several appearances of the rondo theme are mostly wound up by a humorous 'tuning' episode in the strings, progressing in open fifths, but invariably introduced by a kind of refrain:

Ex. 39

strongly reminiscent of a similar 'Kehrreim' in Schumann's fourth *Nachtstück*, Op. 23, bars 1–2. The integration of the tenor-horn introduction into the fabric of the principal *allegro* seems as much indebted to the thematic relationship between movements 1 and 2 in Symphony V as the passionately expanding *cantabile* group ('Mit grossem Schwung,' before cue 15) is to the *cantabile* theme in the first movement of Symphony VI (cue 11). There is also a mysteriously soft chorale episode in the brass, comparable to the chorale theme in Symphony V.

The rondo-finale repeats the processes of its forerunner in Symphony V with tremendous gusto, but with less inward conviction. Its unbuttoned contrast group (cue 23), with its Slavonic lilt and primitive bass pedal, comes perilously near to Lehár's *Merry Widow* waltz —the kind of light Viennese music for which Mahler entertained a furtive admiration. By far the most original of the Symphony's five movements is the scherzo, where Mahler succeeds in creating a new and eerie type of *notturno* music, aptly labelled 'Schattenhaft' (shadowy, spectral) and most impressively expanded in the ghostly episodes oi Symphonies IX and X. The troll-like dialogue between timpani, double bass and brass, recurring as a refrain with ever-increasing vigour, is one of Mahler's most potent inventions. A savage waltz (D major, cue 126) alternates with a trio section (cue 134) of *Wunderhorn* naïvety and harmonic poignancy. Both elements appear as incompatible as fire and water, even where they are combined contrapuntally and where the lyrical trio melody blazes out from the trombones (cue 163, 'Wild'). The shadowy trailing off in the coda anticipates the scherzo-coda of Symphony IX, just as the wide skips in the waltz later became the germ for the second of Alban Berg's *Drei Orchesterstücke* (*Reigen*), Op. 6.

The blindly clod-hopping savagery of this scherzo acts as a link between the first and second 'Nachtmusik,' with which it forms a nocturnal triptych between the loose framework of the Symphony. It is difficult to see a close affinity of this central portion with the two outer movements, and one cannot help feeling that Mahler here failed to weld the *disjecta membra* of symphonic structure into a clearly discernible unity. From Mahler's letter to his wife of June 1910 we know that the two 'Nachtmusiken' were composed in 1904, whereas the sketches for the other three movements existed only as preliminary drafts, to be completed after repeatedly unsuccessful attempts at the end of the summer vacation of 1905. The two 'Nachtmusiken' and the connecting scherzo would have made a *Wunderhorn* serenade of convincing stylistic and thematic unity; it is a pity that Mahler clung too tenaciously to a rigorous pattern to which he failed to do justice in the heterogeneous assortment of movements he chose to call his seventh Symphony. It is interesting to note that he failed to convince even himself in the case of this work. According to Alma he was 'torn by doubts' when he rehearsed it for its first performance in Prague (19th September 1908). By that time he had completed Symphony VIII and finished the first draft of the *Lied von der Erde*. He had in fact moved on artistically to a different plane. He ruthlessly altered the orchestration of Symphony VII from the very time of these rehearsals, and something of the confusion ensuing from constant revisions remains in evidence in the printed full score (published 1909), which bristles with uncorrected misprints.[1] At the Prague performance the work met with only a lukewarm success, unlike earlier symphonies, which had elicited either violent abuse or enthusiastic response. In the same year Mahler conducted the Symphony at Munich and the following year in Amsterdam, continuing to experiment with its stimulating and yet too often intractable problems of scoring. Despite its truly wonderful exploits in the use of fourths, the strange mixture of orchestral colours in its middle movements and the brilliant use of variation technique in the finale, the 'Seventh' remains a rarely performed and misunderstood work.

The sixth Symphony, composed at Maiernigg in the summer of 1903 and 1904, completed in full score on 9th September 1904, first performed at the Tonkünstlerfest of the Allgemeine Deutsche Musikverein at Essen on 27th May 1906 under Mahler's direction and published in the same year, is in every respect an exceptional work. Although sharing certain basic features with Symphonies V and VII —the symbolic cow-bells and the major-minor chord, the exclusion of the human voice and absence of a clearly defined programme— it surpasses both works by its close-knit unity of thematic matter, mood and formal lay-out as well as by its pessimistic character well expressed by its probably authentic nickname the 'Tragic.' Although receiving fewer performances than any other work by Mahler, it has exercised a deep and lasting influence on younger Austrian composers, especially on Schoenberg and Alban Berg, the former praising its feeling for melodic structure and its boldness of harmony, the latter calling it (in a letter to Anton Webern) 'the only Sixth, despite the "Pastoral"'

[1] Cf. the prefaces to the revised scores, issued in 1960 and 1962 (see Appendices B and D).

and absorbing its thematic processes in his own *Drei Orchesterstücke,* Op. 6 (1914). Mahler himself seems to have been aware of its special message for the future, for he wrote to Richard Specht:

My Sixth will propound riddles the solution of which may be attempted only by a generation which has absorbed and truly digested my first five symphonies. . . .

This Symphony did not escape the fate of its neighbours: it was revised again and again during the remaining years of Mahler's life. The most noticeable revision affects the sequence of its four movements, the two middle ones being made to change places soon after the pub-lication of the full score, an alteration which undoubtedly throws the downward trend of the symphony's 'action' into clearer relief. The two outer movements are excessively long—the finale alone lasting fully thirty minutes—and scored for an enormous orchestra completely dominated by the heavy brass and by percussion instruments. Certain moods—the Segantini-like view from glacial heights into verdant vales far below, with cow-bells and impressionistic shimmerings playing over the surface of a distant chorale, the inexorable major-minor motif, with its fateful rhythm, as also the march-like character of many of its leading subjects—are shared by three out of the four movements. Only the reposeful intimacy and idyllic pastoral of the *Andante* holds up the action like a dream intermezzo (comparable to the structural function allotted to the two 'Nachtmusiken' in Symphony VII). The fierce-ness of the first movement's principal theme is offset by the exultant expansiveness of the *cantabile* group (a melody criticized by Specht for its dependence on romantic melody types but, according to Alma, conceived as an idealized portrait of her), as well as by the chorale, first appearing as a link between first- and second-subject groups (cue 7), but later on playing an important part in the development section. The inner meaning of this movement becomes clear from the composer's emphasis on the 'Alma' subject, which bursts out triumphantly in the coda (cues 42 and 45).

A psychological link between the first two movements is derived from the idyllic moods (e.g. the cow-bell passage) of the first, spun out to great length in the second (*Andante*), whose principal melody shows an evident kinship to the *Kindertotenlieder*. It is developed in binary form, like a romantic *Lied*. Pastoral moods, reaching a passionate climax at cue 100, are mainly propelled by two simple motives of great melodic fertility, and there is a bitter-sweet tang about its harmonies and flash-like modulations.

The sinister Hoffmannesque puppet-show of the scherzo is closely related thematically to the first movement, whose mood of defiance it turns into a spookish dance diversion. Its principal motif is nothing but a syncopated version of the Symphony's first bar and the ghostly rococo motif of its trio section ('Altväterisch'—old-fashioned) is a melodic excrescence of it. Another link with the first movement is established by diabolical trills in violins, woodwind and xylophone, taken over from the development section of the first movement (seven bars after cue 14) and here developed into an exotic episode (in F and E flat minor), heralding a catastrophic recapitulation and coda. The unchangeable motif of the major triad turning into the minor cuts off any further argument and the main trio theme is driven in trailing clouds from the scene. The grim discrepancy between the home-liness of its old-style motives and the fiery breath of its lurid orchestra-tion is characteristic of the demoniacal Mahler. This movement is the forerunner of similar antithetically conceived pieces in Symphonies VII and IX.

The colossal finale (which eventually found a worthy successor in the *Marsch* of Alban Berg's Op. 6) is probably the result of telescoping two original drafts of different movements, as in the similarly long first movement of Symphony III, to which it bears certain structural resemblances, with its long, motive-germinating *sostenuto* intro-duction, its three development sections, each collapsing at the height of its climax under the weight of a brutal but steadily weakening hammer-stroke,[1] and its lyrical episodes of expansive beauty. Nothing short of a close thematic analysis could reveal the grand conception of these 114 pages of full score, which form a pocket-symphony in

---

[1] On which Mahler had many afterthoughts, as may be gathered from his letter (BR, No. 310) to Mengelberg, who had evidently suggested a different technical solution.

themselves. Its conclusiveness is emphasized as much by its refer, ences to earlier movement as by the gloomy finality of its new motives, on which the fierce battles of the three development sections hinge.

The famous hammer-strokes in this finale have programmatic connotations. According to Alma the composer here intended to express the destruction of his hero: 'The hero receives three blows from fate, the third of which fells him like a tree. . . .' The three hammer, blows occur at three pivotal points of the finale: at the height of the first development (cue 129), at the height of the second development (cue 140) and finally at the re-intonation of the 'Fate' motif (major, minor) shortly before the beginning of the funereal coda, a moving dirge for trombones. The Symphony ends significantly enough on a plain minor chord, blaring out once more above the fatal rumble of the leading rhythm in the drums.

From Alma's description as well as from Mahler's letters to Mengel, berg we know that the Symphony created a rather forbidding im, pression at its first performance, and that Mahler continued to revise its sometimes overloaded scoring. It has remained something of an enigma ever since and apparently still awaits a generation who, having digested Symphonies I–V, is able and willing to resuscitate it from the state of semi-oblivion into which it has fallen. Nowhere is Mahler greater as an architect of vast movements and as an engineer of intricate polyphonic processes than in this work where—the *Andante* always excepted—he seems farthest removed from the romantic lyricism that is his true domain. Yet it was shortly before and after this Symphony that the Rückert songs were written, which form a lyric counterpart to the fierce instrumentalism of the three middle symphonies.

To establish a reasonably reliable chronology of these ten songs on poems by Rückert is difficult, since their dates seem to vary with the source of reference. They are collected in two sets of five songs each, both published in 1905. It seems that the first three *Kindertotenlieder* were composed together with the first three numbers of *Letzte Lieder* within a fortnight in the summer of 1901. The date is important because it proves that the principal mood of the Rückert poems—

mourning over the death of children the poet, but not the composer, had lost by the time of their conception [1] and withdrawal from the world—attracted Mahler at a time when he was as yet unmarried, childless and at the height of his success as a conductor. This disparity between an actual life-situation and a creative urge to express its exact opposite is characteristic of a dualistic artist who thrived on contrasts such as would probably have completely wrecked others. Even more awkward seems the further fact that *Kindertoten-lieder* Nos. 4 and 5 were composed in the summer of 1904, when Mahler's two children had only recently been born and were enjoying the best of health. The subsequent tragic death of Mahler's elder child, Maria, three years later (5th July 1907), struck Alma as Fate's reply to a wanton challenge. But Mahler's music as a whole is riddled with autobiographical anticipations of this kind.

Of the two remaining Rückert songs, *Um Mitternacht* and *Liebst du um Schönheit*, the latter was composed late in 1903 as a tribute to Alma, and as a token of love. The ten songs share a predilection for poetic moods of great personal intimacy, far removed from the romantic and medieval atmosphere of the *Wunderhorn*. With their gossamer-like orchestration, their insistence on a style of chamber music in the orchestral accompaniments and their very personal intonation in the vocal part they anticipate their confessional lyricism of the *Lied von der Erde* as well as the introspective attitude of the middle and late symphonies.

Perhaps the most daring enterprise of Mahler as a colourist is represented by the score of the curious song *Um Mitternacht*, a midnight reverie accompanied by winds only, backed by timpani and harp. The oboe d'amore plays the part of a mysterious night-bird (cf. Ex. 12, p. 152) and another primeval sound of nature, familiar from *Das klagende Lied,* intercepts the scale-like descending main motif with ghostly monotony. The Ibsenite mood of introspective self-judgment turned into wistful contemplation, results in the musical cobweb

[1] Rückert mourned for them in no less than 428 poems intended for private reading only, and published posthumously in 1872, significant facts in view of Mahler's self-tormenting exhibitionism in setting five of them for public performance.

fabric of *Ich atmet' einen linden Duft*, a song in which out of a total or thirty-four bars the flute plays only the last four with an almost unbearably lovely valediction, re-echoing the oboe's earlier solo. In such intimate whispers did Mahler seek temporary refuge from the oppressive visions of his middle symphonies.

CHAPTER XIII

THE HYMN OF LOVE: SYMPHONY VIII

In his eighth Symphony Mahler reverts, on a higher plane of his spiral development, to the programmatic and philosophically motivated symphonic type of his youth. As a reflection of his unceasing struggle with religious problems this Symphony takes up the thread from Symphony II, and with it shares the hymnic choral finale. According to the late Alfred Mathis, an expert on Mahler's music,[1] the work was originally planned in four movements:

(1) Hymn, 'Veni Creator'; (2) Scherzo; (3) *Adagio Caritas*; (4) Hymn, *The Birth of Eros*. The two instrumental middle movements (one of them a remnant left over from the original draft of Symphony IV) were eliminated and the Eros movement was eventually replaced by the most potent poetical realization of neo-Platonism: the closing scene of Goethe's *Faust*, Part II. Mathis quotes a letter of Mahler's to Alma (dated Munich, June 1910), written during the rehearsals for the first performance of the Symphony, in which he expatiates on the spiritual link between Plato and Goethe:[2]

... In the discourses of Socrates, Plato gives his own philosophy, which, as the misunderstood 'Platonic love,' has influenced thought right down the centuries to the present day. The essence of it is really Goethe's idea that

---

[1] His plan to write an authoritative volume on Mahler, often discussed with the present writer, was frustrated by his premature death in December 1948. See his two articles on Mahler in the *Listener* (February and December 1948), which are utilized here.

[2] See ER, p. 450. In an earlier letter (June 1909) to Alma (cf. ER, p. 430) Mahler had analysed the meaning of the final 'Chorus mysticus' on similar lines.

all love is generative, creative, and that there is a physical and spiritual generation which is the emanation of this 'Eros'. You have it in the last scene of *Faust*, presented symbolically. . . .

The quotation proves the close philosophical connection between Goethe's scene, deeply influenced by Patristic images and ideas, and deliberately using the symbols of the early Christian Church for the dramatic transfiguration of Faust's and Gretchen's love, culminating in the exhortation by the Mater Gloriosa to 'Una poenitentium' (Gretchen):

> Komm! hebe dich zu höhern Sphären!
> Wenn er dich ahnet, folgt er nach.

and in the Patristic hymn 'Veni Creator' (probably the work of Hrabanus Maurus, Archbishop of Mainz, 776–856), with its passionate appeal to the godhead for the granting of universal love:

> Accende lumen sensibus,
> Infunde amorem cordibus.

Mahler, having first composed 'Veni Creator' in three feverish weeks in the early summer of 1906, experienced in a flash, as it were, the close ideological and spiritual affinity between the hymn and Goethe's scene, which he conceived musically as the hymn's tone-poetical corollary, thus establishing close thematic links between the two halves of the Symphony. It is probably this close thematic interdependence which persuaded him to call the whole work 'a symphony,' despite the fact that it is sung from first to last and that the orchestra has no independent and detachable movement to play. Also, the contributory fact that Part I is composed in sonata form, even if in a rather unorthodox variant of its traditional type, with a double fugue as the climax of the development section, which in turn closes directly into a telescoped recapitulation, may have confirmed him in his conviction that the work was symphonic after all.

Mahler composed this gigantically conceived vocal symphony in the amazingly short time of eight weeks (21st June–18th August 1906), interrupted by a Salzburg Festival with a *Figaro* under his direction. According to Alma the work was complete in full score and ready for immediate performance by late summer 1907. Never had Mahler composed more swiftly and more seemingly at the dictates of a demonic urge; never had he mastered so complex and numerically vast a medium of sound with such technical assurance and unerring instinct for the aural effect. While he continued to experiment with the three middle symphonies, he was sure that he had succeeded with Symphony VIII. This feeling of exultation (very rare in him and doubly significant since it precedes his physical collapse of 1907 by less than a year) is reflected by his letter to Willem Mengelberg of 18th August 1906 (see p. 162).

He also said, proudly, that this Symphony was 'a present bestowed upon the nation.' The triumphant success scored by the work at its first performances under Mahler's direction at Munich, on 12th and 13th September 1910, in a hall specially built for the occasion, seemed to confirm the composer's original and immutable feeling towards this work—the last composition of his own he was ever to conduct.

Was Mahler's estimation of the Symphony's importance justified? The passing of over forty years has afforded time for its reassessment, and it is safe to say that to-day it is reckoned to stand somewhere near the bottom of the ladder. On the other hand nobody can deny that it marks a turning-point in the history of music. Like the mammoth scores of Schoenberg's *Gurrelieder* and of Skriabin's *Prometheus*, the eighth Symphony represents both the climax and the collapse of that tendency to increase orchestral sonorities which had started with Beethoven's choral Symphony and gathered momentum in Berlioz's *Requiem* and *Te Deum*. The tradition to employ vast orchestral forces in conjunction with a chorus, split up into different choral sub-divisions, goes back to the late Renaissance and the early baroque era, i.e. to Giovanni Gabrieli and Orazio Benevoli. The latter's colossal Mass of sixteen vocal and thirty-four instrumental parts, written for the consecration of Salzburg Cathedral in 1628, appears to-day almost like an anticipation of Mahler, who knew it well. His orchestral augmentations in numbers and types elicited censorious comment from the beginning and was even ridiculed as his final bid for monumentalization at all costs, especially in a poem published in 1910 in Germany's leading comic paper *Meggendorfer Blätter*:

Maestoso, animato,   Pauken, Harfen, Xylophöner,
Presto, dolce, pizzicato,   Nur Geduld—es wird noch schöner:
Pianissimo, furioso,   Trommeln, Becken, Schell'n, Posaunen,
Lusingando, lamentoso,   Donnerblechzeug und Kartaunen,
Con sordino, con dolore,   Rathausglockenspielgehämmer,
Allegretto, con amore,—   Löwenbrüllen, Schrei der Lämmer,
Vierundsechzigstel-Triolen,   Huppenklang, Propellerschwirren,
Bässe, Tuben und Violen,   Alphornton und Waffenklirren,—
Kanons, Modulationen,   Alles dieses steckt—und wie!—
Quinten, Variationen,   In der Achten Symphonie
Cis-dur, as-moll, soli, tutti,   Gustav Mahlers.—O du mein!
Chöre, Orgel, tutti frutti,—   Wie wird erst die 'Neunte' sein!

It was clearly considered that monster orchestras had reached
saturation point. Mahler, who himself deprecated the slogan of
'Symphony of a Thousand' with which the work was saddled, afterwards sought out different paths and his final works actually led to a
new conception of intimate orchestral music.

Despite the close thematic interdependence between Parts I and II,
the reutilization of certain motives in one part in the poetically different
atmosphere of the other and finally the employment of a very unorthodox sonata form for the hymn, there is little to link this work to
the classical symphonic type.   On the other hand there is very much
to associate it with ecclesiastical choral music and with oratorio.
Part I, in fact, comes far closer to religious choral music of symphonic
proportions, such as Bruckner's Masses and *Te Deum*, than to symphony proper.   The discrepancy of style between the hymn and the
scene from *Faust* has been noticed by nearly every commentator.
It is, together with Mahler's all too persistent adherence to the tonality
of E flat major (turned to E flat minor at the outset of Part II), a
weakness of the work that Part II, sung in Goethe's German after
the Latin of Part I, should so readily succumb to the tradition of
romantic opera and oratorio in a style more reminiscent of *Parsifal*
as well as of Schumann and Liszt, both of whom had composed the
closing scene from *Faust* in works which Mahler may have subconsciously drawn on as models of style.   While the virtuosic handling of chorus and soloists, especially in Part II, does credit to Mahler

as interpreter *par excellence* of romantic opera, this return to a descriptive and hyper-emotional style after the polyphonic rigours of Part I does not make for conceptual unity such as Symphonies II and III had afforded in rich measure.

A close thematic précis could alone reveal the many felicitous touches, melodic beauties and intricate commentaries on Goethe's sibylline poetry in which Mahler's score abounds, a score written for a truly staggering array of executants.[1]   Here are the main orchestral forces, not counting certain accessory instruments:

Piccolo	8 Horns	Bells
4 Flutes	4 Trumpets	Glockenspiel
4 Oboes	4 Trombones	Celesta
Cor Anglais	Bass Tuba	Pianoforte
3 Clarinets	3 Timpani	Harmonium
Clarinet in E♭	Bass Drum	Organ
Bass Clarinet	Cymbals	2 Harps
4 Bassoons	Gong	Mandoline
Double Bassoon	Triangle	Strings

In contrast to these colouristic intricacies the thematic subject-matter is of breathtaking simplicity and marked diatonicism, as may be seen from the orchestra's telescoped and self-imitative rejoinder to the choir's first invocation of the creative spirit.   Example 24 (p. 163) contains as a germinal cell most of the motives destined to have an organic function in both parts of the work.   Motif *x*, prolonged by a new one, *b*, and combined with *a* 1, becomes the material of the first part's double-fugal development section, proceeding in relentless march rhythm towards the recapitulation:

Ex. 40

[1] In which it is, however, surpassed by the original version of Schoenberg's *Gurrelieder*, the latter asking, for instance, for twenty-five instruments of heavy brass where Mahler is content with a mere paltry seventeen.

Two other motives of Part I, the sudden outburst of the 'Accende' theme as well as the final fanfare on the hymn's concluding 'Gloria in saeculorum' (given out by boys' chorus and trumpets in the distance), fertilize the main motives of Part II. The former is transformed into the motive of the mystical mountain of anachorites who strive in contemplative solitude on different planes of consciousness towards the light of love that theme had evoked so exultantly. Again, an enunciation of distant trumpets (Part I, cue 91) is ingeniously turned into the enthusiastic exclamation from the Doctor Marianus, appealing to the Mater Gloriosa to reveal her splendour to the human eye; and what had been a mere germinal cell at first, expressing but the faint stirrings of mystic communion with the godhead, blossoms out in the melody of the final *chorus mysticus*, 'Alles Vergängliche ist nur ein Gleichnis,' one of Mahler's most admirable inspirations, revealing a deep affinity with the final hymn of his early 'Resurrection' Symphony (No. II).

If Part I is easy to take in despite its imposing array of sonorities and its occasional complexities, caused by Mahler's unorthodox part-writing, the sequel of semi-dramatic situations conjured up in the final scene of *Faust* is bewildering in its complexity. Part II is a dramatic oratorio (somewhat in the manner of Liszt's *St Elisabeth*), containing moments of real drama in a kaleidoscopic change of situations, but with very little symphonic content,[1] except for those few sections which appear as exact quotations from Part I in the manner of a recapitulatory gesture while shedding light on the undercurrent of conceptual unity linking both poems. The introductory orchestral prelude (*Poco adagio*, E flat minor) to Part II contains— almost in the manner of an operatic overture—all the thematic elements destined to further evolution. The passionate grandeur of this initial section changes to the brilliant luminosity and *scherzando* rhythms of the scene in which the younger angels triumphantly carry Faust's 'immortal soul' into the lofty heights of heaven. The appearance of the Mater Gloriosa is heralded by Doctor Marianus's ecstatic invocation

---

[1] Some analysts, like R. Specht (1913) and E. Stein (1953), have tried to discover the three traditional movements of the *Adagio*, scherzo and finale in this Part II, but I believe this to be an interpretation *a posteriori*.

and finally expressed by a romantic melody in E major stretching over fully twenty-five bars, played by violins alone, *pianissimo,* to arpeggios for harp and harmonium, marking its most delicate effect in this symphony of massive sonorities.

The following adoration of the Mater Gloriosa, first by the chorus alone, then canonically intertwined by the 'great sinners,' Magra peccatrix, Mulier Samaritana and Maria Aegyptiaca, and finally by Una poenitentium (Gretchen), is intercepted by the joyful strains of the chorus of celestial youths. Mary's exhortation to Gretchen is re-echoed in the rousing hymn 'Blicket auf' intoned by Doctor Marianus and followed up by the chorus. It fades away in an orchestral inter-lude of strange luminosity (cues 197 ff.), skilfully combining the etherealized sonorities of harmonium, celesta, pianoforte, harps, organ, piccolo and clarinet, and weaving them into a fabric of unearthly beauty. It gradually fades off with the solemn strain of the *Chorus mysticus,* starting as a simple four-part chorale and culminating in a last symphonic climax of all the forces, including distant trumpets and trombones, giving out (not unlike the final chorale in Bruckner's Symphony V),[1] in broad augmentation, exultantly altering the inter-val of the seventh (Ex. 41 *z*) to a ninth, as if trying to reach the stars:

Ex. 41

Mahler's eighth Symphony (dedicated to his wife) was the first work of his to be published by Universal Edition. It was also the last to be seen through the press by the composer himself. The vocal score appeared in time for the Munich performance of 1910, while the full score was issued in 1911, pocket-size only, a few weeks after Mahler's death.

---

[1] See Ex. 6 (*b*), p. 54.

CHAPTER XIV

THE THREE POSTHUMOUS SYMPHONIES

THE three major works occupying Mahler's creative energies during the three final years of his life are closely related to each other, not only by thematic affinities and a similarity of mood, but also through the 'programme' they have in common: the composer's farewell to life and preparation for death. Ever since the fatal day in July 1907, when, following closely on the tragic death of his elder child, a country doctor by chance discovered a dangerous heart disease, Mahler had lived, as it were, under sentence of death. He believed himself doomed and probably estimated his expectation of life even lower than events were to prove. Under medical orders he had to change his way of life and, having savagely taxed his physical energies in times gone by, he became a valetudinarian. The necessity to find a new *modus vivendi* coincided with his departure from the Vienna Opera (December 1907). Oncoming illness and a feverish will to live clashed head-on and created a crisis in his existence which somehow seemed to awaken new impulses. He was in a state of almost hysterical euphory at times, alternating with fits of the deepest depression. This is reflected in a letter to Bruno Walter, written from New York early in 1909, which reads like a commentary on the three works under discussion and reflects the composer's state of mind during the completion of *Das Lied von der Erde* and the planning of the ninth Symphony:

... I have been going through so many experiences (for the last year and a half) that I can hardly discuss them. How should I attempt to describe such a colossal crisis? I see everything in such a new light and am in such continuous fluctuation; I shouldn't be surprised to discover that I had acquired a new body (as Faust does in the final scene). I am thirstier than ever for life and I find the 'habit of life' sweeter than ever. These days are just like the Books of the Sybils. ...

'I am thirstier than ever for life . . .': the artist confiding this only two years before his death felt compelled to express the inner conflict between his desire to live and his deep-seated conviction of impending death in these last works, all of them revolving round the word and the experience of 'Farewell' and all of them conceived in a truly vale-dictory spirit. The *Song of the Earth* culminates in a sixth vocal move-ment called 'The Farewell,' a telescoped version of two different Chinese poems the following verses of which might have been written by Mahler himself as a true reflection of his resigned state of mind under the growing shadows of death:

> O my friend, while I was in the world
> My lot was hard.
> Where do I go? I go, to wander in the mountains,
> I seek but rest, rest for my lonely heart.
>
> .   .   .   .   .   .
>
> I shall no longer seek the far horizon,
> My heart is still and waits for its deliverance. . . . [1]

Symphony IX is pervaded by the same atmosphere of autumnal farewell. In the short score of its first movement the restatement of the first-subject group (cue 8) carries the significant headline: 'O vanished days of youth, O scattered love. . . .' Its third movement (*Rondo-Burleske*) is headed in the sketch by the words 'Meinen Brüdern in Apoll' ('To my brethren in Apollo'), and the final *Adagio* fades away 'ersterbend' ('dying away') in a similar spirit of utter extinction—dissolving, as it were, in the infinity of the universe as the *Lied* does on its final chord, 'gänzlich ersterbend' ('totally dying away'), characterized by its added sixth. Messages of farewell are scattered all over both works, sometimes couched in seemingly enigmatic symbols to be grasped only by a penetrating and thoroughly sympathetic mind. Most significant in this connection is the evidently deliberate allusion to Beethoven's Sonata, Op. 81a (*Les Adieux*), at the point where its *Leitmotiv*, 'Lebe wohl,' becomes so strangely blurred in dissonant canon, fading off in the increasing distance of

---

[1] Translation by Sir Steuart Wilson.

the final bars of the first movement. To quote the motif used by Mahler:

Ex. 42

is to show that he made this allusion quite deliberately and was fully conscious of its implications. Similarly at the parallel passage ('Sehr zögernd,' p. 59, pocket score) shortly before the end of the movement, where two canonic strands of this 'Farewell' motif are interlocked in a last romantic echo of Beethoven's Sonata.

The same mood, combining a sense of the quickly fading past and a relentless future, emanates from the pages of the fragmentary tenth Symphony, the sketches for whose fourth movement end with marginal notes of exclamatory interjections and signs of violent emotion coming near to insanity—words that might be used as a motto theme for the whole of this chapter: 'Leb' wohl, mein Saiten-spiel . . .' ('Farewell, my lyre . . .')

How unmistakably the imprint of death had stamped Symphony IX even while its creator was still alive is to be gathered from an unpublished letter of Alban Berg, who was privileged to study the full score of the first movement in the summer of 1910 and gave the following penetrating analysis in a letter [1] to his future wife, an analysis such as only a kindred spirit is capable of, anticipating uncannily the circumstances of Mahler's death a year later:

. . . Once again I have played through the score of Mahler's ninth Symphony: the first movement is the most heavenly thing Mahler ever wrote. It is the expression of an exceptional fondness for this earth, the longing to live in peace on it, to enjoy nature to its depths—before death comes.

For he comes irresistibly. The whole movement is permeated by pre-monitions of death. Again and again it crops up, all the elements of terrestrial dreaming culminate in it . . . most potently of course in the colossal passage where this premonition becomes certainty, where in the

---

[1] The original letter is reproduced in its entirety in the German edition of my book on Alban Berg (Vienna, 1957, pp. 88 ff.).

midst of the *höchste Kraft* of almost painful joy in life Death itself is announced *mit höchster Gewalt.* . . .

Mahler's attitude towards this trilogy of Farewell was morbid, contradictory and at times almost pathological. He was sure of the special value of these last works, proudly writing to Bruno Walter about the *Lied* in 1908: 'To me a lovely time was granted, and I believe it is the most personal thing I have created up to now. . . .' A year later, in another letter to Walter, he called the ninth Symphony 'a very welcome increase in my little family.' Nearly every other day during these last two years he played parts of the *Lied* to Alma, who says she knew it by heart long before it was performed and published. Yet he refused to publish or to perform either work, although the full scores of both were ready to print by the summers of 1909 and 1910, respectively. It was as if he were afraid of them, and in superstitious fear of death he even tried to play Fate a trick by avoiding, as it were, the composition of a fatal ninth symphony altogether, conscious of the mysterious finality inherent in that number in connection with the lives of his symphonic predecessors. He called the song-cycle of *Das Lied von der Erde* 'a symphony,' thus cheating himself into the belief that he was really composing a 'tenth' symphony while he was sketching No. IX, which he steadfastly refused to call by its actual dreaded number. When in the last summer of his life he started to compose Symphony X, which, according to his trick, now really represented No. XI, he felt safe at last. But death was blind to Mahler's subterfuges and felled him before he could complete Symphony X. Thus Symphony IX remained, as with Beethoven, Schubert, Bruckner and Dvořák, his last completed work.

But are these two works of 1908–10 complete in the sense of the foregoing? Would Mahler have left them in the state in which their scores were published posthumously? Nobody conversant with his never-ceasing revisions would dare to answer this in the affirmative. It is certainly curious to observe that the man who eagerly asked the Vienna Philharmonic Orchestra to play through the sixth Symphony in the spring of 1906, before its first performance at Essen, never heard a note of the *Lied* or Symphony IX in performance. It looks as if he had dreaded the hidden message of these works which such a hearing might have divulged to him. He even assumed the same attitude of fear and shyness towards the sketch of Symphony X, which in the last months of his life, contrary to his lifelong habit of completing and orchestrating the sketches of the summer during the following winter months, he refused to touch. Mahler, who—according to himself—had never in his life written a note that did not ring utterly true, instinctively felt his last music was his own death-warrant and could not bear to be reminded of it. But there is no doubt that this dread to be confronted with it deprived it of its final perfection. Although it seems inconceivable that he could have felt constrained to make major alterations in so perfect a score as the *Lied*, in Symphony IX he might have had second thoughts, especially with regard to the second movement (*Ländler*), which certainly is not on the same high level of inspiration as the rest of the work. As for Symphony X, I personally doubt that Mahler would have passed the sketches of three of its planned five movements, had he taken up work on them in conditions of physical and mental health. Yet that conjectural thought seems futile if related to the actual nature of these sketches, for they are the true reflection of a death-struggle and even in their most inspired moments (*Adagio*) suggest approaching dissolution. I firmly believe that even the second movement (*Purgatorio*), which he left complete in a kind of short score, would ultimately have been replaced by another more worthy of Mahler's genius and showing his stylistic fingerprints less openly as being applied without the impetus of real inspiration.

Mahler's three posthumous symphonies originated in close proximity to one another. They were sketched in the three successive summers of 1908-9-10 at Alt-Schluderbach near Toblach (Dobiacco) in the Dolomites, on the borders of eastern Tyrol and Carinthia, in alpine surroundings of rare beauty and magnificence. The *Lied*, the first sketch of which possibly dates back to the tragic summer of 1907, was ready in full score by October 1909, and the fair copy of Symphony IX was completed shortly before 1st April 1910, in New York. The sketches of Symphony X were written at Toblach in the summer weeks of 1910, preceding the final rehearsals for Symphony VIII at Munich. Both the *Lied* and Symphony IX were posthumously published in 1911 and 1912, the first performances under Bruno

Walter taking place at Munich on 20th November 1911 (*Lied*) and in Vienna in June 1912 (Symphony IX). Two movements of Symphony X were performed for the first time in 1924, at a concert of the Vienna Opera, conducted by Franz Schalk. It is a supreme irony of fate that these three posthumous works, none of which Mahler ever heard or conducted, should be among the chief favourites of his modern audiences and that even the fragment of Symphony X has recently secured more live performances than the middle symphonies. In the case of the *Lied* posterity's verdict has coincided with Mahler's own conviction: it has been his most popular success ever since the day of its first performance under the composer's favourite disciple.

Mahler had received from his old friend, Theobald Pollak, a copy of the recently published anthology of ancient Chinese poems in a German translation by Hans Bethge, entitled *Die chinesische Flöte.* The stark contrast between abject pessimism and a love of wine and nature, which characterizes most of these poems, especially those attributed to Li-Tai-Po, must have struck a chord in Mahler's wounded heart. He chose six poems (or rather seven, since *Der Abschied* fuses two different ones) and composed them at first quite independently of each other; but later on he discovered their affinity of mood and finally extended them into a more symphonic shape by the insertion of orchestral interludes.[1] The structure of *Das Lied von der Erde* (whose title was at first intended to be *Die Flöte aus Jade* and then *Das Lied vom Jammer der Erde*) is typical late Mahler. Funereal lamentation, solitude and approach of death (Nos. 2 and 6) establish a kind of framework for three brightly coloured middle movements (Nos. 3, 4 and 5) dealing with the brittle splendours of life: youth, beauty and intoxication by wine and spring. But Mahler's true state of mind is most forcibly expressed in the introductory song, perhaps the most powerful and original piece of music that ever came from his pen. *Das Trinklied vom Jammer der Erde* (*The Drinking-Song of*

[1] According to Alma (ER, p. 152) this had taken place before 1907 and Mahler had started to compose some of the poems in the summer of that year; but the Bethge volume did not appear till 1908. P. Stefan (see Bibliography), p. 148, footnote 20. Alma must here have become the victim of a slip of memory.

Earth's Misery), couched in the gorgeous colours of a subtly orien-
talized orchestra, has three stanzas concluded by the same refrain,
reiterated each time a semitone higher and presenting, as it were at
the threshold of the composer's death, a kind of motto *a posteriori* to
his creative life: 'Dunkel ist das Leben, ist der Tod.' The colouristic
qualities of this song are especially noteworthy through the novel
treatment of woodwind and trumpets (flutter-tongue), the highly
differentiated percussion and the delicate use of the harp. There are
two complementary pentatonic motives acting as determinants for the
harmonic bent of the whole work and contributing to the diffuseness
of tonality that is so obvious in many parts of it.

The alternating frenzied defiance and dreamy self-abandonment of
the *Trinklied* change to utter resignation in No. 2 (*Autumn Loneliness*),
which has become a model for chamber-musical delicacy for later
composers, with its solitary plaint in the oboe, backed only by the
ubiquitous rustling of the violins moving restlessly and noiselessly
about within the narrow limits of the pentatonic scale. The full
maturity of idiom here reached by Mahler may best be assessed if the
impersonal bird-cry of the oboe's initial melody is compared with its
humanization and thematic extension at the turn to B flat major
(*fliessend,* cue 5), when the motif is divided between horn and cello:

Ex. 43

The hymn-like outburst and its desperate questioning addressed to
Fate (cue 18), 'O love's warm sunshine, have you gone for ever . . .'
trails off in the bird-like expressionless ultimate phrase, 'Mild
aufzutrocknen,' linking the heart's passionate and vain appeal with
the inexorability of the autumnal mists enveloping the banks of the
beloved lake.

The sparkling gaiety of Nos. 3, 4 and 5 is as though seen at a

distance through a telescope. Their lovable artificiality and unob-
trusive *chinoiserie* turns them into reflections of a world far distant from
the symphony's 'narrator.' Their poignancy is in the first place one
of contrast, by implication, to Nos. 1, 2 and 6. The playfulness of
pentatonic motives is matched by the exotic sonorities of mandoline,
harp and tambourine in brittle tone-clusters, especially in the picturesque orchestral interlude of No. 4, painting the equestrian sport of
high-spirited youths longingly watched by the furtive glances of
beautiful maidens.

No. 5 has all the ambivalence of Mahler's earlier music. It is
vulgar and philosophical, passionate and dreamy. The music depicts
not only physical intoxication but also the ecstatic exuberance of an
artist inspired by his vision. The tender dialogue between the poet
slowly awakening from his drunken sleep and a bird announcing the
coming of spring is among Mahler's noblest and most lovable inspirations (cues 6–8). The solemnity of the visionary passage 'Aus
tiefstem Schauen lauscht' ich auf . . .' ('I look and look and listen
hard . . .'), with its echo in the bird's high-pitched reply (flute), is
offset by the noisy exuberance of the poetical drunkard, whose
phrase-endings on the highest possible note try to drown in raucous
shouting the irrepressible achings of the heart.

No. 6 (*The Farewell*), the longest movement of the whole work, is a
solo cantata of epic proportions, running through the whole gamut
of valediction and in its climaxes reaching a sombre grandeur.
Funereal sounds, as of clods of earth falling into an open grave, begin
it, and later interrupt its structural sections, some of which are composed in a recitative-like narration, sparingly underlined by long
pedal-points and a *continuo*-like cello, held up only occasionally by
the rhythmic irresponsibilities of bird-cries. These bird-cries, which
permeate the whole movement, and especially its pastoral and descriptive sections, are more or less derived from the initial turn of the
oboe:

Ex. 44

The longest cohesive orchestral section is an interlude which links the ecstatic nostalgia of the first poem (cue 34–5) with the scene of farewell enacted between two friends in the second. The orchestral interlude, occasionally producing deliberately harsh dissonances, is dominated by two motives which play an integral part in the whole movement, and are here used in the manner of an *ostinato*. The presentiment of the movement's ultimate end and the disintegration of its music, as indeed of all human flesh, in the infinity of the eternal blue horizon are wonderfully expressed through the subtle introduction of new musical elements: the whole-tone scale, six bars before cue 58, and the silvery ripple of the celesta five bars before cue 62, accompanying the word 'ewig' (eternal), which is repeated no less than nine times in a soft downgrade curve of three notes of the pentatonic scale while the remaining two are supplied by flute and cello. This represents a perfect abbreviation of the chief thematic elements in No. 1, and a rounding-off of the whole work with an indescribable feeling of final completion, and, at the same time, heart-searing and unconquerable longing for the unattainable—the romantic union of Life and Death.

The ninth Symphony is built on lines not dissimilar to the structure of the *Lied*. The ubiquitousness of death is here even more noticeable than in the former work. Alban Berg understood the first movement as expressing the premonition of impending death. His programmatic commentary [1] may be extended to three-quarters of the Symphony, for movements 3 and 4 are also dominated by the image of approaching dissolution. That being so, the *allegro* movements had to be surrounded by music of mourning and foreboding. The division into the four customary movements of the traditional symphony in this work corresponds closely to the psychological arrangement of the six movements in the *Lied*, where three *allegro* movements are flanked by the *lento* movements 2 and 6. Mahler here again discards the voice, as in the fourth Symphony, because words are no longer necessary to establish the principal mood.

The creative emphasis is on the two slow movements. The first

---

[1] See p. 220.

is a long and as it were peripatetic *Andante* with a beautiful principal subject like a melody sung while walking,[1] interrupted by truly terrifying combats with death (cue 9, 'mit Wut'; eight bars before cue 16, and finally in the funeral-march episode, 'Wie ein schwerer Kondukt,' twelve bars after cue 16).

All these conflicting and contrasting elements grow organically out of the germinal idea contained in the movement's initial bars, with their dreamy waywardness and its continuation. Thematic fragments are later developed into the farewell atmosphere of significant episodes, until the movement's most stirring final stage is reached in the deep, breath-taking extension of the 'Lebewohl' motif into a perfect cadence. The visionary power of this first movement, with its folktune-like meanderings, rudely interrupted by nerve-shattering climaxes and its haunted, shadowy thematic re-emergences, is unique among Mahler's work, and the whole movement is perhaps the composer's most convincing utterance next to *Das Trinklied vom Jammer der Erde*.

None of the succeeding three movements is a match for it, and the whole structure thus shows a certain top-heaviness. This becomes the more noticeable because the wonderful final *Adagio*, which is clearly woven from threads left dangling from the rich fabric of the first and third movements as well as from the *Lied*, is all too short and too much in the manner of an epilogue to counterbalance the weight of the first and the length of the two middle movements. But its derivative character—as far as one of its leading motives is concerned—is also one of its most telling features, making for close cohesion with the middle movements, for the roots of the *Adagio* are to be found in the *Rondo-Burleske* (A flat section, nine bars before cue 36), in which that movement's main thematic material (i.e. the defiant rondo theme and its counterpoint in the brass) undergoes a climactic transformation foreshadowing a 'chorale' episode (D major, p. 134, pocket score) which in itself presents, as it were, an anticipation of the *Adagio*. The limpid beauty of the final pages of

---

[1] See Berg's letter on the ninth Symphony (1910), referred to on p. 220, and E. Stein's analysis (see Bibliography), p. 19.

this *Adagio*, with its curiously broken phrases suggestive of a story trailing off in the death agony of its narrator, forms a strange, almost unbearable contrast to the defiant harshness and garish hilarity of the *Rondo-Burleske*, whose main subject harks back to the similarly turbulent second movement of Symphony V. But whereas the rondo is in form and content truly unique among Mahler's 'Mephisto-phelian' movements, the *Ländler* scherzo of this Symphony cannot claim the same high standard of originality. Technically a first-class achievement and full of felicities of scoring and thematic combination, it might be called an epitome of all the Mahlerian scherzo types, especially in view of the fact that, as Erwin Stein has pointed out, it consists of a *Ländler* movement alternating with a waltz and minuet (trios I and II). The respective movements of Symphonies I, V, VI and VII come readily to mind, and it is this movement's failure that it cannot obliterate the memory of its predecessors within Mahler's own creative work. Even the ultimate falling-off with broken phrases, as though scattered about and finally engulfed by the dusk, cannot compare with the very similar scherzo coda in Symphony VII. The movement is—perhaps for the first time in Mahler's career—like the work of a Mahlerian rather than of Mahler himself.

The same verdict would have to be passed on four out of the five planned and sketched movements of Mahler's unfinished Symphony X, if the fragment were really fit for comparison with its forerunners on anything like equal terms. But this is certainly not the case, and opinions will continue to clash over the question whether Alma did well to publish this torso. Specht eventually withdrew his original statement that Mahler had expressed a wish that the sketch should be burnt after his death; still, it seems unlikely that he should have desired a performance of parts of it in the condition of utter incompleteness in which he had perforce to leave it. The facsimile reproduction of the original, however, published in 1924, has benefited scholarship and enabled the student to watch Mahler's titanic struggle with recalcitrant thematic material and with terrifying Dantesque visions in the last year of his ebbing life.

Two of the five movements were completed in short score, one of them (the *Adagio* in F sharp major) even in full score, although both remain incomplete in view of Mahler's habitual self-criticism, and full of gaps not easy to bridge. Ernst Křenek, who in the early 1920s became Alma's son-in-law, made a practical score of these two move-ments (*Adagio* and *Purgatorio*) with the advice of Franz Schalk and Alban Berg. They were first performed by Schalk in Vienna and subsequently found their way into concert programmes. The facsimile reprint of the original was not followed up by a printed pocket score until 1951. It not only fails to refer back to the facsimile of 1924, but does not even clearly indicate the exact amount of the considerable additions made by an anonymous editor.[1]

The plan of the Symphony can be easily traced: like Symphonies V and VII it was to consist of five movements, several of which were expressly planned as scherzos. Mahler would perhaps have called the whole 'Dante' or 'Inferno' Symphony later on. That he was haunted by Dantesque visions when he conceived it may be gathered not only from the allusion to Dante in the heading of the third move-ment, but also from marginal commentaries jotted down between the staves. Specht even goes so far as to speak of four scherzos, leaving the introductory *Adagio* as the only movement of a different type—obviously a plan difficult to realize, even for a composer of Mahler's stature. The three scherzo-like movements were called:

(2) Scherzo-Finale.

(3) *Purgatorio* (or *Inferno*)

(4) The devil dances it with me. . . .
    Madness, take hold of me, cursed one. . . .
    Destroy me that I may forget that I am . . .
    That I cease to be, that I . . .

Of these No. 4 was originally planned as No. 1, later on as a last movement, and the title 'Scherzo (first movement)' was eventually crossed out. It is fully sketched and the music is in the *Ländler* manner of Symphonies V and IX, without, however, the former's melodic distinction. No. 2 (Scherzo-Finale) reads like a replica of the *Rondo-Burleske* of Symphony IX. It contains an allusion to the F sharp major *Adagio* (movement 1) similar to that movement's anti-cipation in the *Rondo-Burleske* (chorale episode in D major). Its

[1] Cf. p. 274, footnote 1.

thematic material is curiously unimpressive and derivative. The same applies to the finale, in which reminiscences from the *Lied von der Erde*, from Symphony VII and from the *Purgatorio* abound.

Movements 4 and 5 contain allusions to Alma ('You alone know the meaning of this. . . . Farewell, my lyre . . .'), the former ending with the single stroke of a muffled drum and thereby reflecting an experience they both had in New York,[1] the latter ending with a phrase accompanied by the words 'Almschi: To live for you, to die for you . . .' being obviously a reminiscence of a motif from movement 3 (*Purgatorio*), where the score bears exclamations such as 'Have mercy! O Lord! Why hast Thou forsaken me? Thy will be done. . . .' The fact that the finale refers back to the *Purgatorio* suggests that the latter was planned as the pivotal movement of the whole Symphony. This would also explain its psychological background, illuminated by Mahler's letters to Alma written in August 1910 from Toblach and reflecting his pathological reattachment to her after a matrimonial crisis fully discussed in her reminiscences. These letters, in which Alma is often addressed as 'mein Saitenspiel' (cf. the end of movement 4), give a clue to the underlying programme of this Symphony, culminating in the *Purgatorio*. This movement, again, despite its ostensible completeness, is a disappointment for the true Mahler lover because of the utterly derivative character of its principal motives. It is pervaded by a restless figure re-echoing the spookish *Wunderhorn* song *Das irdische Leben*, just as the oboe's chief tune seems to re-echo the world of the early symphonies and their scherzo-like middle movements.

The first movement (*Andante-Adagio*) can alone be called a musical creation worthy of the composer of *Das Lied von der Erde*. But even this deeply moving, abjectly melancholy, hopelessly nostalgic movement, with its beauty almost visibly turning to ashes, could not have come into being without the coda of *The Farewell* (*Lied von der Erde*), without the two outer movements of Symphony IX and indeed without the *Adagio* (*Abschied vom Leben*) of Bruckner's own incomplete Symphony IX, which acted as a kind of model for the wide

---

[1] BR, No. 420.

skips and the fiery trombone-background of the movement's main subject:

Ex. 45

The movement starts with a long unaccompanied solo for the viola (one of the most striking ideas of the whole plan), which in turn becomes the 'lighter' contrast group, recalling the manner in which Bruckner alternates between his 3–4 contrast subject and the main chorale subject in the *Adagio* of his Symphony VII. The latter might also be regarded as one of Mahler's subconscious stylistic models for the *Adagio* of his Symphony X. The beautiful transformation of the viola solo into a lilting second subject of melancholy grace (cue 3, U.S. score), together with the terrifying shriek of the isolated high trumpet in the *Inferno* episode (cue 28), alone make one wonder what Mahler might have achieved in this work, had he been granted a few more years of creative life. More perhaps than any other of his later works this *Adagio* left its imprint on Schoenberg and his disciples. Mahler's simultaneous employment of theme and inversion (Ex. 45. (*a*) and (*b*)), as well as his obvious predilection for melodic skips of the ninth and tenth, undoubtedly found a creative echo in the later music of Schoenberg, and Alban Berg,[1] the coming of which can be felt in every bar of Mahler's ultimate symphonic 'Farewell.'

---

[1] Cf. my book on Alban Berg (see Bibliography).

231

APPENDICES

APPENDIX A

(Figures in brackets denote the age reached by the person mentioned during the year in question.)

Year	Age	Life	Contemporary Musicians
1824		Joseph Anton Bruckner born, Sept. 4, at Ansfelden, in Upper Austria, son of Anton Bruckner, sen. (1791–1837), a village schoolmaster, and his wife Theresia, born Helm (1801–60), eldest of eleven children.	Cornelius born, Dec. 24; Reinecke born, June 23; Smetana born, March 2. Adam aged 21; Auber 42; Balfe 16; Beethoven 54; Bellini 23; Berlioz 21; Boieldieu 49; Catel 51; Cherubini 64; Chopin 14; Clementi 74; Czerny 33; Dargomizhsky 11; Donizetti 27; Field 42; Flotow 12; Franck 2; Franz 9; Gade 7; Glinka 21; Gossec 90; Gounod 6; Gyrowetz, 61; Halévy 25; Heller 9; Henselt 10; Hérold 33; Hiller 13; Hummel 46; Kirchner 1; Lalo 1; Lesueur 64; Liszt 13; Loewe 28; Marschner 29; Mendelssohn 15; Mercadante 29; Meyerbeer 33; Moniuszko 4; Nicolai 14; Offenbach 5; Paer 54; Raff 2; Rossini 32; Schubert 27; Schumann 14; Serov 4; Spohr 40; Spontini 50; Thomas (A.) 13; Verdi 11; Vieuxtemps

Year	Age	Life	Contemporary Musicians
			4; Wagner 11; Weber, 38; Zelter 66.
1825	1		Strauss (J. ii) born, Oct. 25.
1826	2		Weber (40) dies, June 4–5.
1827	3		Beethoven (57) dies, March 26.
1828	4		Schubert (31) dies, Nov. 19.
1829	5		Gossec (95), dies, Feb. 16; Rubinstein born, Nov. 28.
1830	6		Catel (57) dies, Nov. 29; Goldmark born, May 18.
1831	7		
1832	8		Clementi (80) dies, March 10; Zelter (74) dies, May 15.
1833	9	B.'s confirmation, his cousin J. B. Weiss (1813–50) acting as godfather.	Brahms born, May 7; Hérold (42), Jan. 19.
1834	10		Boieldieu (59) dies, Oct. 8; Borodin born, Nov. 12; Ponchielli born, Sept. 1.
1835	11	Has up to date received first musical tuition from his father, whom he occasionally assists in his educational duties. In the spring he is sent to cousin J. B. Weiss at Hörsching near Linz for a more systematic musical education.	Bellini (34) dies, Sept. 24; Cui born, Jan. 18; Saint-Saëns born, Oct. 9; Wieniawski born, July 10.
1836	12	Receives tuition in organ playing and composition from Weiss, who acquaints him also with Mozart's music. First attempts at composition, modelled on the music of Weiss.	Delibes born, Feb. 21.
1837	13	B.'s father falls dangerously ill and dies, June 7. The	Balakirev born, Jan. 12; Field (55) dies, Jan. 11.

Year	Age	Life	Contemporary Musicians
		property at Ansfelden is sold and B. transferred, on Weiss's recommendation, to the Augustinian foundation of St Florian. He starts as a chorister although his voice is breaking. Organ Prelude in E flat composed.	
1838	14	Chorister at St Florian. B.'s teachers are Gruber (violin), Kattinger (organ and piano), and Bogner (thorough-bass).	Bizet born, Oct. 25; Bruch born, Jan. 6.
1839	15		Mussorgsky born, March 21; Paer (68) dies, May 3; Rheinberger born, March 17.
1840	16	Passes his first official examination with distinction and becomes an assistant schoolmaster on Oct. 1. In the autumn he enrols for the *Präparandenkurs* at Linz. He continues his study of musical theory there under Dürrnberger.	Götz born, Dec. 17; Svendsen born, Sept. 3; Tchaikovsky born, May 7.
1841	17	Second examination on July 30. B. is declared fit to teach as an assistant for elementary schools. In Oct. he is appointed assistant schoolmaster at Windhaag o/Maltsch, near Freystadt (Upper Austria).	Chabrier born, Jan. 18; Dvořák born, Sept. 8; Pedrell born, Feb. 19.
1842	18	Bitter experiences in this first post. In addition to being deputy-organist and sexton, B. is asked to do	Boito born, Feb. 24; Cherubini (82) dies, March 15; Massenet born, May 12; Sullivan born, May 13.

Year	Age	Life	Contemporary Musicians
		menial jobs in the fields. Plays the fiddle at country inns and at wedding celebrations in weaver Sücka's little band. First Mass, in C major, composed.	
1843	19	Serious clash with his superior Fuchs. Prior Arneth of St Florian transfers him in Jan. to the even smaller village of Kronstorf near Steyr. The appointment is a great improvement and enables B. to perfect himself as organist under L. von Zenetti of Steyr. Assiduous organ practice and study of J. S. Bach. *Tantum ergo* in D and *Libera* in F composed.	Grieg born, June 15; Sgambati born, May 28.
1844	20	Masses in E flat and F composed.	Rimsky-Korsakov born, March 18.
1845	21	Successful competitive examination, May 29. B. becomes a fully salaried schoolmaster. On Sept. 25 he is appointed teacher and assistant organist at St Florian. He perfects himself as improviser on the organ. Composes small items of secular and ecclesiastical choral music.	Fauré born, May 13.
1846	22	*Tantum ergo* and some male-voice choruses composed.	
1847	23		Mackenzie born, Aug. 22; Mendelssohn (38) dies, Nov. 4.

Year	Age	*Life*	*Contemporary Musicians*
1848	24	Enrols as 'Nationalgardist' during the revolution and takes part in military exercises.	Donizetti (51) dies, April 8; Duparc born, Jan. 21; Parry born, Feb. 27.
1849	25	*Requiem* in D, B.'s first large-scale composition, completed and first performed at St Florian, March 13. He is appointed temporary organist at the foundation with an increased salary.	Chopin (39) dies, Oct. 17; Nicolai (39) dies, May 11
1850	26	Joins a 2-year course at the Unter-Realschule of Linz, to perfect his education. He also learns Latin.	
1851	27	Starts work in the district law courts of St Florian as a temporary assistant and clerk. Goes to Vienna and calls on Ignaz Assmayer (1790–1862).	d'Indy born, March 27; Lortzing (49) dies, Jan. 21; Spontini (77) dies, Jan. 14.
1852	28	Intensified creative work: *Magnificat* in B flat, Psalms CXIV and XXII composed. Also pieces for piano duet and cantatas for mixed chorus.	Stanford born, Sept. 30.
1853	29	Applies in July for a permanent post in the civil service, but without success.	
1854	30	*Missa solemnis* in B flat completed and first performed at St Florian, Sept. 14. Second journey to Vienna, Oct. B. is examined by Assmayer, Preyer and Sechter, who take a benevolent interest in him.	Humperdinck born, Sept. 1; Janáček born, July 3.

Year	Age	Life	Contemporary Musicians
1855	31	Successful examination at Linz, Jan. 25–6. B. is now made a fully qualified teacher for senior schools. He obtains from Robert Führer (Prague) a flattering testimonial as organist (April 27). He is at last appointed first organist of St Florian. Third journey to Vienna, July. Simon Sechter (1788–1867) accepts him as pupil. B. beats his competitors at the preliminary competition for the post of first organist at Linz Cathedral in succession to W. Pranghofer. He is appointed temporary organist (Nov. 9).	Chausson born, Jan. 21.
1856	32	Succeeds in the main competition for the post of organist at Linz Cathedral, Jan. 25. He is definitely appointed on April 25 with a salary of *c.* 520 fl. and free lodgings. He thereby terminates all his appointments at St Florian. He meets Bishop Rudigier, his future benefactor. *Ave Maria* for chorus and organ composed. B. becomes a member of the Liedertafel 'Frohsinn.'	Martucci born, Jan. 1; Schumann (46) dies, July 29; Sinding born, Jan. 11; Taneyev born, Nov. 25.
1857	33	Officiates as organist at the cathedral and the parish church of Linz. He gives	Elgar born, June 2; Glinka (54) dies, Feb. 15.

Year	Age	Life	Contemporary Musicians
		piano lessons and travels each year for *c.* 6 weeks to study with Sechter in Vienna. He gives up composition for about 5 years.	
1858	34	Completes harmony course with Sechter and begins simple counterpoint.	Leoncavallo born, March 8; Puccini born, June 22.
1859	35	He completes simple counterpoint.	Spohr (75) dies, Oct. 22.
1860	36	Double counterpoint studied with Sechter. B.'s mother dies, Nov. 11. He begins Psalm CXLVI for chorus and orchestra. Gustav Mahler born, July 7, at Kališt. (Bohemia), near the Moravian border, son of Bernhard Mahler (1827–89), a brandy distiller and merchant, and his wife Marie, born Hermann (1837–89). He is one of 12 children. In Dec. the family moves to Jihlava (Iglau).	Albeniz born, May 29; Wolf born, March 13. Auber 78; Balakirev 23; Balfe 52; Berlioz 57; Bizet 22; Boito 18; Brahms 27; Bruch 22; Chabrier 19; Chausson 5; Cornelius 36; Cui 25; Dargomizhsky 47; Delibes 24; Duparc 12; Dvořák 19; Fauré 15; Franck 38; Franz 45; Gade 43; Goldmark 30; Götz 20; Gounod 42; Grieg 17; Halévy 61; Heller 45; Henselt 46; Hiller 49; Humperdinck 6; d'Indy 9; Lalo 37; Liszt 49; Loewe 64; Mackenzie 13; Marschner 65; Martucci 4; Massenet 18; Mercadante 65; Meyerbeer 69; Mussorgsky 21; Offenbach 41; Parry 12; Pedrell 19; Ponchielli 26; Raff 38; Reinecke 36; Rheinberger 21; Rimsky-Korsakov 16; Rossini 68; Rubinstein 31; Saint-Saëns 25; Serov 40;

Year	Age	*Life*	*Contemporary Musicians*
			Smetana 36; Stanford 8; Strauss (J. ii) 35; Sullivan 18; Taneiev 4; Tchaikovsky 20; Thomas (A.) 49; Verdi 47; Wagner 47.
1861	B. 37 M. 1	B. studies canon and fugue with Sechter; passes his final examination, with distinction, March 20. Eighth and final examination at the organ of the Piarists' Church in Vienna, Nov. 22. The examiners, Herbeck among them, are unanimous in their praise. *Ave Maria* in 7 parts; first performed May 12, at Linz. First performance of offertory *Afferentur* there, Dec. 14, together with Psalm CXLVI. B. resumes composition. Appointed librarian and conductor of Liedertafel 'Frohsinn' (Linz). Starts his studies of orchestration and musical form with Otto Kitzler (1834–1915) at Linz.	MacDowell born, Dec. 18; Marschner (66) dies, Dec. 14; Thuille born, Nov. 30.
1862	B. 38 M. 2	B. composes festival cantata *Preiset den Herrn* and pieces for orchestra. Cantata performed under his direction. String Quartet in C minor composed.	Debussy born, Aug. 22; Delius born Jan. 29; Halévy (63) dies, March 17.
1863	B. 39 M. 3	B. composes Psalm CXII, Overture in G minor, Symphony in F minor and men's chorus *Germanenzug*.	Mascagni born, Dec. 7.

Year	Age	Life	Contemporary Musicians
		Applies unsuccessfully for post of organist-designate at imperial court chapel, Vienna. He hears Wagner's *Tannhäuser* for the first time, Feb. 20. Passes his final examination under Kitzler, July 10. Visits Franz Lachner (1803–90) at Munich, who takes interest in F minor Symphony.	
1864	B. 40 M. 4	B. completes his first mature masterpiece, Mass in D minor, Sept. 29. First performance at Linz, Nov. 20. Starts work on Symphony 'O.'	d'Albert born, April 10; Meyerbeer (73) dies, May 2; Strauss (R.) born, June 11.
		M. plays soldiers marches on an accordion and sings about 200 folk tunes which he learns from a maid.	
1865	B. 41 M. 5	B. hears the first *Tristan* at Munich (June); meets Wagner and Bülow, also establishes personal contact with Liszt and Berlioz in Vienna and Budapest. Symphony I begun.	Dukas born, Oct. 1; Glazunov born, Aug. 10; Sibelius born, Dec. 8.
1866	B. 42 M. 6	B. completes Mass in E minor, Nov. 25, and Symphony I, April 14. He hears Beethoven's choral Symphony for the first time in Vienna.	Busoni born, April 1; Satie born, March 17.
		M. learns the piano and gives piano lessons to an	

Year	Age	Life	Contemporary Musicians
		older boy, goes to the elementary school at Jihlava.	
1867	B. 43 M. 7	B. suffers a serious nervous breakdown; goes for a 3 months' cure to Bad Kreuzen, May–Aug.; begins Mass in F minor. Mass in D performed under Herbeck at the imperial court chapel. B. renews his application for the post of court organist at the court chapel. First application for the post of university lecturer in Vienna.	Granados born, July 29. Sechter dies, Sept. 10.
1868	B. 44 M. 8	B.'s Symphony I first performed at Linz, May 9. Mass in F minor completed, Sept. 9. Herbeck's visit to B., May 24. Appointed professor for thorough-bass, counterpoint and organ at the Vienna Conservatory, in succession to Sechter, with 800 fl. annual salary, July. B. starts work in Vienna on Oct. 1. He retains his post at Linz Cathedral for another 2 years. Appointed organist-designate at the imperial court chapel, Vienna, Sept. 9. M. borrows music from a lending library. Gets musical tuition from conductor Viktorin and from piano teacher Brosch.	Bantock born, Aug. 7; Rossini (76) dies, Nov. 15; Schillings born, April 19.

Year	Age	Life	Contemporary Musicians
1869	B. 45 M. 9	B. plays the organ of St Epvre, Nancy, and of Notre-Dame, Paris, April. Achieves much success and meets César Franck, Saint-Saëns and other French musicians. First performance of Mass in E minor at Linz Cathedral, Sept. 29. Completion of Symphony 'O,' Sept. 12.	Berlioz (66) dies, March 8; Dargomizhsky (56) dies, Jan. 17; Loewe (73) dies, April 20; Pfitzner born, May 5; Roussel born, April 5.
1870	B. 46 M. 10	B. appointed piano teacher at the Seminary St Anna in Vienna with 500 fl. annual salary. His sister Anna, who had acted as his housekeeper, dies, Jan. 16. M. becomes a pupil at the 'Gymnasium' at Jihlava; is temporarily transferred to Prague.	Balfe (62) dies, Oct. 20; Mercadante (75) dies, Dec. 17; Novák born, Dec. 5; Schmitt (Florent) born, Sept. 28.
1871	B. 47 M. 11	B. plays the organ in London at the Albert Hall, Aug. He is especially successful as an improviser. Involved in a disciplinary action at St Anna, Oct. Starts to compose Symphony II, Oct. 11.	Auber (89) dies, May 12; Serov (51) dies, Feb. 1.
1872	B. 48 M. 12	B.'s Mass in F first performed in the Augustines' Church, Vienna, June 16, with Brahms, Hanslick and Dessoff attending. Completion of Symphony II, Sept. 11.	Skriabin born, Jan. 4; Vaughan Williams born, Oct. 12.

Year	Age	Life	Contemporary Musicians
1873	B. 49 M. 13	Symphony III begun Feb., completed (version 1), Dec. 31. Visit to Marienbad and Bayreuth, where Wagner accepts dedication of Symphony III, Aug-Sept. First performance of Symphony II, Vienna, Oct. 26.	Rakhmaninov born, April 1; Reger born, March 19.
1874	B. 50 M. 14	B. loses his post at St Anna with disastrous effects on his financial situation; he has to borrow money at interest. The Vienna Philharmonic orchestra refuses to perform Symphonies II and III. Symphony IV (version 1) completed, Nov. 22.	Cornelius (50) dies, Oct. 26; Holst born, Sept. 21; Schoenberg born, Sept. 13; Suk born, Jan. 4.
1875	B. 51 M. 15	B. appointed unpaid lecturer in harmony and counterpoint at Vienna University, Nov. 8; also appointed vice-archivist and deputy singing-master at the court chapel, June. Begins Symphony V, Feb. 14. M. loses his brother Ernst. M. arrives in Vienna, accompanied by his father. Julius Epstein (1832–1926) at once accepts him as pupil at the Conservatory. His tutors there are Epstein (piano), Fuchs (harmony), Krenn (composition).	Bizet (37) dies, June 3; Ravel born, March 7.
1876	B. 52 M. 16	B. attends the first performance of Wagner's *Ring* at Bayreuth, summer.	Falla born, Nov. 23; Götz (36) dies, Dec. 3; Wolf-Ferrari born, Jan. 12.

Year	Age	Life	Contemporary Musicians
		Completion of Symphony V, May 16. Works on revisions of Symphonies II and III.	
		M. wins prizes for piano playing and composition (1st movement of a piano Quartet). Composes Sonata for violin and piano (lost).	
1877	B. 53 M. 17	Disastrous first performance of B.'s Symphony III in Vienna under his own direction. Rättig decides to publish it; Mahler and Krzyzanowski are commissioned to make a 4-hand piano arrangement. Beginning of friendly relations between B. and M. First revision of Symphony V started.	Dohnányi born, July 27.
		M. wins another prize for piano playing; composes piano Quintet and other works (partly lost). His most intimate friends are Hugo Wolf and Hans Rott; he shares a room and at times a bed with the former.	
1878	B. 54 M. 18	B. appointed a full member of the court chapel, Jan. Starts thorough revision of Symphony IV (with 2 new movements). Symphony III published (Rättig).	Schreker born, March 23.

Year	Age	*Life*	*Contemporary Musicians*
		M. leaves the Conservatory, July 11, with diploma. His piano Quintet (Scherzo) is performed in public on that day. Begins to compose an opera, *Herzog Ernst von Schwaben*, on a book by Joseph Steiner (lost). His piano arrangement of B.'s Symphony III is published. He passes his matriculation at Jihlava late summer; attends lectures at Vienna University. Begins composition of *Das klagende Lied* (still planned as an opera) and composes a number of other works (destroyed or lost).	
1879	B. 55 M. 19	B.'s string Quintet completed, July 12. Symphony VI begun, Sept. 24.	Bridge (Frank) born, Feb. 26; Ireland born, Aug. 13; Karg-Elert born, Nov. 21; Medtner born, Dec. 24; Respighi born, July 9; Scott (Cyril) born, Sept. 27.
		M. lives partly in Moravia, partly in Vienna and Hungary; returns to Vienna, Sept. 29. Gives lessons and composes.	
1880	B. 56 M. 20	B. travels to Oberammergau and visits Switzerland. Symphony IV (2nd version) completed.	Bloch born, July 24; Offenbach (61) dies, Oct. 4; Pizzetti born, Sept. 20.
		M. completes *Das klagende Lied* (version 1), Nov. He competes for the Beethoven prize with it. The work is rejected by Brahms, who is	

Year	Age	Life	Contemporary Musicians
		a member of the jury. Conducts musical farces during the summer at Bad Hall (Upper Austria). M. plans an opera, *Die Argonauten*.	
1881	B. 57 M. 21	B.'s Symphony VI completed Sept. 3. Symphony VII begun, Sept. 23. First performance of Symphony IV (version 2) under Richter in Vienna, Feb. 20. First (incomplete) performance of string Quintet in Vienna. *Te Deum* begun.	Bartók born, March 25; Miaskovsky born, April 20; Mussorgsky (42) dies, March 28.
		M. conductor at the theatre of Ljubljana (Laibach); works at an opera, *Rübezahl* libretto still in existence in 1908; music lost.	
1882	B. 58 M. 22	B. attends the first performance of *Parsifal* at Bayreuth, summer: sees Wagner for the last time. Mass in D revised.	Kodály born, Dec. 16; Malipiero born, March 18; Raff (60) dies, June 24-5; Stravinsky born, June 17; Szymanowski born, Oct. 6; Turina born, Dec. 9.
		M. works at a *Nordic Symphony* (destroyed).	
1883	B. 59 M. 23	B.'s Symphony VII completed, Sept. 5. *Te Deum*, 2nd version, begun, Sept. First performance of Symphony VI (middle movements) in Vienna, Feb. 11.	Bax born, Nov. 6; Casella born, July 25; Wagner (69) dies, Feb. 13; Webern born, Dec. 3; Zandonai born, May 28.
		M. appointed conductor at Olomouc, Jan. 20. Conducts *Carmen* and makes his	

Year	Age	Life	Contemporary Musicians
		mark as a brilliant conductor. Chorus master for Italian opera season, Carl Theatre, Vienna, summer. Attends performance of *Parsifal* at Bayreuth. Engagement as musical director of Court Theatre, Cassel, June. Also chorus master at Munich. Passion for Johanne Richter. *Lieder eines fahrenden Gesellen* begun, Dec.	
1884	B. 60 M. 24.	B.'s *Te Deum* (version 2) completed, March 7. Symphony VII first performed under Nikisch at Leipzig, Dec. 30. B. attends and is enthusiastically acclaimed. B. plays the organ at the Rudolfinum in Prague. Symphony VIII begun, summer. M. continues at Cassel, composes incidental music for a stage version of Scheffel's *Trompeter von Säckingen,* June. Visit to Dresden and its opera. Sees Ernst von Schuch and tries to obtain appointment; also tries unsuccessfully to become Bülow's assistant. First sketches for Symphony I.	Smetana (60) dies, May 12.
1885	B. 61 M. 25	B.: Successful first performance of Symphony VII at Munich (Levi), March 10.	Berg born, Feb. 9; Hiller (74) dies, May 10; Wellesz born, Oct. 21.

Year	Age	Life	Contemporary Musicians

First performance of *Te Deum* (with piano accompaniment) in the Wagner Verein, May 2. Symphony III performed in New York (Seidl), Dec. 6. First draft of Symphony VIII completed; Mass in E revised.

M. conducts music festival at Cassel, June 29–July 1. Leaves Cassel for good, July 1; conducts for a month 'on trial' at Municipal Theatre, Leipzig; appointed 1886. Appointed as second conductor at the Deutsches Theater in Prague, Aug. 1. *Lieder eines fahrenden Gesellen* completed by Jan. 1. They reflect M.'s unhappy love affair with Johanne Richter. M. in financial straits throughout the year.

1886 B. 62 · M. 26 — B.: First performance of *Te Deum* and first performance in Vienna of Symphony VII (Richter), March 21; *Te Deum,* Munich (Levi), April 2. Receives the Franz Joseph Order, July 9, and is received by the emperor, Sept. 23. Visit to Bayreuth, where he attends *Tristan* and plays the organ at Liszt's funeral, Aug. 3.

Kaminski born, July 4; Liszt (75) dies, July 31; Ponchielli (52) dies, Jan. 16.

Year	Age	Life	Contemporary Musicians
		Second version of Symphony VIII started, summer. *Te Deum* published.	
		M. second conductor at Leipzig (under Nikisch and Stägemann) Meets Weber's grandson and falls deeply in love with his wife.	
1887	B. 63 M. 27	B. appointed member of the Maatschappij tot Bevordering der Toonkunst, Amsterdam. Second version of Symphony VIII completed, June. First sketch for Symphony IX begun, Sept. 21. Symphony VII first performed in London (Richter), May 23. Deep disappointment, caused by Levi's rejection of Symphony VIII, autumn. Deterioration of psychic condition.	Borodin (53) dies, Feb. 28; Toch born, Dec. 7.
		M. deputizes for the indisposed Nikisch as conductor of Wagner's *Ring*. Estrangement between them; passionate love affair with Frau von Weber. Practical edition of Weber's opera fragment *Die drei Pintos* started in collaboration with Hauptmann von Weber. M. meets R. Strauss, autumn. First sketches for Symphony II.	

Year	Age	Life	Contemporary Musicians
1888	B. 64 M. 28	B.: Symphony VII in Prague under Muck, Jan. 15. *Te Deum* and Symphony IV (version 4) in Vienna under Richter, Jan. 22. Symphony IV in New York (Seidl), April 4. Third revision of Symphony III and third version of Symphony VIII started. Fourth revision of Symphony IV (started in 1887) completed, Jan. M.: Arrangement of *Drei Pintos* completed; first performance in Leipzig, Jan. 20. Symphony I completed, March. Disagreement with Staegemann. M. is in indifferent health, undergoes an intestinal operation at Munich, summer, visits Bayreuth and later Vienna, where he conducts negotiations with Budapest Opera. Appointed musical director of Budapest Opera, Oct. 18.	Heller (74) dies, Jan. 14.
1889	B. 65 M. 29	B. appointed hon. member of the Richard Wagner Verein. Symphony VII performed in Vienna (Richter). Symphony IV (version 4) published in Vienna. Third version of Symphony III completed, Feb. 11.	Henselt (75) dies, Oct. 10.

Year	*Age*	*Life*	*Contemporary Musicians*
		M.: Death of father, Feb. 18, and mother, Oct. 11. M.'s sister Justine becomes his housekeeper. Conducts the first performance of *Walküre* and *Rheingold* in Hungarian. Symphony I first performed in Budapest, Nov. 20, meets with chilly reception. Indifferent health and repeated surgical treatment.	
1890	B. 66 M. 30	B.: Gradual deterioration in health; on sick-leave until Jan. 15, 1891. Honorary member of Upper Austrian Diet, from which he receives a stipend. Plays the organ for the emperor at Ischl, Oct. 20. Third version of Symphony VIII completed, March 10. Work in progress on Symphony IX. Final revision of Symphony I started, March 12 (completed by April 18, 1891). Last revision of Mass in F. Masses in E and F published. Symphony III (3rd version) published, and first performed in Vienna, Dec. 21. Great success of Symphony IV (4th version) at Munich (Fischer), Dec. 12. M. journeys to Vienna and to Italy, where he recuperates. Return to Budapest,	Franck (68) dies, Nov. 8; Gade (73) dies, Dec. 21.

Year	Age	Life	Contemporary Musicians
		Aug. Increasing administrative difficulties despite his success as conductor.	
1891	B. 67 M. 31	B.: Retirement as Professor at the Conservatory, Jan. 15. Attends the Berlin performance of *Te Deum* (S. Ochs), May 31. First performance of Symphony I (revision) (Richter), Dec. 13. Hon. doctor's degree conferred by Vienna University, July 4.	Bliss born, Aug. 2; Delibes (55) dies, Jan. 16; Prokofiev born, April 23.
		M.: Intendant Beseczny, M.'s patron, resigns, Jan. His successor, Count Zichy, quarrels with M. M. resigns, March 14. Budapest Opera has to pay substantial compensation for breach of contract. M. starts his new appointment as first conductor of the Hamburg Opera, April 1. Becomes friendly with Bülow, plays to him the first movement of his Symphony II, but without success. Conducts Bruckner's Mass in D at Hamburg, March 31. Friendship with Anna Mildenburg and J. B. Foerster.	
1892	B. 68 M. 32	B. resigns from the court chapel. Last visit to Bayreuth, summer. Composition of Psalm CL; first performed in Vienna, Nov.	Franz (77) dies, Oct. 24; Honegger born, March 10; Jarnach born, July 26; Lalo (69) dies, April 22; Milhaud born, Sept. 4.

Year	Age	Life	Contemporary Musicians

13. Publication of Symphony VIII (revision), of Symphony II (last revision), of Psalm CL and Mass in D minor. First performance of Symphony VIII (revision) in Vienna (Richter), Dec. 18.

M. highly successful as opera conductor at Hamburg. Conducts German opera at Drury Lane, London, summer. Spends his vacations for the next years mainly in Steinbach (Attersee), where his friendship with Natalie Bauer-Lechner develops. Three books of early songs published. Performances of Symphony I, of *Humoresken* (*Wunderhorn* songs) in Hamburg and Berlin. M. deputizes for the ailing Bülow as conductor of some of the 'Bülow Concerts,' Dec. Bruno Walter appointed chorus master at Hamburg Opera. Some *Wunderhorn* songs composed at Hamburg and Steinbach.

1893 B. 69 B. composes the symphonic chorus *Helgoland*; first performed in Vienna, Oct. 9. Falls gravely ill with dropsy, summer. His condition is considered so serious that he

M. 33

Gounod (75) dies, Oct. 18; Tchaikovsky (53) dies, Nov. 6.

Year	Age	Life	Contemporary Musicians
		is persuaded to make his will, Nov. 10. Symphony I (final version) published. B. is created hon. member of the Society of Friends of Music in Vienna.	
		M.: Bülow resigns because of ill health and M. is appointed his successor at Hamburg. At Steinbach he continues to work at Symphony II and the *Wunderhorn* songs.	
1894	B. 70 M. 34	B. rallies once more and is able to travel to Berlin, Jan. (in the company of Hugo Wolf) to attend performance of Symphony VII, *Te Deum* and string Quintet. But his health gives way, spring; he is unable to attend the first performance of Symphony V at Graz (Schalk), April 8. He recovers sufficiently once more to travel to Steyr, where his seventieth birthday is celebrated, Sept 4. Gives his last university lecture, Nov. 12. Given the freedom of Linz, Nov. 15. Completes the first three movements of Symphony IX, Nov. 30; he starts finale, Dec.	Chabrier (53) dies, Sept. 13; Pijper born, Sept. 8; Rubinstein (65) dies, Nov. 20.
		M.: Symphony I performed	

Year	Age	Life	Contemporary Musicians
		at Music Festival of Weimar, June 29; Symphony II completed in Steinbach, July 25. Visit to Brahms at Bad Ischl.	
1895	B. 71 M. 35	B., whose health continues to give way gradually, moves to lodgings in Belvedere, July, offered him by the emperor. He works fitfully at the finale of Symphony IX.	Hindemith born, Nov. 16.
		M.: R. Strauss conducts the first 3 movements of Symphony II in Berlin. M. himself conducts the first performance of the complete Symphony there, Dec. 13. At Steinbach M. begins with the sketch for Symphony III, summer. Becomes official conductor of the Bülow Concerts at Hamburg.	
1896	B. 72 M. 36	B. attends the last concert of his music in Vienna: *Te Deum* (Perger), Jan. 12. He suffers increasingly from religious mania; his mind becomes overclouded at times and his physical condition takes a turn for the worse. Symphony V is published under F. Schalk's supervision. B. fails to complete the finale of Symphony IX. He dies, Oct.	Thomas (A.) (85) dies, Feb. 12. Albéniz aged 36; Balakirev 59; Bantock 28; Bartók 15; Bax 14; Berg 11; Bliss 5; Bloch 16; Boito 54; Brahms 63; Bridge (Frank) 17; Bruch 58; Busoni 30; Casella 13; Chausson 41; Cui 61; Debussy 34; Delius 34; Dohnányi 19; Dukas 31; Duparc 48; Dvořák 55; Elgar 39;

Year	Age	Life	Contemporary Musicians

11. Solemn funeral in the Carl Church, Oct. 14. His remains subsequently transferred to St Florian.

M. conducts his Symphony I and the *Lieder eines fahrenden Gesellen* in Berlin. Nikisch, Weingartner and Schuch conduct single movements of Symphonies II and III. M. completes Symphony III at Steinbach, Aug. 6. He also composes *Lob des hohen Verstandes,* June 21, and Nietzsche's *Midnight Song,* summer. Frequent visits to Austria (Vienna and Bad Ischl), where he negotiates discreetly with the administrators of the Vienna Opera and continues to enlist Brahms's support.

Falla 20; Fauré 51; Glazunov 31; Goldmark 66; Granados 29; Grieg 53; Hindemith 1; Holst 22; Honegger 4; Humperdinck 42; d'Indy 45; Ireland 17; Karg-Elert 17; Kirchner 73; Kodály 14; Leoncavallo 38; MacDowell 35; Mackenzie 49; Malipiero 14; Martucci 40; Mascagni 33; Massenet 54; Medtner 17; Miaskovsky 15; Milhaud 4; Novák 26; Parry 48; Pedrell 55; Pfitzner 27; Pizzetti 16; Prokofiev 5; Puccini 38; Rakhmaninov 23; Ravel 21; Reger 23; Respighi 17; Rheinberger 57; Rimsky-Korsakov 52; Roussel 27; Saint-Saëns 61; Satie 30; Schmitt 26; Schoenberg 22; Scott (Cyril) 17; Sibelius 31; Sinding 40; Skriabin 24; Stanford 44; Strauss (J. ii) 72; Strauss (R.) 32; Stravinsky 14; Suk 22; Sullivan 54; Svendsen 56; Szymanowski 14; Taneiev 40; Vaughan Williams, 24; Verdi 83; Webern 13; Wolf 36.

1897 M. 37 — Symphony II and *Lieder eines fahrenden Gesellen* published. Parts of Symphony II performed in Berlin (Weingartner). M. conducts

Brahms (64) dies, April 3; Korngold born, May 29.

Year	Age	Life	Contemporary Musicians
		concerts in Moscow, March. He asks for release from his Hamburg contract early in the year. Conversion to Roman Catholic Church early spring. Visit to Vienna and to Brahms, shortly before the latter's death. Appointed *Kapellmeister* in Vienna, May 1. M. conducts *Lohengrin* on trial, May 11. Appointed deputy director, next to W. Jahn, July 21. Life appointment as artistic director of Vienna Opera in succession to Jahn, Oct. 8. Throat trouble; vacation at Kitzbühel.	
1898	38	Appointed conductor of Vienna Philharmonic concerts. Performances of Symphonies I and II at Dresden and Liège. Symphonies I and III published. Revision of *Das klagende Lied*.	Rieti born, Jan. 28.
1899	39	Purchases a plot of land at Maiernigg am Wörthersee and begins to build a chalet. Composition of Symphony IV started at Alt-Aussee (Styria), *c*. Aug. 20. *Das klagende Lied* published. M. conducts performance of his Symphonies I and II at Frankfort o/M. and Vienna. Composition of last	Chausson (44) dies, June 10; Poulenc born, Jan. 7; Strauss (J. ii) (74) dies, June 3.

Year	Age	Life	Contemporary Musicians
		Wunderhorn songs (*Revelge, Tamboursg'sell*) during the summer vacation.	
1900	40	Symphony IV completed at Maiernigg, Aug. 5. Performance of Symphony II at Munich. M. conducts five concerts with the Vienna Phil. Orch. in Paris at the world exhibition. They fall flat. His relations with the orchestra become increasingly strained.	Křenek born, Aug. 23; Sullivan (58) dies, Nov. 22.
1901	41	Conducts first performance of *Das klagende Lied* in Vienna, Feb. 17. Bruno Walter appointed conductor at the Opera, spring. M. suffers a haemorrhage, and goes on sick leave to Abbazzia, March. Meanwhile the Philharmonic Orchestra appoints Hellmesberger, jun., as his successor, behind his back. M. resigns, April. He meets Alma Schindler, his future wife, Nov. Conducts the first performance of Symphony IV in Munich, Nov. 25. Symphonies II and IV performed in Berlin and Dresden. Symphony IV published. Symphony V begun at Maiernigg, summer. *Kindertotenlieder* 1–3 and two further songs to	Rheinberger (62) dies, Nov. 25; Verdi (88) dies, Jan. 27.

Year	*Age*	*Life*	*Contemporary Musicians*
		poems by Rückert (*Ich atmet' einen linden Duft; Ich bin der Welt abhanden gekommen*) composed, summer.	
1902	42	Conducts for the first time in Vienna Symphony IV (together with *Das klagende Lied*), Jan. 12. Marries Alma Schindler after short, passionate engagement, March 9. M. conducts first performance of the complete Symphony III at Music Festival of Crefeld, June. Symphony V completed, autumn. Birth of his elder daughter Maria Nov. 3. Late in year M. conducts concerts in Russia.	Walton born, March 29.
1903	43	Conducts Symphony II in minster at Basle and Symphony III in Amsterdam (Concertgebouw). Beginning of M.'s friendship with Willem Mengelberg and his orchestra. Performances of Symphonies I and IV at Darmstadt and Düsseldorf. Symphony VI begun at Maiernigg (2 movements). Rückert's song *Liebst du um Schönheit* composed for Alma. Birth of younger daughter Anna, June 15.	Wolf (43) dies, Feb. 22.
1904	44	Conducts first performance of Symphony V at Cologne, Oct. 18, also performances of Symphonies II and IV in	Dvořák (63) dies, May 1.

Year	Age	Life	Contemporary Musicians
		Amsterdam and of Symphony I at The Hague. Symphony VI completed at Maiernigg, Sept. 9; Symphony V published, Symphony VII started. *Kindertotenlieder* 4 and 5 composed, and the cycle completed.	
1905	45	Numerous performances of Symphonies I, II, IV, V, and the songs. M. completes Symphony VII during the summer months, revises Symphony V and finishes the orchestration of Symphony VI, May. M.'s song cycles performed by the Vereinigung schaffender Tonkünstler in Vienna organized by Zemlinsky and Schoenberg. M.'s interest in Schoenberg increases. Symphony V performed at Strasbourg at the Alsatian Music Festival, and in Vienna, Dec.	
1906	46	Conducts first performance of Symphony VI at Essen, May 27; performances of Symphony VI given in Amsterdam and Vienna, May 27. Symphony VIII completed in sketch on Aug. 18 at Maiernigg. Numerous performances of M.'s symphonies under Nikisch, Mengelberg, Fried. Symphony VI published.	Shostakovich born, Sept. 25.

Year	Age	Life	Contemporary Musicians
1907	47	M.'s elder daughter, Maria Anna, dies, July 5. Dr Blumenthal diagnoses M.'s heart disease. Growing intrigue against M. undermines his position at the Opera. He asks to be released from his contract by Dec. 31. He accepts an invitation from the Metropolitan Opera, New York, to conduct Mozart and Wagner. The orchestration of Symphony VIII completed, summer; first sketches for *Das Lied von der Erde* probably begun at Alt-Schluderbach. M. leaves with wife and daughter and sails for U.S.A., Dec. 9.	Grieg (64) dies, Sept. 4; Thuille (46) dies, Feb. 5.
1908	48	Spectacular success as a conductor in New York, where apart from opera he performs Symphony II. Returns to Vienna, May. First performance of Symphony VII in Prague, Sept. 19, with rather indifferent success. *Das Lied von der Erde* completed at Toblach (Dobbiacco), autumn. Symphony VII published. Return to U.S.A., late autumn.	MacDowell (47) dies, Jan. 24; Rimsky-Korsakov (64) dies, June 21.
1909	49	Appointed conductor of a newly founded Philharmonic Society in New York.	Albéniz (49) dies, June 16; Martucci (53) dies, June 1.

Year	*Age*	*Life*	*Contemporary Musicians*
		He confines himself mainly to concert work; conducts 46 concerts in the winter of 1909–10. Returns to Europe, spring; stay with friends in Moravia. He conducts Symphony VII in Amsterdam. Begins to compose Symphony IX, summer. Return to U.S.A. on his third visit, Oct.	
1910	50	Returns to Europe, April 7. He conducts Symphony II at the Châtelet in Paris; meets Debussy and Dukas. Return to Vienna, where a general contract for the publication of his works is concluded with Universal Edition. He purchases a plot of land near Breitenstein (Semmering), south of Vienna, summer, and starts to build a house there, the completion of which he will never live to see. Deterioration of his health. Angina and emotional disturbances in his marital life. Flying visit at Leyden to Sigmund Freud, whose psychoanalytical treatment restores the balance of his matrimonial relations with Alma. M. conducts the first performances of Symphony VIII at Munich, Sept. 12–13. M. starts to compose	Balakirev (74) dies, May 30; Reinecke (86) dies, March 10.

Year	Age	Life	Contemporary Musicians

Symphony X, the sketches of which reflect the deep emotional disturbance from which he was suffering, July. He thoroughly revises Symphonies IV and V, winter 1910–11, but refrains from performing his new works. Symphony X remains fragment. M. leaves for U.S.A., Nov. 15. He conducts 48 concerts out of a total of 65 during the last winter of his life.

1911   51   Friction with his orchestra in New York hastens M.'s physical collapse. He conducts his last American concert, Feb. 21, and takes to his bed immediately after. A few days later Fraenkel diagnoses mortal illness. M. returns to Europe gravely ill (Paris), April. He returns finally to Vienna, where he dies, May 18. The full score of Symphony VIII is published at the time of his death, the *Lied von der Erde* soon after. Its first performance in Munich is conducted by Bruno Walter, Nov. 20.

d'Albert aged 54; Bantock 43; Bartók 30; Bax 28; Berg 26; Bliss 20; Bloch 31; Boito 69; Bridge (Frank) 32; Busoni 45; Casella 28; Cui 76; Debussy 49; Delius 49; Dohnányi 34; Dukas 46; Duparc 63; Falla 35; Fauré 66; Glazunov 46; Goldmark 81; Granados 44; Hindemith 16; Holst 37; Honegger 19; Humperdinck 57; d'Indy 60; Ireland 32; Jarnach 19; Kaminski 35; Kodály 29; Korngold 14; Křenek 11; Leoncavallo 53; Malipiero 29; Mascagni 48; Massenet 69; Medtner 32; Miaskovsky 30; Milhaud 19; Novák 41; Parry 63; Pedrell 70; Pfitzner 42; Pijper 17; Pizzetti 31; Poulenc 12;

Appendix A—Calendar

Prokofiev 20; Puccini 53; Rakhmaninov 38; Ravel 36; Reger 38; Respighi 32; Rieti 13; Roussel 42; Saint-Saëns 76; Satie 45; Schmitt (Florent) 41; Schoenberg 37; Schreker 33; Scott (Cyril) 32; Shostakovich 5; Sibelius 46; Skriabin 39; Stanford 59; Strauss (R.) 47; Stravinsky 29; Suk 37; Szymanowski 29; Taneiev 55; Toch 24; Turina 29; Vaughan Williams 39; Walton 9; Webern 28; Wellez 26; Wolf-Ferrari 35; Zandonai 28.

APPENDIX B

BRUCKNER

Large-scale Sacred Works

Short Chorale Mass, C major, for contralto, chorus and 2 horns (*c.* 1842).

Chorale Mass, F major, for unaccompanied four-part chorus for Maundy Thursday (1844).

Mass, E flat major, for chorus and orchestra (fragment) (*c.* 1846).

Requiem, D minor, for chorus, orchestra and organ (1848-9; revised 1854 and 1894; published 1931).

Magnificat, B flat major, for solo voices, chorus and orchestra (1852).

Psalm CXIV, for five-part chorus and 3 trombones (1852-3).

Psalm XXII, for four-part chorus and pianoforte (1852).

Missa solemnis, B flat minor, for solo voices, chorus and orchestra (1854, published 1934).

Psalm CXLVI, for solo voices, chorus and orchestra (1860). (Unpublished.)

Psalm CXII, for double chorus and orchestra (1863). (Incomplete.)

Mass, D minor, for chorus and orchestra (composed 1864; revised 1876 and 1881; published 1892. Revision ed. L. Nowak, published 1957).

Mass, E minor, for eight-part chorus and wind instruments (composed 1866, revised 1876-85; published 1890. Revision of 1876-85, ed. L. Nowak, published 1959).

Mass, F minor (*Grosse Messe*), for solo voices, chorus, orchestra and organ (1867-8; revised 1876, 1881, 1883 and 1890; published 1890; O.V. published 1944, ed. R. Haas. Second revision, ed. L. Nowak, published 1960).

Te Deum, C major, for solo voices, chorus, orchestra and organ (first version, 1881; second version, 1883-4; published December 1885. Original version of 1884, ed. L. Nowak, published 1962).

Psalm CL, for soprano solo, chorus, orchestra and organ (1892; published 1892).

Smaller Sacred Works

Pange lingua, C major, for four-part chorus (1835 or 1842; revised 1891).

Tantum ergo, D major (1843).

Libera, F major, for four-part chorus and organ (1843).

Litanei, for four-part chorus and brass (1843–5).

Herz Jesu-Lied, for four-part chorus and organ (*c.* 1845).

Two *Asperges me*, four-part chorus and organ (1845–6).

O du liebes Jesukind, for voice and organ (*c.* 1845).

Tantum ergo, D major, for five-part chorus (1846).

Five *Tantum ergo* for four-five-part chorus (No. 5 with organ) (1846; revised 1888; published 1888).

Chorale (*Dir Herr will ich mich ergeben*) (*c.* 1847).

Chorale, F minor (*In jener letzten der Nächte*) (1848).

Tantum ergo, A major, for four-part chorus and organ (*c.* 1849).

Libera, F minor, for chorus, trombones, cellos, double bass and organ (1854).

Ave Maria, for four-part chorus and organ (1856; published in Bruckner's lifetime).

Ave Maria, for seven-part chorus unaccompanied (1861).

Offertory, *Afferentur*, for four-part chorus and trombones (1861).

Offertory, *Inveni David*, for male-voice chorus and 3 trombones (1868).

Hymn, *Jam lucis orto sidere* (Phrygian) (1868; published 1868).

Pange lingua, for chorus only (Phrygian) (1868; published 1885).

Asperges me, F major, for chorus only (1866).

Gradual, *Christus factus est*, D major, for six-part chorus and 3 trombones (1879; published 1886).

Gradual, *Christus factus est*, D major, for seven-part chorus unaccompanied (1884).

Locus iste, for four-part chorus (1869).

Gradual, *Os justi*, for chorus unaccompanied (1879; published 1879).

Ave Maria, for contralto and organ (1882).

Antiphon, *Tota pulchra es*, for tenor, chorus and organ (1878; published 1884).

Ave Regina, for harmonized plainsong (1879).

Salvum fac populum (Faburden), for chorus only (1884).

Virga esse floruit (Gradual), for four-part chorus (1885; published 1886).

Ecce sacerdos, for chorus, 3 trombones and organ (1885).

Vexilla regis, for chorus only (1892).

Orchestral Works

March, D minor (1862). (Unpublished.)

Three pieces (E flat major, E minor, F major) (1862).

Overture, G minor (1862–3; published 1921).

Symphony, F minor (student work) (1863; published 1932, piano arrange-ment only; full score unpublished, except *Andante*. Vienna, 1913).

2 Marches for military band (E flat major and *Apollomarsch*) (both *c.* 1865).

Symphony 'O,' D minor (1863–4; revised 1869; published 1924, revision only).

Symphony I, C minor (1865–6; revised 1890–1. Revised version pub-lished 1893; 'Linz' version published 1939, ed. R. Haas; 1953, ed. L. Nowak).

Symphony II, C minor (1871–2; revised 1875–6, and later; last revision after 1891; revision published 1892; O.V. published 1938, ed. R. Haas).

Symphony III, D minor ('Wagner' Symphony) (version 1, 1873, un-published; version 2, 1876–7, published 1878, republished 1950 (ed. F. Oeser); version 3, 1888–9, published 1959, ed. L. Nowak; version 4, published 1890; revision published 1962, ed. H. F. Redlich).

Symphony IV, E flat major ('Romantic') (version 1, 1874; version 2, 1877–8, with new finale; version 3 (1878–80), with new 'Hunt' scherzo; version 4, 1887–8, published 1889; amalgamation of versions 2 and 3, score of 1881, published 1936, ed. R. Haas, together with parts of earlier versions; version 3, revision ed. L. Nowak, published 1953; version 4, revision ed. H. F. Redlich, published 1955).

Symphony V, B flat major (1875–6; several revisions 1876–8 and after; published 1896 without Bruckner's participation; O.V. published 1939, ed. R. Haas; republished and revised 1951, ed. L. Nowak).

Symphony VI, A major (1879–81; published 1899; O.V. published 1935, ed. R. Haas; republished and revised 1952, ed. L. Nowak).

Symphony VII, E major (1881–3; published 1885; O.V. published 1944, ed. R. Haas; republished and revised, ed. L. Nowak, 1954; published version of 1885 revised, ed. H. F. Redlich, 1958).

Symphony VIII, C minor (version 1, 1884–5; version 2, 1886–7; version 3, 1888–90; version 3 published 1892; version 2 published 1935, ed. R. Haas; republished and revised, ed. L. Nowak, 1955).

Symphony IX, D minor (movements 1–3, 1887–94, Finale incomplete, 1894–6; published 1903, ed. F. Löwe; O.V. published 1934, together with the sketches for the Finale, ed. A. Orel; republished and revised, ed. L. Nowak, 1951).

Cantatas for Mixed Chorus

Vergissmeinnicht (Marinelli), with solo quartet and piano, 3 versions (1845).

Entsagen (from O. Redwitz's 'Amaranth'), with solo voices and organ (*c.* 1851).

Das edle Herz (c. 1851).

Zwei Totenlieder, F major and D major, unaccompanied (1852).

Auf Brüder, auf, zu hohen Festen (Marinelli), with solo quartet and brass (*c.* 1852).

Festive song, *St Jodok, Spross aus edlem Stamm,* with solo voices and piano 1855).

Auf Brüder, auf, die Saiten zur Hand (Marinelli) (1855).

Du bist wie eine Blume (Heine), with solo quartet (1862).

Festive Cantata, *Preiset den Herrn* (Pammesberger), with solo voices, male chorus, brass and woodwind instruments and timpani (1862).

Male-voice Choruses

An dem Feste, 1843 (later *Tafellied,* 1893).

Das Lied vom deutschen Vaterland (1845).

Ständchen (c. 1846).

Festlied (c. 1846).

Der Lehrerstand (c. 1847).

Sternschnuppen (c. 1848).

Two Mottoes (1851).

Die Geburt (1852).

Vor Arneths Grab (1854).

Lasst Jubelklänge laut erklingen, with brass instruments (1854).

Des Dankes Wort sei mir gegönnt (1855).

Am Grabe (Grabgesang) (1861).

Germanenzug (Silberstein), with brass instruments (1863; published 1865).

Herbstlied (F. Sallet), with 2 sopranos and piano (1864).

Um Mitternacht I (S. Mendelssohn), with solo quartet and piano (1864).

Trauungslied (Proschko), with organ (1865).

Der Abendhimmel (Zedlitz) (? 1866) (male quartet only).

O könnt' ich dich beglücken (1866).

Vaterlandsliebe (Silberstein), with 2 soloists (1866).

Vaterländisches Weinlied (1866).

Das hohe Lied (Mattig), with 3 soloists (1876).

Trösterin Musik (A. Seuffert), with organ (1877) (originally called *Nachruf*).

Zur Vermählungsfeier (Silberstein), with tenor solo (1878).

Abendzauber (Mattig), with baritone solo and 4 horns (1878).

Sängerbund (Kerschbaum) (1882).

Um Mitternacht II (R. Prutz), with tenor solo (1886).

Appendix B—Catalogue of Works

Träumen und Wachen (Grillparzer), with tenor solo (1890).
Das deutsche Lied (E. Fels), with brass instruments (1892).
Helgoland (A. Silberstein), with brass instruments (1893).

Chamber Music

Aequali for 3 trombones (1847).
String Quartet, C minor (1862; published 1955, ed. L. Nowak).
String Quintet, F major (1878–9; published 1884).
Intermezzo for string quintet (composed 1879; published 1913).
Abendklänge for violin and piano (1866).

Organ Music

Four Preludes (*c.* 1836).
Prelude in E flat major (*c.* 1837).
Prelude and Fugue, C minor (1847).
Two pieces, D minor (*c.* 1852).
Fugue, D minor (1861).
Prelude, C major (1884).

Piano Music

Lancier-Quadrille (*c.* 1850).
Steiermärker (*c.* 1850).
Three pieces for piano duet (1852–4).
Quadrille for piano duet (1856; republished 1943, ed. H. Lemacher).
Klavierstück, E flat major (*c.* 1856).
Stille Betrachtung an einem Herbstabend (1863).
Erinnerung (1866).
Fantasy in E flat (*c.* 1868).

Songs

Frühlingslied (1851).
Amaranths Waldeslieder (O. Redwitz) (*c.* 1858; published in *Die Musik*, Berlin 1902).
Im April (Emanuel Geibel) (*c.* 1868).
Mein Herz und deine Stimme (*c.* 1868).
Herbstkummer (*c.* 1868).

Note.—Fragments, lost or spurious works are not included in this list. For them the catalogue of Max Auer (*Anton Bruckner*, Zurich-Vienna,

1923, and its subsequent revisions), the bibliographical references in R. Haas's Bruckner biography (Potsdam, 1934) and F. Blume's article in his encyclopaedia, *Musik in Geschichte und Gegenwart* (Cassel, 1949 ff.; vol. ii, 1952) should be consulted. The majority of the smaller sacred works and all compositions for piano and organ solo are reprinted in Göllerich-Auer's Bruckner biography in 4 vols. (Ratisbon, 1938). The sacred motets of 1870–92 have been reprinted, Vienna, 1927, ed. E. F. Schmid. There have also been some separate reprints of otherwise inaccessible smaller works. For these the author's article and catalogue of works in Grove's *Dictionary of Music and Musicians* (5th edition, ed. Eric Blom, 1954) should be consulted.

MAHLER

Symphonies and Choral Works

Das klagende Lied, for soprano, contralto, tenor, chorus and orchestra (words by the composer) (1878–99), published 1899. First version, with the subtitle 'Märchenspiel,' in 3 parts, completed November 1880; revised in 2 parts (with Part I, 'Waldmärchen,' eliminated[1]), 1888; again revised before 1896; rescored 1898.

Symphony I, D major (temporarily entitled *Titan*), 4 movements (1884–8), published 1898.

Symphony II, C minor, 5 movements, with soprano, contralto and chorus (*c.* 1887–29th June 1894), published 1897.

Symphony III, D minor, 6 movements, with soprano, contralto and chorus (summer 1893–6th August 1896), published 1898.

Symphony IV, G major, 4 movements, with soprano solo (*c.* 20th August 1899–5th August 1900), published 1901, last revision, 1910, unpublished.

Symphony V, C sharp minor, 5 movements (1901–summer 1902, repeatedly revised, 1907–*c.* 1909), published 1904 ff. by C. F. Peters, Leipzig, who issued at least three revisions during Mahler's lifetime, last revision unpublished.

Symphony VI, A minor, 4 movements (1903–9th September 1904, scoring completed May 1905), published 1906, in two versions.

Symphony VII, E minor, 5 movements (summer 1904–summer 1905),

---

[1] This part is unpublished, but in existence in U.S.A. A sketch of Part II, 'Spielmann,' dated 21st March 1880, is in the Vienna City Library.

published 1908; republished 1960 as first volume of a critical complete edition, issued by the International Gustav Mahler Society, Vienna. The volume is edited by Erwin Ratz. A different reprint, ed. H. F. Redlich, was published 1962.

Symphony VIII, E flat major, 2 parts, with 8 solo parts, double chorus and boys' chorus (sketch completed 18th August 1906; scoring completed in 1907), published 1910.

Das Lied von der Erde, symphony in 6 movements, with contralto and tenor solo (words from Hans Bethge's *Die chinesische Flöte*) (summer 1907–autumn 1908), published 1911.

Symphony IX, D major, 4 movements (summer 1909–1st April 1910), published 1912.

Symphony X, unfinished (sketched summer 1910).[1]

Songs

Lieder und Gesänge aus der Jugendzeit, for voice and piano (before and *c.* 1883), three books: I published 1885, II and III published 1892:

I. 1. *Frühlingsmorgen* (R. Leander).
    2. *Erinnerung* (Leander).
    3. *Serenade aus 'Don Juan'* (Tirso de Molina).
    4. *Phantasie aus 'Don Juan'* (Tirso de Molina).
    5. *Hans und Grete* (text by the composer).[2]
II. 6. *Um schlimme Kinder artig zu machen.*
    7. *Ich ging mit Lust.*
    8. *Aus! Aus!*
    9. *Starke Einbildungskraft.*   (From *Des Knaben*
III. 10. *Zu Strassburg auf der Schanz.*   *Wunderhorn.*)
    11. *Ablösung im Sommer.*
    12. *Scheiden und Meiden.*
    13. *Nicht Wiedersehen!*
    14. *Selbstgefühl.*

---

[1] Two movements, completed by Ernst Křenek, performed 1924; a facsimile reproduction of Mahler's MS. was published in 1924. Published (in a different edition), New York, 1951. A complete reconstruction of the whole work, for which Deryck Cooke was responsible, was broadcast by the B.B.C., London, in February 1961. Further performances have been prohibited by Mahler's widow. The reconstruction is excellent and has a truly authentic ring.

[2] Composed 5th March 1880 under the title *Maitanz im Grünen*.

Appendix B—Catalogue of Works

Lieder eines fahrenden Gesellen, for voice and orchestra (1883–1st January 1885), published 1897. Republished with foreword by H. F. Redlich, 1959.

1. *Wenn mein Schatz Hochzeit macht.*
2. *Ging heut' morgen übers Feld.*
3. *Ich hab' ein glühend Messer.*
4. *Die zwei blauen Augen.*

(Words by the Composer.)

Lieder aus 'Des Knaben Wunderhorn,' for voice and orchestra (originally entitled *Humoresken*) (1888–99), published 1905:

I.
 1. *Der Schildwache Nachtlied* (composed Leipzig, 1888).
 2. *Verlor'ne Müh'.*
 3. *Trost im Unglück* (composed 6th April 1892).
 4. *Wer hat dies Liedel erdacht?*
 5. *Das irdische Leben* (composed 1892).

II.
 6. *Des Antonius von Padua Fischpredigt* (composed Steinbach, Attersee, 1st August 1893).
 7. *Rheinlegendchen* (originally 'Tanzlegendchen') (composed Steinbach, Attersee, 10th August 1893).
 8. *Lied des Verfolgten im Turm* (composed 1895).
 9. *Wo die schönen Trompeten blasen.*
 10. *Lob des hohen Verstandes* (composed 21st June 1896).
 11. *Es sungen drei Engel* (from Symphony III) (composed 1895).
 12. *Urlicht* (from Symphony II) (composed 1893–4).

Wir geniessen die himmlischen Freuden for soprano and orchestra (from *Des Knaben Wunderhorn*) (from Symphony IV). (12th March 1892.)

O Mensch, gib Acht! for contralto and orchestra (Friedrich Nietzsche) (from Symphony III) (summer 1896).

Revelge (from *Des Knaben Wunderhorn*) (c. 1899), published 1905.

Der Tamboursg'sell (from *Des Knaben Wunderhorn*) (c. summer 1899), published 1905.

Kindertotenlieder, for voice and orchestra (Friedrich Rückert), Nos. 1–3 composed summer 1901 in Maiernigg, the rest in 1904, published 1905; 1, republished with foreword by H. F. Redlich, 1962.

1. *Nun will die Sonn' so hell aufgeh'n.*
2. *Nun seh' ich wohl.*
3. *Wenn dein Mütterlein.*
4. *Oft denk' ich, sie sind nur ausgegangen.*
5. *In diesem Wetter.*

Appendix B—Catalogue of Works

Fünf Lieder nach Rückert, for voice and orchestra, Nos. 1 and 4 composed summer 1901, No. 2 composed summer 1903, published 1905:

1. *Ich atmet' einen linden Duft.*
2. *Liebst du um Schönheit.*
3. *Blicke mir nicht in die Lieder.*
4. *Ich bin der Welt abhanden gekommen.*
5. *Um Mitternacht.*

Juvenilia

Sonata for violin and piano (Jihlava, 12th September 1876), destroyed.

Quartet for strings and piano (Vienna, 10th July 1876), believed lost in Russia; first movement and sketch of Scherzo recovered and one page published in facsimile by D. Mitchell, *op.cit.,* 1958.

Quintet for strings and piano (Vienna, 11th July 1878), destroyed.

Opera *Herzog Ernst von Schwaben* (? after Uhland) (1878–9), destroyed.

Opera *Die Argonauten* (? after Grillparzer) (*c.* 1880), destroyed.

Opera *Rübezahl* (1881–3), libretto still in existence in 1908, music probably lost.

Nordic Symphony (*c.* 1882–3), lost.

Incidental music for a dramatic version of Scheffel's *Trompeter von Säckingen* (June 1884), ? lost.

Symphony, lost in Russia.

Symphony in A minor, 3 movements still in existence in 1896.

Songs, lost. (5 preserved, partly fragmentary).

Arrangements and Editions

Weber's opera fragment, *Die drei Pintos* (libretto in collaboration with Hauptmann von Weber) (1887), published 1888.

Weber's *Euryanthe* (with new libretto by Mahler) (1903–4).

Mozart's *Figaro* (1906), published 1906.

Weber's *Oberon* (with new libretto by Mahler) (*c.* 1906), published 1919.

Suite by J. S. Bach (1909), published 1909.

Symphonies by Beethoven (rescored by Mahler), still in MS.

Symphonies by Schumann (rescored by Mahler), still in MS.

APPENDIX C

Adler, Guido (1855–1941), Austrian musicologist, born in Moravia. He was reader in musical history at the German University of Prague and succeeded E. Hanslick in the chair for music at the University of Vienna (1898–1927). He was founder and chief editor of the *Denkmäler der Tonkunst in Oesterreich*. He was a pupil of Bruckner at the Conservatory in Vienna (until 1874) and a friend of Mahler, whom he met in the later 1870s.

Arnim, Achim von (1781–1831), German poet of the Romantic movement. He edited with Clemens Brentano (q.v.) the collection of German folk poetry *Des Knaben Wunderhorn* and married his sister Bettina.

Assmayer, Ignaz (1790–1862), Austrian organist and notable composer of music for the Roman Church. He was a pupil of Michael Haydn and a friend of Schubert. He lived in Vienna, where he was appointed court organist in 1825 and succeeded Weigl in 1846 as second court conductor.

Auer, Max (born 1880), Austrian biographer of Bruckner.

Bahr-Mildenburg, Anna (1872–1947), Austrian dramatic soprano, famous for her interpretation of the great heroines of Wagner and Strauss. She sang under Mahler at Hamburg (1895–7) and followed him later to Vienna, where she became one of the celebrated members of the Opera (until 1917). She married the Austrian playwright and essayist Hermann Bahr (1863–1934) in 1909, and lived with him, first at Salzburg, later on (from 1919 onwards) in Munich, where she died.

Bauer-Lechner, Natalie (1859–1923), Austrian violinist; played second violin in the Soldat-Roeger Quartet (until 1914). The first performance of Hugo Wolf's string Quartet took place in her house. She was a close friend of Mahler's sisters and of Mahler (especially in the years before 1902).

Brentano, Clemens (1778–1842), German poet of the Romantic movement. Friend and brother-in-law of Achim v. Arnim (q.v.).

Decsey, Ernst (1870–1941), Austrian musicographer, pupil of Bruckner. He published biographies of Hugo Wolf and Bruckner.

Dessoff, Otto (1835–92), German conductor. From 1860 to 1875 he was conductor at the Vienna Opera, professor at the Conservatory of the Gesellschaft für Musikfreunde and chief conductor of the Philharmonic concerts in Vienna. Later on he went to Karlsruhe and Frankfort on Main in similar positions. His daughter, Margarethe Dessoff, went to New York in 1923, where she founded the Dessoff Choir.

Dorn, Ignaz, theatre conductor at Linz, friend of Bruckner. He introduced Liszt's 'Faust' Symphony to him. Bruckner used to relate that Dorn had appeared to him in a dream and had given him the principal subject of the first movement of Symphony VII.

Dürrnberger, August (1800–80), musical educationist and teacher at Linz, Bruckner's first tutor in harmony and thorough-bass (1841 ff.). He played a great part in connection with Bruckner's appointment as organist of Linz Cathedral.

Eckstein, Friedrich (1861–1939), pupil and friend of Bruckner, a notable musical amateur and a 'character' in Viennese musical circles at the turn of the century. He published valuable memoirs.

Epstein, Julius (1832–1926), notable Austrian piano teacher and one of the editors of the Collected Edition of Schubert's works. His wife and his son, Richard Epstein, were also pianists.

Fischer, Franz (1849–1918), originally violoncellist in Hans Richter's orchestra in Budapest, he became assistant conductor in Munich and Bayreuth under Wagner. Later on he occupied leading posts as court conductor at Mannheim and Munich.

Förster, Joseph Bohuslav (1859–1951), notable Czech composer, son of Joseph Förster (1833–1907), husband of the dramatic soprano Berta Lauterer, who sang under Mahler, first at Hamburg (1892–7) and later in Vienna (1903–18). Both returned to Prague in 1918, where Förster became professor and eventually director of the Conservatory (1922). Förster was a staunch friend of Mahler during the Hamburg years. He was a prolific composer of operas, symphonies and of intimate piano music.

Fuchs, Johann Nepomuk (1842–99), a Styrian; like his brother Robert, he became opera conductor in 1864. From 1880 on he was conductor at the Vienna Opera and from 1888 teacher (and eventually director) at the Conservatory of the Gesellschaft für Musikfreunde in Vienna. He is still remembered as editor of Handel's *Almira* and of comic operas by Gluck.

Fuchs, Robert (1847–1927), teacher of harmony at the Vienna Conservatory. Among his pupils were Hugo Wolf and Mahler. As a composer he achieved some success with his Serenades for small orchestra. He was the brother of Johann Nepomuk Fuchs (q.v.), a conductor at the Vienna Opera and one of Mahler's earliest antagonists there.

Führer, Robert (1807–61), notable organist and composer of Roman Catholic Church music in Prague and Vienna. He wrote about 100 masses.

Göbler, Georg (1874–1954), German conductor and composer of somewhat academic bent. He was one of the earliest partisans of Mahler's music.

Göllerich, August (1859–1923), pupil and friend of Bruckner and of Liszt. He wrote valuable biographies of both. His biography of Bruckner was completed by Max Auer.

Grünfeld, Alfred (1852–1924), Austrian pianist, renowned for his elegant interpretation of the waltzes of Johann Strauss (son) and of Schubert's chamber music. His brother, Heinrich G. (1855–?) was a popular cellist in Berlin.

Haas, Robert (1886–1960), Austrian musicologist and for many years director of the music section of the Vienna State Library, besides being a distinguished member of Vienna University. He edited many valuable issues of the Austrian *Denkmäler* and issued (with few exceptions) the original versions of Bruckner's works. He published a scholarly book on Bruckner (1934). He has distinguished himself also as a thoughtful editor and interpreter of the music of the early seventeenth century.

Hellmesberger, Joseph (father) (1828–93), prominent Austrian conductor, violinist, educationist and leader of a famous string quartet. He was director of the Vienna Conservatory of the Gesellschaft fur Musikfreunde (from 1851 on), besides being the society's conductor until 1859. It was there that Bruckner taught and Mahler studied. He took an erratic interest in Bruckner's music, commissioned the Quintet and seems to have appreciated Mahler's gifts. His tragi-comical conflict with Hugo Wolf, however, led to the latter's forcible exclusion from the Conservatory.

Hellmesberger, Joseph (son) (1855–1907), son of the above. He played in his father's quartet and made a career as violinist, violin leader and conductor. In 1884 he was appointed ballet conductor at the Vienna Opera, and in 1901 he became—for a short time only—Mahler's successor as chief conductor of the Philharmonic concerts in Vienna. He composed operettas and ballets with moderate success.

Appendix C—Personalia

Herbeck, Johann (1831–77), Austrian conductor. He became the elder Hellmesberger's successor as conductor of the Gesellschaftskonzerte (1859) and was appointed director of the Vienna Opera in 1870, with which he had been connected since 1863. He resigned, however, in 1875. Herbeck was responsible for Bruckner's appointment in Vienna and remained one of his greatest benefactors.

Hynais, Cyril, faithful pupil and follower of Bruckner. He witnessed Bruckner's last will, acted as his copyist during the last years and bears chief responsibility for the posthumous publication of Symphony VI and of parts of the 'Studiensymphonie' in F minor.

Jahn, Wilhelm (1835–1900), Austrian conductor and Mahler's predecessor at the Vienna Opera (1881–97).

Kalbeck, Max (1850–1921). Austrian music critic, author of the first full-scale biography of Brahms and translator of opera librettos. His poetical gifts were appreciated by Mahler. Bruckner, however, suffered from his unrelenting hostility.

Kattinger, Anton, organist at St Florian and Bruckner's first organ teacher. Bruckner succeeded him in that post in 1855.

Kitzler, Otto (1834–1915), German conductor who became Bruckner's tutor at Linz (1861–3). He was a progressive musician and an early champion of Wagner, whose *Tannhäuser* he first conducted at Linz. In his later years he taught and conducted at Brno.

Křenek, Ernst (born 1900), Austrian composer who emigrated to the U.S.A. in 1938. He married Mahler's surviving daughter, Anna, in the early 1920s and issued a practical edition of two movements of Mahler's tenth Symphony in 1924. He also collaborated with Bruno Walter in a book on Mahler (1941). As a composer he achieved a sensational but transient success with his jazz opera *Jonny spielt auf* (1927). He employed twelve-note technique in the opera *Karl V* (1933) and in many of his later works.

Krenn, Franz (1818–97), Austrian composer and musical theorist. He was teacher for harmony, counterpoint and composition at the Vienna Conservatory, and among his pupils were Hugo Wolf and Mahler.

Krismann, Franz Xaver (1726–95), famous Austrian organ builder, born in Carniola. He constructed the organ at St Florian (Collegiate Church), completing it in 1774. This was Bruckner's instrument. It was rebuilt by M. Mauracher in 1873–5. A reconstruction of the original disposition was completed in 1951.

Krisper, Anton (?–1914), Austrian musician. He was an intimate friend of Mahler and Hans Rott.

Krzyzanowski, Rudolf (? 1859–1911), Austrian conductor, a close friend of Mahler in his early days. He was court conductor at Weimar (1898–1907).

Lachner, Franz (1803–90), Bavarian conductor and composer. He was a friend of Schubert, a pupil of Sechter and was liked by Beethoven. His brilliant career as a conductor culminated in his appointment to Munich (1852). This was terminated prematurely in 1865 because of his antagonism to Wagner. His suites and symphonies achieved great success during his lifetime.

Levi, Hermann (1839–1900), German conductor, originally a friend of Brahms, later on strongly attached to Wagner, whose *Parsifal* he first conducted in 1882. In later years he became one of the first leading conductors genuinely interested in Bruckner's music. His notable Mozart interpretations (edition of *Così fan tutte*) anticipated the Mozart revival of this century.

Löwe, Ferdinand (1865–1925), Austrian conductor and faithful apostle of Bruckner, whose Symphony IX he edited, published and first performed in 1903. He made his mark as a distinguished musician of classical bent in leading posts in Munich and Vienna.

Marschalk, Max (1863–1940), German composer and music critic of the *Vossische Zeitung*. He became Gerhart Hauptmann's brother-in-law and composed incidental music for various plays of his.

Mathis, Alfred (Alfred Rosenzweig) (1897–1948), Austrian music critic of the *Wiener Tag*. He emigrated to England in 1938. Among his writings are an unpublished biography of Elisabeth Schumann and a monograph on Toscanini's *Fidelio* production at Salzburg (1937).

Neumann, Angelo (1838–1910), Austrian singer and theatre director. He organized the first travelling Wagner theatre (1882), which received the composer's blessing. In 1885 he was appointed director of the Deutsche Landestheater in Prague.

Nottebohm, Martin Gustav (1817–82), German musicologist. He was a pupil of Mendelssohn, Schumann and Sechter, and established himself in Vienna as an esteemed music teacher (1845). He was a leading Beethoven scholar and received high praise from Brahms.

Nowak, Leopold (born 1904), Austrian musicologist. He was a pupil of Robert Haas (q.v.), whom he succeeded in 1945 as director of the music section of the Austrian National Library in Vienna. He has begun to issue a new critical Complete Edition of Bruckner's works.

Ochs, Siegfried (1858–1929), German choral conductor. He founded the Philharmonic Choir in Berlin and gave early and successful performances of Bruckner's *Te Deum* and of choral works by Hugo Wolf and Max Reger. He was sincerely attached to Bruckner in the 1890s.

Pollini, Bernhard (1838–97), German singer, impresario and theatre director. From 1874 onwards he directed the Hamburg Municipal Theatre with Hans von Bülow and Mahler among its chief conductors.

Popper, David (1843–1913), Hungarian violoncellist and notable composer for his instrument. On Bülow's recommendation he was appointed solo cellist at the Vienna Opera.

Preyer, Gottfried (1807–1901), Austrian organist, musical theorist and composer of church music. From 1833 to 1848 he was director of the Conservatory of the Gesellschaft der Musikfreunde. In 1853 he was appointed conductor at the cathedral of St Stephan, Vienna.

Rosé, Arnold (1863–1946), Austrian violinist, of Rumanian birth, leader of a famous string quartet (since 1883), leader of the Viennese Philharmonic Orchestra and of the orchestra of the Vienna Opera (1881–1938). He married Mahler's sister Justine in 1902 and remained one of Mahler's most faithful followers. In 1938 he emigrated to England, where he died. His son, Alfred Rosé (born 1902) has become an American citizen. His elder brother, Eduard (1859–?) started as violoncellist in his string quartet. He became a notable cellist in his own right later on and received leading appointments in Budapest, Vienna and Weimar. He married Mahler's youngest sister, Emma.

Rott, Hans (1859–?81), son of a Viennese actor, favourite pupil of Bruckner. He studied counterpoint and composition with Krenn, and was appointed organist of the Piarist Church, Vienna, in 1877. He was a close friend of Mahler in the later 1870s and continued to value his music highly. Rott died in a lunatic asylum.

Rückert Friedrich (1788–1866), German poet and orientalist. He belongs to the younger romantics. A prolific versifier and a virtuoso in the handling of difficult forms and metres (specializing in the Turkish ghazal), he had a special appeal for Schumann, Mahler and other composers of the later nineteenth century.

Schalk, Franz (1863–1931), Austrian conductor. He was Bruckner's pupil and most ardent follower, exercising at times great influence on the ageing master. He conducted the first performance of Bruckner's Symphony V (Graz, 1894) and was responsible for its first publication in the year of the composer's death. His memoirs, published posthumously in 1935, contain valuable data of Bruckner's life and work. Schalk was intimately connected with the Vienna Opera for more than thirty years, starting as Mahler's assistant in 1900 and appointed artistic director in November 1918 (until 1924 in collaboration with Richard Strauss). For many years he was also the conductor of the Gesellschaftskonzerte in Vienna and he specialized in authentic performances of the symphonies and choral works of Bruckner and Mahler. His brother Joseph (1857–1901) was also a pupil of Bruckner. His influence on the composer was greater still. He propagated the cause of Bruckner by means of piano arrangements, lectures, programme notes and pamphlets. He also championed the music of Hugo Wolf.

Sechter, Simon (1788–1867), Bohemian-born Austrian organist and musical theorist. He was appointed court organist in Vienna in 1824 and became professor at the Conservatory in 1851. As a teacher of counterpoint he was held in high esteem. Schubert intended to become his pupil in 1828. Sechter was for many years teacher and musical mentor of Bruckner, who in turn became his successor at the Conservatory in 1868. Sechter's theoretical treatise *Grundsätze der musikalischen Komposition* (published 1853–4) has retained its value to the present day.

Seidl, Arthur (1863–1928), German writer on matters of musical aesthetics, notable music critic and musical educationist. He did valuable spadework for a better understanding of the artistic aims of Strauss, Mahler and Pfitzner.

Specht, Richard (1870–1932), Viennese music critic and author of biographical essays on Mahler, Strauss, Puccini, Brahms and others. He published thematic analyses of Mahler's late works, some of which were based on information from the composer.

Tappert, Wilhelm (1830–1907), musical theorist and influential music critic. He was an ardent partisan of Wagner and published in 1887 the notorious *Wagner-Lexikon*, in which all verbal injuries, attacks and innuendos against the master of Bayreuth were carefully listed. He also did some valuable research and collected a library which was later on incorporated in the Berlin State Library.

Traumihler, Ignaz (1825–84), Regens Chori of St Florian from 1852 and a friend of Bruckner, who dedicated the four-part *Ave Maria* to him. He also composed the gradual *Os justi* in 1879, following a suggestion of Traumihler's, to whom this too was dedicated. In 1877 Bruckner recommended Hans Rott to him as possible successor to the deceased organist Seiberl.

Weinwurm, Rudolf (1835–1911), Austrian choirmaster and composer. He was a close friend of Bruckner, especially during the Linz period. Weinwurm founded the Akademische Gesangverein in Vienna (1858), was appointed conductor of the Singakademie in 1864 and musical director of the University in 1880. As an inspector of music he did much to raise the level of musical tuition at state-subsidized schools and colleges.

Weiss, Johann Baptist (1813–50), teacher, organist and composer at Hörsching, near Linz. He was a first cousin to Bruckner, his mother being a sister of Bruckner's father. In 1833 he became Bruckner's godfather. He also gave him first musical tuition (1835–7). Weiss composed masses and smaller pieces for liturgical use which became important as models for Bruckner's first essays in composition.

Witt, Franz Xaver (1834–88), Catholic priest and composer for the Church. In 1867 he founded the Caecilienverein, bent on improving the quality of Roman Catholic Church music in Germany; he also edited the periodical *Musica sacra*, which published in 1885 Bruckner's *Tantum ergo* and *Pangue lingua* of 1868. Witt was a stout Palestrinian and pleaded for the total exclusion of the orchestra from devotional music.

Wöss, Joseph Venantius von (1863–1943), Austrian composer and music teacher. He issued many piano arrangements of symphonies and choral works by Bruckner and Mahler. He also published smaller choral works of Bruckner for the first time and wrote a memoir of Bruckner, with whom he was personally acquainted.

Zemlinsky, Alexander von (1872–1942), notable Austrian conductor and composer. He was the only teacher of Schoenberg, who became his brother-in-law, marrying his sister Mathilde in 1901. Mahler appreciated his gifts and performed his opera *Es war einmal* in 1900. Zemlinsky's later music made a deep impression on Alban Berg. As a conductor Zemlinsky held important posts in Vienna, Mannheim and Prague, where he was appointed chief of the German Opera in 1920. From 1927 to 1932 he conducted at the Berlin Kroll-Oper. Later on he returned to Vienna and finally emigrated to New York in 1938.

Zenetti, Leopold von, organist and music teacher at Enns, Upper Austria. Bruckner became his pupil in 1843. Zenetti drew Bruckner's attention specially to J. S. Bach.

Zichy, Géza, Count (1849–1924), Hungarian aristocrat and famous one-armed pianist and composer. He was a pupil of Liszt and played in later life an important part in the musical politics of his country. In 1891 he became intendant of the Hungarian State Opera (as successor to Bezeczny). His meddlesomeness was chiefly responsible for Mahler's premature departure from Budapest in the following year. In 1892 Zichy was appointed president of the Hungarian Musical Academy in Budapest. He remained in that post until 1918. His operas were performed in Austria-Hungary, also in Germany, especially at the turn of the century.

APPENDIX D

BIBLIOGRAPHY

(a) BRUCKNER

Auer, Max, 'Anton Bruckner: sein Leben im Werk.' (Vienna, 1923; 2nd ed., Leipzig, 1934; 6th ed., Vienna, 1949.)

——, 'Anton Bruckner als Kirchenmusiker.' (Ratisbon, 1927.)

Blume, Friedrich, article 'Bruckner' in *Die Musik in Geschichte und Gegenwart*, Vol. II. (Cassel, 1952.)

Brahms, Johannes, 'J. Brahms im Briefwechsel mit Heinrich und Elisabet v. Herzogenberg,' ed. by Max Kalbeck. (Berlin, 1907.)

Bruckner, Anton, 'Gesammelte Briefe,' ed. by F. Gräflinger. (Ratisbon, 1924.)[1]

——, 'Gesammelte Briefe, neue Folge,' ed. by Max Auer. (Ratisbon, 1924.)[2]

——, 'Vorlesungen über Harmonielehre und Kontrapunkt an der Universität Wien,' ed. by E. Schwanzara. (Vienna, 1951.)

Chord and Discord, 'Journal of the Bruckner Society of America,' 1945 ff.

Decsey, Ernst, 'Bruckner: Versuch eines Lebens.' (Berlin, 1920.)

Doernberg, E., 'The Life and Symphonies of Anton Bruckner.' (London 1960.)

Eckstein, Friedrich, 'Erinnerungen an Bruckner.' (Vienna, 1923.)

Göllerich, August, and Auer, Max, 'Anton Bruckner: ein Lebens- und Schaffensbild,' 4 vols. (Ratisbon, 1924-36.)

Grüninger, Fritz, 'Anton Bruckner: der metaphysische Kern seiner Persönlichkeit und Werke.' (Augsburg, 1930.)

——, 'Der Ehrfürchtige: Anton Bruckners Leben dem Volke erzählt.' (Freiburg i. B., 1937.)

Haas, Robert, 'Anton Bruckner' (in *Die grossen Meister der Musik*, ed. E. Bücken). (Potsdam, 1934.)

Hanslick, Eduard, 'Aus dem Tagebuch eines Musikers,' Vol. VI. (Berlin, 1892.)

---

[1] Referred to as 'Briefe, I.'   [2] Referred to as 'Briefe, II.'

Klose, Friedrich, 'Meine Lehrjahre bei Bruckner: Erinnerungen und Betrachtungen.' (Ratisbon, 1927.)

Krohn, Ilmari, 'Anton Bruckners Symphonien: Untersuchung über Formenbau und Stimmungsgehalt,' 3 vols. (Helsinki 1955–7.)

Kurth, Ernst, 'Bruckner,' 2 vols. (Berlin, 1925.)

Laux, Karl, 'Anton Bruckner: Leben und Werk.' (Leipzig-Wiesbaden, 1947.)

Newlin, Dika, 'Bruckner—Mahler—Schoenberg.' (New York, 1947.)

Oeser, Fritz, 'Die Klangstruktur der Bruckner-Symphonie.' (Leipzig, 1939.)

——, Introduction to his edition of Symphony III (2nd version, 1878). (Wiesbaden, 1950.)

Orel, Alfred, 'Bruckner-Brevier (Briefe, Dokumente, Berichte).' (Vienna, 1953.)

——, 'Entwürfe und Skizzen zur IX. Symphonie.' (Vienna, 1934.)

Redlich, Hans Ferdinand, 'Bruckner-Entdeckungen' (*Der Auftakt,* Prague, XIV/10, 1934; *Schweiz. Musikzeitung,* Year 74, No. 24, 1934.)

——, 'Vom unbekannten Bruckner' (Symphony IX, O.V.). (*Frankfurter Zeitung,* 1st January 1935.)

——, 'Bruckner's Choral Music.' (*The Listener,* London, 6th November 1947.)

——, 'The Finale of Bruckner's Symphony IX.' (*Monthly Musical Record,* LXXIV, 1949.)

——, 'Bruckner's Forgotten Symphony, No. "O."' (*Music Survey,* II, 1949.)

——, article 'Bruckner' in Grove's *Dictionary.* (5th ed., 1954.)

——, Introduction to a revision of Symphony IV (version 4). (Eulenburg Miniature Scores, London, 1955.)

——, 'Bruckner and Brahms Quintets in F,' *Music and Letters,* Vol. 36, No. 3, pp. 253 ff. (July 1955.)

——, Introduction to a revision of Symphony VII, Eulenburg Miniature Scores. (London, 1958.)

——, Introduction to a revision of the Te Deum, Eulenburg Miniature Scores. (London, 1960.)

——, Introduction to a revision of Symphony III, Version 4, Eulenburg Miniature Scores. (London, 1962.)

Schalk, Franz, 'Briefe und Betrachtungen.' (Vienna-Leipzig, 1935.)

Appendix D—Bibliography

Schwanzara, Erich, 'Anton Bruckners Stamm und Urheimat.' (Ratisbon, 1937.)

Sharp, Geoffrey, 'Anton Bruckner: Simpleton or Mystic?' (*Music Review*, III, 1942.)

Simpson, Robert, 'Bruckner and the Symphony.' (*Music Review*, VII, 1946.)

——, 'The VIIth Symphony by Bruckner: an Analysis.' (*Music Review*, VIII, 1947.)

Wellesz, Egon, 'Anton Bruckner and the Process of Musical Creation.' (*Musical Quarterly*, July 1938.)

Wolff, Werner, 'Anton Bruckner: Rustic Genius.' (New York, 1942.)

N.B. This is deliberately selective: it contains only books and papers of importance to this volume. For additional biographies and analytical works on Bruckner consult F. Blume's article in M.G.G., II and the writer's article in Grove (5th ed., 1954).

(b) MAHLER

Adler, Guido, 'Gustav Mahler.' (*Biographisches Jahrbuch und deutscher Nekrolog*, Vol. XVI, Vienna, 1914; in book form, Vienna, 1916.)

Adorno, Theodor W., Mahler. Eine musikalische Physiognomik. (Frankfurt-am-Main, 1960.)

Bauer-Lechner, Natalie, 'Erinnerungen an Gustav Mahler.' (Vienna, 1923.)

Berg, Alban, 'Verbindliche Antwort auf eine unverbindliche Anfrage.' (*UE Jahrbuch*, Vienna, 1926.)

Bekker, Paul, 'Mahlers Sinfonien.' (Berlin, 1921.)

——, 'Die Symphonie von Beethoven bis Mahler.' (Berlin, 1918.)

Bülow, Hans von, 'Neue Briefe' (ed. by Richard Graf du Moulin-Eckart). (Munich, 1927.)

Decsey, Ernst, 'Stunden mit Mahler.' (*Die Musik*, July–August 1911.)

Eckstein, Friedrich, 'Alte, unnennbare Tage.' (Vienna, 1936.)

Engel, Gabriel, 'Gustav Mahler: Song-Symphonist.' (New York, 1932.)

Förster, Josef Bohuslav, 'Aus Mahlers Werkstatt.' (*Der Merker*, I.)

Hollaender, Hans, 'Unbekannte Jugendbriefe Mahlers.' (*Die Musik*, XX/11, August 1928.)

Karpath, Ludwig, 'Begegnung mit dem Genius.' (Vienna, 1934.)

Klemperer, Otto, Meine Erinnerungen an Gustav Mahler. (Zürich, 1960.)

Kralik, Heinrich von, Das grosse Orchester. Die Wiener Philharmoniker und ihre Dirgenten. (Vienna, 1952.)

Mahler, Alma Maria, 'Gustav Mahler: Erinnerungen und Briefe.'[1] (Amsterdam, 1940; English ed., 'Memories and Letters,' trans. by Basil Creighton, London, 1947.)

——, (assisted by E. B. Ashton), *And the Bridge is Love.* (New York, 1958; London, 1959.)

——, Introduction to the facsimile edition of Symphony X. (Vienna, 1924.)

Mahler, Gustav, 'Briefe, 1879–1911,' ed. by Alma Maria Mahler.[2] (Berlin-Vienna-Leipzig, 1924.)

'Mahler—Symphonien: Meisterführer No. 10' (collected thematic analyses), ed. by Edgar Istel. (Berlin, 1910.)

'Gustav Mahler: ein Bild der Persönlichkeit in Widmungen,' ed. by Paul Stefan. (Munich, 1910.)

Mathis, Alfred (Rosenzweig, Alfred), 'Gustav Mahler: Composer-Conductor.' (*The Listener,* 5th February 1948, referring especially to Symphony VIII.)

——, 'Mahler's Unfinished Symphony' (Symphony X). (*The Listener,* 11th November 1948.)

Mitchell, Donald, 'Gustav Mahler: The Early Years.' (London, 1958.)

Mittag, Erich, 'The Vienna Philharmonic.' (Vienna, 1950.)

Newlin, Dika, 'Bruckner—Mahler—Schoenberg.' (New York, 1947.)

Pamer, Fritz Egon, 'Die Lieder Gustav Mahlers.' (Vienna, 1922.)

Redlich, Hans Ferdinand, 'Gustav Mahler: eine Erkenntnis.' (Nuremberg, 1919.)

——, 'Die Welt der V. VI. und VII. Symphonie.' (Mahler issue, *Der Anbruch,* II/7–8, April 1920.)

——, 'Mahlers Wirkung in Zeit und Raum.' (*Der Anbruch,* XII/3, March 1930.)

——, *Alban Berg—Versuch einer Würdigung.* (Vienna, 1957.)

——, *Alban Berg—The Man and his Music.* (London, 1957.)

——, Introduction to a revision of *Songs of a Wayfarer,* Eulenburg Miniature Scores. (London, 1959.)

---

[1] Referred to here as 'ER.'   [2] Referred to here as 'BR.'

Redlich Hans Ferdinand, Article 'Gustav Mahler' in *Die Musik in Geschichte und Gegenwart*, Vol. VIII. (1960.)

——, Introduction to a revision of Symphony VII, Eulenburg Miniature Scores. (Zürich, 1962.)

——, Introduction to a revision of *Kindertotenlieder* Eulenburg Miniature Scores. (London, 1962.)

Reik, Theodore, 'The Haunting Melody.' (New York, 1953.)

'Richard Strauss—Jahrbuch.' (Bonn, 1953.)

Roller, Alfred, 'Die Bildnisse Gustave Mahlers.' (Leipzig, 1922.)

Schaeffer, Alfred, 'Gustav Mahlers Instrumentation.' (Düsseldorf, 1935.)

Schönfeldt, Christl, Die Wiener Philharmoniker. (Vienna 1957.)

Schoenberg, Arnold, 'Style and Idea.' (London, 1951.)

——, 'Harmonielehre.' (Vienna, 1911.)

Sharp, Geoffrey, 'Gustav Mahler' (in *The Symphony*, ed. by Ralph Hill). (Pelican Books, London, 1949.)

Specht, Richard, 'Gustav Mahler.' (Berlin, 1913.)

——, Thematic analyses of Symphony VIII and 'Lied von der Erde.' (Vienna, 1910–11.)

——, Introduction to Mahler's Symphony X. (Vienna, 1924.)

Stefan, Paul, 'Gustav Mahler: eine Studie über Persönlichkeit und Werk' (4th ed., Munich, 1912.)

Stein, Erwin, 'Orpheus in New Guises.' (London, 1953.)

Steinitzer, Max, article on Mahler (Mahler issue of *Der Anbruch*, II/7–8, May 1920.)

Tischler, Hans, 'Mahler's "Das Lied von der Erde."' (*Music Review*, X/2, 1949.)

——, 'Mahler's Impact on the Crisis of Tonality.' (*Music Review*, XII/2, 1951.)

Walker, Frank, 'Hugo Wolf.' (London, 1951.)

Walter, Bruno, 'Gustav Mahler.' (Vienna, 1936.)

—— (with Ernst Křenek), 'Gustav Mahler.' (New York, 1941.)

——, 'Theme and Variations,' autobiography. (London, 1950.)

Wellesz, Egon, 'The Symphonies of Gustav Mahler.' (*Music Review*, I/1–2, 1940.)

N.B. For additional books on Mahler consult the author's article in *Die Musik in Geschichte und Gegenwart*, Vol. VIII, 1960.

INDEX

INDEX

293

Index

Index

Index

Index